Law and Philosophy Library

Volume 109

The Law and Philosophy Library—, which has been in existence since 1985, aims to publish cutting edge works in the philosophy of law, and has a special history of publishing books that focus on legal reasoning and argumentation, including those that may involve somewhat formal methodologies. The series has published numerous important books on law and logic, law and artificial intelligence, law and language, and law and rhetoric. While continuing to stress these areas, the series has more recently expanded to include books on the intersection between law and the Continental philosophical tradition, consistent with the traditional openness of the series to books in the Continental jurisprudential tradition. The series is proud of the geographic diversity of its authors, and many have come from Latin America, Spain, Italy, the Netherlands, Germany, and Eastern Europe, as well, more obviously for an English-language series, from the United Kingdom, the United States, Australia, and Canada.

More information about this series at http://www.springer.com/series/6210

Åke Frändberg

From *Rechtsstaat* to Universal Law-State

An Essay in Philosophical Jurisprudence

Springer

Åke Frändberg
Faculty of Law
Uppsala University
Uppsala
Sweden

ISSN 1572-4395 ISSN 2215-0315 (electronic)
ISBN 978-3-319-38027-8 ISBN 978-3-319-06784-1 (eBook)
DOI 10.1007/978-3-319-06784-1
Springer Cham Heidelberg New York Dordrecht London

Printed on acid-free paper

Springer is part of Springer Science+Business Media (www.springer.com)

For my children.
Iucundi acti labores. (Cicero)

Acknowledgements

Four chapters in this book are substantially rewritten versions of articles published previously, as follows:

Chapter 5

"Legal Equality", *Perspectives on Jurisprudence. Essays in Honor of Jes Bjarup*, P. Wahlgren (ed.) Scandinavian Studies in Law Vol. 48, Stockholm, 2005, pp. 83–97.

Chapter 6

"Om rättssäkerhet", *Juridisk Tidskrift*, 2000–2001, pp. 269–280. Reprinted in Å. Frändberg, *Rättsordningens idé. En antologi i allmän rättslära*, Uppsala, 2005, pp. 283–295.

Chapter 7

"Legal Accessibility", *Festskrift till Anders Fogelklou*, Å. Frändberg, S. Hedlund, T. Spaak (eds.), Uppsala, 2008, pp. 33–47

Chapter 9

"Rättsstatens organisation", *Changing Positions. Essays Dedicated to Lars Lindahl on the Occasion of his Fiftieth Birthday*, P. Needham, J. Odelstad (eds.), Philosophical Studies Published by the Philosophical Society and the Department of Philosophy, University of Uppsala, No 38, 1986, pp. 21–43. Reprinted in Å. Frändberg, *Rättsordningens idé. En antologi i allmän rättslära*, Uppsala, 2005, pp. 265–281.

I would like to thank Torben Spaak for valuable comments and Robert Carroll for checking my English. I am indebted to Stanley L. Paulson, who commented upon the manuscript with a view to matters of English style. Further I would like to thank two anonymous reviewers for Springer for thought-provoking comments. I also wish to acknowledge a debt of gratitude to the Royal Academy of Arts and Sciences of Uppsala for a generous grant that made the project possible.

Thanks are also due to Hodder & Stoughton for their permission to quote from *Gaudy Night* (1935) by Dorothy L. Sayers.

Contents

About the Author

Åke Frändberg is Emeritus Professor of Jurisprudence at Uppsala University, Sweden. He is the author of several books and articles in Swedish. He has also published in English, Chinese, German and Spanish. He is a member of the Royal Uppsala Academy of Arts and Sciences. He has been visiting professor at University of Minnesota, Minneapolis, and lecturer at the European Academy of Legal Theory, Brussels.

Chapter 1
The Basic Idea

Quis custodiet ipsos custodes?
(Juvenal)

Mr. Black is tortured in prison. Mrs. Brown is denied the opportunity to acquaint herself of evidence brought forward against her by her adversary in a trial. A tax of 50 % of the profit Mr. White has made in a business transaction is retroactively imposed on him, although, according to the tax law in force at the time of the transaction, he should have paid a tax of only 25 %. The bishop of the see receives a less severe punishment than unemployed Mr. Grey for stealing, in each case, a tin of tuna-fish in the supermarket, and that for no other reason than his higher position in society.

What, if there be any, are the common denominators of these four situations?

There are three, to wit: (i) they all have to do with the law, (ii) they are all instances of wrong-doing (unfairness, immorality) and (iii) this wrong-doing is performed, not by fellow-citizens, but by state authorities, and even judicial ones (policemen, courts of law, a legislative body).

In the ideological reaction to phenomena of the kind exemplified, and in the endeavour of creating legal devices capable of preventing them, we find the germ of the idea of *the Rule of Law* in the Anglo-American tradition as well as the idea of the *Rechtsstaat* in the German or Continental tradition.

Early in the history of law certain ideas of an evaluative character emerge, pertaining not to the content of particular parts of the law such as civil law or criminal law, but to the very handling—the *good* handling—of legal orders as such, through legislation and administration of justice. What I have in mind are ideas giving expression to such values as legality, legal equality and legal certainty. Occidental law is by origin inherited from the Romans, but the fundamental ideas concerning its good handling belong to a great extent to our heritage from the ancient Greeks. A pregnant formulation of legalism in Greek is νόμος βασιλεύς (*nómos basileús*), "the Law is the King". Man shall be ruled by law, not by men, as has been said. Another very important idea in Greek legal thinking is that of isonomy, equality before the law.

These old ideas are preserved—and by Germanic influence even reinforced—in medieval legal thinking. Legalism was of crucial importance in the Middle Ages.

Å. Frändberg, *From Rechtsstaat to Universal Law-State,* Law and Philosophy Library 109,
DOI 10.1007/978-3-319-06784-1_1, © Springer International Publishing Switzerland 2014

The supremacy of law rendered even kings subject to the laws of the land. The cluster of ideas thus inherited receives its first more penetrating and systematic expression in John Locke's *Second Treatise of Government* (1690), a work whose ideas were further developed by Montesquieu and representatives of the Enlightenment movement such as Voltaire, Beccaria, and Bentham.

When in the nineteenth century the German *Rechtsstaat* ideology as well as the British ideology of *the Rule of Law* emerge, they offer little innovation in terms of basic ideas. They can best be regarded as two viable branches in full leaf found on a venerable old tree extant over a long period of time.

The word "*Rechtsstaat*" appears, probably for the first time, in a work published by Robert von Mohl in 1855.[1] In 1864, a book by Otto Bähr was published, having the very title of *Der Rechtsstaat*.

Already some decades earlier, that is, before the breakthrough of the *Rechtsstaat* ideology, Paul Johann Anselm von Feuerbach had presented his classic Latin formulation of the principles of legality in criminal law: *Nullum crimen, nulla poena sine lege poenali, Nullum crimen sine poena legali, Nulla poena legalis sine crimine.*[2]

The foundation of the German doctrine of the *Rechtsstaat* is twofold. On the one hand, it has a basis in classical seventeenth and eighteenth century natural law and Enlightenment ideas—emerging as a reaction to arbitrary and uncontrolled exercises of power by absolute rulers in European autocracies during the sixteenth and seventeenth centuries. Legalism (the rule of law), equality before the law, legal certainty and, not least of all, legal security against uncontrolled exercise of violence on the part of the state are core values defended by the Enlightenment thinkers. On the other hand, it is firmly rooted in the specifically nineteenth century world of ideas found in the German Historical School of Law, characterised by conservatism and a romantic conception of the state as an organism. This double foundation of *Rechtsstaat* thinking no doubt explains why it was embraced both by conservatives (such as Stahl) and liberal thinkers (such as Otto Bähr and Rudolf Gneist).

The conservative strand lends to *Rechtsstaat* thinking its special flavour as compared with, first of all, the British idea of the Rule of Law. This German feature is given its most forceful expression in the writings of the monarchical philosopher of state, Friedrich Julius Stahl, a Christian conservative. The state, according to him, is a divine institution,[3] and "the monarchical principle" is the foundation of German constitutional law and German political wisdom.[4] He distrusts the English "parliamentary principle". The *Rechtsstaat* in Stahl's version demarcates a legal sphere where individuals can claim rights against the state. This sphere includes on the one hand a "*Privat-Rechtszustand*", encompassing (among other things) civil law and criminal law, and on the other the individual's "freedom against state power as far

[1] *Geschichte der Literatur der Staatswissenschaften*, vol. I (1855), pp. 296 ff.

[2] *Revision der Grundsätze und Grundbegriffe des positiven peinlichen Rechts*, Part I (1799), pp. 146 ff.

[3] *Die Philosophie des Rechts nach geschichtlicher Ansicht*, vol II, *Rechts- und Staatslehre auf der Grundlage christlicher Weltanschauung*, 2nd ed. (1845–1846), p. 144.

[4] Op. cit., p. 364.

as this freedom consists in legal relations", e.g., the rules of compulsory military service and school attendance.[5] The "path of the civil law" (*der Civil-Rechtsweg*) is, in Stahl's opinion, open only for claiming rights within the *Privat-Rechtszustand*, not for claiming rights pertaining to individuals within the public law sphere exclusively.

This leads us to an important difference between the *Rechtsstaat* doctrine and the idea of the Rule of Law. In this respect French law plays a decisive role, due to the development in France of a modern administrative law (*droit administratif*) at the beginning of the nineteenth century. According to Gaudemet[6], this administrative law is characterised by two factors: (i) The administrative bodies in France are not supervised by the general courts of law, and (ii) the existence of special administrative courts of law (the *Conseil d'État* was established in 1800). The German *Rechtsstaat* conception is greatly influenced by the development of French administrative law.

A crucial question in the nineteenth century discussion on the *Rechtsstaat* and Rule of Law is this: Shall the individual's legal protection against state power be regulated within civil law or within public law? Is "the path of the civil-law" or "the path of the public-law" or some combination of the two to be chosen? This question is answered in strikingly different ways in Germany and in England, respectively.

In 1885 the first edition of Dicey's classic *Introduction to the Study of the Law of the Constitution* was published. In this famous work, legally valid English principles that concern the individual's protection against the state, are described—or, rather, reconstructed and dogmatised—under the comprehensive term *the Rule of Law*.

This expression covers ideas such as[7]:

(1) Legality. Strict obedience to law by those exercising state power, including supreme power, as opposed to arbitrary, discretionary use of power.

(2) Legal equality. No individual is above the law, and everyone is subject to the general laws of the land and the jurisdiction of the general courts of law.

(3) The general principles of the British "constitution" (e.g., the right to personal freedom and freedom of assembly) is the result of individual judgments, handed down by courts, in which the rights of private persons have been established. These rights do not emanate, as is the case elsewhere, from generally formulated principles in a written constitution. In this lies, in Dicey's opinion, the supremacy of civil law: "… the principles of private law have with us been by the action of the courts and Parliament so extended as to determine the position of the Crown and of its servants; thus the constitution is the result of the ordinary law of the land".[8] Dicey strongly contrasts the Rule of Law, representing "the path of the civil-law", with the French *droit administratif*, representing "the path of the public-law". The

[5] Op. cit., p. 336.

[6] E. Gaudemet, "*Droit administratif* in France", in A.V. Dicey, *Introduction to the Study of the Law of the Constitution*, 10th ed. (1959), Appendix 1, p. 482.

[7] A.V. Dicey, *Introduction to the Study of the Law of the Constitution*, 10th ed. (1959), pp. 187 ff.

[8] Op. cit., p. 203.

comparison no doubt favours the former, although Dicey is not at all blind to the advantages of the latter.[9]

From one point of view the Rule of Law principles belong—Dicey states it a bit more precisely—to the ordinary civil and criminal law, but from another point of view they belong to constitutional law, namely when the rules of civil and criminal law regulate the relations between individual citizens and the executive—the distinction between civil law and public law is, in fact, nothing other than two different aspects of the same thing.[10]

The Rule of Law in Dicey's version includes a good bit of what is nowadays called human rights. In connection with the right to personal freedom he discusses, among other things, the important Habeas Corpus Acts of 1679 and 1816.

Lending to Dicey's conception of the Rule of Law its special flavour is the (certainly not unproblematic) coupling together of the Rule of Law and the notion of parliamentary sovereignty—an idea unfamiliar to the German conception of the *Rechtsstaat*.[11]

The very concept "*Rechtsstaat*" has been attacked by Kelsen.[12] He sees it as an instrument for legitimising the state. As such, however, it is "completely inappropriate, since every state must be a *Rechtsstaat*—if one understands by '*Rechtsstaat*' a state that 'has' a legal system"—a view, however, that very few would be inclined to accept! Kelsen grants that the concept can be used in the "ordinary" way, but to "perceive a 'true' legal system only in a system of norms fashioned along these lines is a prejudice of natural law".

This objection falls far short of the mark. Far from being instrumental in legitimising any legal order whatsoever, the *Rechtsstaat* ideology is a device for the criticism of legal orders—it offers a standard against which existing such orders can be measured from certain moral points of view. The *Rechtsstaat* idea rests upon the presupposition that there are states (legal orders) that are not *Rechsstaaten*. Whether a state is a *Rechtsstaat* or not is a matter of contingency. There are also *Unrechtsstaaten*. The concept "*Rechtsstaat*", as it was developed in nineteenth century Germany, is not a defining element of the concept of law, and, hence, "*Rechtsstaat*" is no natural law concept within that tradition.

The development after the Second World War is characterised by a very considerable degree of convergence between the *Rechtsstaat* and the Rule of Law doctrines—or, if you like, a return to the classical Western tradition of legalism and values attached thereto, shorn of some nineteenth century German and English peculiarities. A contributing factor in this development has been the appearance of international conventions of human rights, more or less effectively realised by

---

[9] Op. cit., ch. XII.

[10] Op. cit., p. 285.

[11] Op. cit., ch. XIII. For an illuminating comparison between the Rule of Law and the *Rechtsstaat* ideas, see D. N. MacCormick, "Der Rechtsstaat und die rule of law", *JuristenZeitung* (1984), pp. 65–70.

[12] *Introduction to the Problems of Legal Theory*. A Translation of the First Edition of the *Reine Rechtslehre* by B. Litschewski Paulson and S. L. Paulson (1992), p. 105.

institutions created for that very purpose. (A more accurate title of the present book would therefore have been "From *Rechtsstaat* and Rule of Law to Universal Law-State", but I have found it too clumsy a formulation for a book-title.)

I am certainly not claiming that ideas such as those mentioned are to be found exclusively in the Western tradition of legal thinking. We find similar ideas in, e.g., Chinese and Indian cultural traditions. However the respective traditions may differ, it is my intention in this monograph to present a clarification of universally applicable "Law-State" values.

In this connection I find it important to state explicitly that the present work is not a study in the history of ideas; it is a study in philosophical jurisprudence (or philosophy of law). My ambitions are of a clarifying nature and I am concerned with conceptual, not terminological problems.

The term "*law-state*", used as the title of this book, is a literal translation of the German word *Rechtsstaat*.[13] It is taken to cover a general set of ideas concerning the handling of legal orders, which are (i) based on what I called above "the classical Western tradition of legalism and values attached thereto" and (ii) claimed to be universally applicable. This set of ideas—constituting a universal conception of a law-state—is the subject of explication in this monograph.

In the current political and legal debate we often find references to ideas of the type mentioned. A proposed bill, for instance, is criticised for threatening the law-state by endangering legal certainty, or predictability ("*Rechtssicherheit*" in German) in society—whereupon adherents of the bill reply that, on the contrary, it strengthens the law-state by giving citizens a greater degree of legal security or equality before the law than they had had before. Some people even talk ominously about the decline here and there of the law-state in our time.

But what is the meaning of terms such as "law-state", "legal certainty", "legal security" and "equality before the law", and what kind of ideas are hidden behind the rather vague wording "the ideas (values, ideals) of the law-state"?

The purpose of this monograph is to analyse and cast into some order the fundamental conceptions tied to the word "law-state"—conceptions given visible expression in the legal dogmatic literature and in judicial reasoning, as well as in the political and general topical debate. We shall try to construct a general framework of thought which, if successful, enables us to deal with this cluster of interrelated ideas with greater perspicuity and consideration to nuances than is usually the case. In this endeavour we shall tread in the venerable footsteps of John Locke, who,

---

[13] I am well aware of the fact that the term "law-state" is not a common one at all—as a matter of fact, I have seen it used only once before, as a translation of, and together with, the German term "*der Rechtsstaat*", namely in S. Strömholm, *A Short History of Legal Thinking in the West* (1985), p. 195. However, I have found it suitable for my purposes not to identify altogether the set of ideas investigated in this essay with either the Rule of Law or the *Rechtsstaat* doctrines, although its core constitutes the essentials of both. The term "law-state" has been approved—and used—by N. MacCormick in *Questioning Sovereignty*, 1999, see p. 9, at note 12. See also N. MacCormick and R. Summers (eds.), *Interpreting Precedents. A Comparative Study*, 1997, p. 549.

according to a Swedish scholar, was able to "make already extant disparate fragments and isolated ideas crystallise, as it were, into a clear pattern".[14]

The ideas associated with the term "law-state" can be conceived of as a way of thinking—let us refer to it as *law-state thinking*. This thinking contains as components (i) evaluations qualifying certain states of affairs as (positive) values, (ii) normative principles aimed at the realisation of these values, (iii) arguments justifying these evaluations and principles, and (iv) conceptions of social reality on which such arguments are based. The evaluative component, however, forms the core of law-state thinking and lends to it its distinctive mark.

The values defended by law-state ideology are several in number, and they are mutually and closely related. Law-state thinking can be regarded as an amalgamation of distinct values clustered around one fundamental value, which we might call the nucleus of this kind of thinking: *that the individual enjoy legal protection against violations caused by the exercise of power on the part of the state* (*the Government, the public power*). The purpose of this monograph is to clarify this idea.

Historically, legal orders are older than states in Western societies. In Europe, the establishment of nation-states and their consolidation by a centralised power capable, to a large extent, of efficient control over its territory began in the Middle Ages and extended over half a millennium. But long before that, legal rules, even in statutory form, governed the lives of men and the courts of law (e.g., in the Germanic world the *Thing*) settled disputes between them. What was lacking was an efficient means of executing judgments—the winning party was reduced to self-help—as well as an efficient police force capable of preserving order. Today we live in the era of the nation-state. For millions of people the state is something taken for granted—the state is conceived as a "natural" political unit—and millions of people have lived—and died—for the purpose of subjecting their corner of the world to a state-organisation. Now, however, at the turn of the millennium, we might discern signs of a possible dissolution, or at least transformation, of the nation-state hegemony.[15] We have international, or supranational, organisations and state-transcending economic regions, as well as separatist movements within nation-states. But there are also tendencies in the opposite direction, not least with regard to such separatist movements: efforts to create new nation-states, more closely adapted to what is conceived as "a nation". Whether the nation-state will survive the next century or two is an open question. Law is, as I remarked above, older than the state, and it might well happen that law survives the state. In whatever shape *supreme* power will appear, though, it seems most likely that it will retain its "public" character (parliamentary assemblies, civil service agencies, military forces—all financed by general taxation), rather than a private nature (limited companies etc., financed by voluntary economic participation). However that may be, the basic idea of the law-state ideology is not likely to lose its importance in the future.

In its relation to law the state appears with a Janus-face. On the one hand, the state is a powerful resource in the service of law. Hobbes's social philosophy is based upon a philosophical anthropology, often (with a somewhat undue simplification)

[14] Strömholm, op. cit., p. 195.

[15] See N. MacCormick, *Questioning Sovereignty* (1999).

summarised in the slogan *homo hominis lupus*, and although this is certainly not the whole truth of mankind, it is a part of it and, from the viewpoint of the law, an important part at that.[16] The state provides law with an organisation capable, at best, of keeping peace among men and upholding order in society. Locke stresses the point that the single individual, however clearly he may be in the right, nevertheless cannot realise his right by his own strength alone. To achieve that purpose, he must have recourse to some collective body, i.e. the state.[17]

On the other hand, however, Locke more clearly than anyone before him has also discerned the other, darker face of the state: the state as an actual or potential abuser of law. The collective strength of the state, far stronger than the strength of a single individual, can be a frightful weapon against that single individual. *Res publica hominis lupus*.

The state—that is a lesson of the twentieth century—can become a machine aimed at mass murder, as it was in the hands of Hitler, Lenin, Stalin and Mao, as well as Nicolae Ceausescu, Deng Xiaoping, Idi Amin, Ayatollah Khomeini, Pol Pot, Hendrik Verwoerd, Saddam Hussein and Kim Il-sung. But to reject for this reason the idea of the state altogether would, of course, be a foolish thing to do. The state has also provided no small part of the world's population with a degree of education, health and security unknown earlier in the history of mankind, without making most people less free than before, but rather the opposite, as is the case in the democratic welfare-states—that is still another lesson of the twentieth century. But these two faces of the state are not distinct phenomena. They can appear as a kind of double exposure of the same face, the bright face of the state borrowing features of its darker side. The values of law-state thinking do not dwell in a protected garden in any place; they can be violated to a greater or lesser extent anywhere.

The purpose of legal orders—or, rather, the goal aimed at by the handling of legal orders—is often said to be that of settling disputes, preserving order (very generally speaking: to protect individual human beings from their fellow-beings and groups of such) and of organising co-operation among men. This purpose is something outside the legal order itself—the latter being a means of obtaining the former.

Law-state thinking, however, works on another level than that of this general purpose of legal orders. It focuses not on that purpose but on the very handling of the legal orders by their functionaries—that is, not on the goals but on the means. The law-state ideology is about protection of individuals from *the threat which lies in the very existence of legal orders* (and states, as their organs). Law-state thinking is directed against *abuse of legal orders by their own functionaries*. If there were no legal orders, the law-state thinking would not be necessary and, would be, indeed, meaningless.

With this in mind, we can formulate two fundamental tasks for legal functionaries (i.e., legislators, draftsmen, judges, advocates, prosecutors, policemen, etc.) operating in a "law-state":

(1) To contribute to achieving the general purpose of legal orders.

---

[16] T. Hobbes, *Leviathan* (1651).

[17] J. Locke, *Two Treatises of Government*. The Second Treatise (1689).

(2) In so doing, to adhere to the values of the law-state.

Now, a common justification, even in honest societies, for violations of (2) is that otherwise one would not fulfil (1) in an efficient manner. Since arguments of that kind often are persuasive on the face of it, there is all the more reason to be observant when such arguments are adduced.

The law-state is threatened not only by the ill-disposed. Its values can, indeed, also be violated by the thoughtless, the ignorant, the unfeeling, the naïve, the over-reacting, the prejudiced and those playing on prejudice, the obsessed and the far too benevolent.

The central claim of law-state thinking can be formulated thus: Upholding civilisation shall be achieved by civilised means.

Chapter 2
Legal Orders

2.1 Introduction

Since law-state thinking deals with the abuse of legal orders, it is no doubt called upon to explicate, at least roughly, our notion of "legal order" before we proceed with an analysis of the ways in which the law-state ideology concerns itself with legal orders.

Allow me, right at the outset, to make an important remark concerning the use of the term "legal order". In everyday language, and in legal practice, it is often used in the sense of "legal directive" or "legal command". In jurisprudence, however, it is not infrequently used in a more general way, where it is understood as roughly comparable to "legal system". This becomes apparent in such uses as "the legal order of Scotland". In some instances the two terms, "legal order" and "legal system", are used more or less synonymously, in other instances legal orders are regarded as a species of legal system or as something closely related to that. In this book, as you will see, I treat legal systems as integral parts of legal orders.

I regard legal orders as abstract entities, created by men. They are products of human culture, not something inherent in human or extra-human "nature". I profess a humanistic conception of legal orders. More precisely, I see them as inter-personal structures of normative ideas, maintaining their temporal permanence through language. Like other human ideas, legal ideas and, hence, legal orders can be morally good or bad. Indeed, if they could not be bad, the law-state ideas would be superfluous. This conception of legal orders belongs to the family of positivistic theories of law.

I also regard legal orders as instruments for achieving goals outside the legal orders themselves. Legal orders have many and varied social functions. These instruments are handled by professional functionaries of various kinds. The relationship between a legal order and the juridical handling of it is a highly complex phenomenon. One might, of course, deny that there are such things as abstract legal orders at all, looking upon "law" as a certain kind of practice, or certain type of behaviour. However, although legal behaviour—both that of the public and that of the functionaries—is, after all, what really matters, this conception of law is, in my opinion, an over-simplification. Legal behaviour is idea-governed behaviour and

Å. Frändberg, *From Rechtsstaat to Universal Law-State,* Law and Philosophy Library 109,
DOI 10.1007/978-3-319-06784-1_2, © Springer International Publishing Switzerland 2014

the explanatory component of law and legal life is not legal behaviour but the very ideas guiding it. These ideas exclusively are what make law law. No doubt it is true that, when looking upon legal orders as separate and discernable entities, we ascend to a very high and lofty level of abstraction. But in order to formulate a satisfactory "general conception of law" we inevitably have to reach this level of abstraction.

Legal orders can be studied from many different points of view. The main task of legal science is of course to study them from the point of view of their *content*. The study of the law-content (i.e., *the law*) is in the first place the task of legal dogmatics (civil law, criminal law, procedural law, etc., also including comparative studies in these fields).

But legal orders can also be studied on a more general and "formal" level than can legal dogmatics. The most basic branch of legal science is *the ontology of legal orders*: what kind of entities are they (or, rather, their elements)? Closely related to the ontology of legal orders is *the morphology of legal orders*: which elements constitute a legal order, which is the logical structure of the different kinds of norms forming such elements and which are the legal-technical relationships between the different elements (a question closely connected to the logical question)?[1]

The clarification of conceptions related to legal orders in operation, i.e., how they influence the public and how their functionaries handle them, belongs to the *praxeology of legal orders*. Within praxeology, legal orders are studied in the social context in which they function. Praxeological concepts are concepts about *the handling of legal orders* by the general public as well as by the legal functionaries.

Praxeology, on its part, is based upon certain more basic ideas concerning the general goals of legal orders. The study of these foundations of praxeology belongs to *the teleology of legal orders*.

In Sect. 2.2 I shall present an outline of some basic ideas in the fields of the morphology and ontology of legal orders and in Sect. 2.3 ideas in the fields of praxeology and teleology.

2.2 Some Morphological and Ontological Points of View

I regard the concept of an (advanced) *legal order*, *LO*, as a (binary) relation *LO(N,O)* (i.e., a set of ordered couples {<*N,O*>}) between a set of norms (legal rules), *N*, and an organisation (a set of legal positions), *O*, such that

(i) norms of *N* constitute *O*
(ii) the function of *O* is (mainly) to handle (create, apply, execute) norms of *N*, i.e., it is the task of the functionaries of *O* to handle norms of *N*
(iii) the function of *N*, in its totality, is to regulate, by the handling of *N* by functionaries in *O*, social life in its fundamental parts and in a comprehensive way

[1] Å. Frändberg, "Morphological levels as a tool for the general study of law", in *Justice, Morality and Society. A tribute to Aleksander Peczenik on the occasion of his 60th birthday 16 November 1997*, A. Aarnio, R. Alexy, G. Bergholtz, eds. (1997), pp. 147–158.

(iv) some part of *O* (i.e., some organs within the organisation system *O*) has the function of settling disputes among persons in accordance with norms in *N* and to take a standpoint to alleged non-compliance with obligations or prohibitions in *N* (i.e., courts of law)

(v) some part of *O* has the function to impose and execute sanctions (punishment, damages, etc.) on persons under certain conditions, stated by *N*, as the ultimate resource for obtaining the goals of the rules of *N*.

A legal system is any such set, *N*, of norms.

A legal norm is any member, *n*, of a legal system.

A legal organisation is any such organisation (or constellation of organisations), *O*. As being a special set of legal positions, *O*, as well as *N*, has a normative character (see below). *A particular legal order* (e.g., the Swedish legal order), then, is a legal order-relation holding between a certain system of norms and a certain organisation. The nature of this relationship is roughly indicated by clauses (i)–(v).

The study of *legal systems* from the formal viewpoint of structure and technical function is primarily a concern of general jurisprudence, and has been so since Bentham and Austin laid the foundations of that discipline.[2] Examples of such morphological analyses of legal systems are Merkl's and Kelsen's genetic-hierarchical *Stufenbau*[3], Hart's distinction between primary and secondary rules (and within the latter category between rule(s) of recognition, rules of change, and rules of adjudication), the discerning of norms of competence (or power-conferring rules) as a separate norm-type[4] and the distinction between rules and principles.[5] Most legal theorists (myself included) are, I think, of the opinion that any entity being an integral part of a legal system in the last analysis has a normative character (although there are certain divergencies of opinion concerning permissions, statutory definitions and principles). It might therefore be justifiable to regard all members of legal systems as (different kinds of) norms.

The nature and make-up of *legal organisations*, and the requirements that the law-state ideology lays down on them, will be dealt with in further detail in Chap. 9. Let me here just briefly hint at what I have in mind when I talk about legal organisations.

In a society that has a legal order—or, in other words, in a legally organised society—there are certain typical bodies (authorities, but also private institutions) which are to be found in every (advanced) legal order: courts of law, legislative bodies, police, prosecutors, advocates, etc.[6] They all belong to the legal organisation

---

[2] J. Bentham, *Of Laws in General*, ed. H.L.A. Hart, (1970), J. Austin, *The Province of Jurisprudence Determined and the Uses of the Study of Jurisprudence*, ed. H.L.A. Hart (1954).

[3] A.J. Merkl, "Prolegomena einer Theorie des rechtlichen Stufenbaus", in *Gesellschaft, Staat und Recht*. Festschrift für Kelsen (1931), pp. 252–294. H. Kelsen, *General Theory of Law and State* (1945), *Reine Rechtslehre*, 2nd ed. (1960).

[4] A. Ross, *On Law and Justice* (1958), H.L.A. Hart, *The Concept of Law* (1961), J. Raz, *The Concept of a Legal System* (1970).

[5] R. Dworkin, *Taking Rights Seriously* (revised ed., 1978).

[6] Cf. M.P. Golding, *Philosophy of Law* (1975), ch. 1.

of that society. But also a parliamentary assembly, a government, and administrative authorities are parts of the legal organisation (in a wider sense), since they are constituted by legal norms. The state belongs to, and is the main constituent of, the legal organisation.

What, then, is the ontological status of such "bodies"?

Legal systems fulfil their social tasks by creating normative relations between individuals. An individual standing in some such relationship to another individual is in *a legal position* (towards that other).[7] Such legal positions, or relationships, are, e.g.:

(a) *A* has the obligation to pay rent to *B*
(b) *C* is married to *D*
(c) *E* owns the cow Rosita
(d) Judge *F* shall sentence *G* to imprisonment.

The relationship between legal positions and legal norms is a deductive one.[8] Sentences about legal positions are deduced from (perhaps unstated) sentences expressing legal norms in conjunction with sentences about certain operative facts, e.g.:

Example (a')

(1) Anyone who rents a house has an obligation to pay rent on the day of maturity
(2) *A* rents a house from *B* and the day of maturity has arrived
(3) Thus: *A* has the obligation to pay rent to *B*.

Example (b')

(1) Anyone who has completed a marriage ceremony [along with certain other operative facts] is married
(2) *C* and *D* have together completed a marriage ceremony [along with such operative facts]
(3) Thus: *C* is married to *D*.

Example (c')

(1) Anyone who has bought a thing [along with certain other operative facts] owns that thing
(2) *E* has bought the cow Rosita [along with such operative facts]
(3) Thus: *E* owns the cow Rosita.

Example (d')

(1) Any judge who finds the defendant guilty of theft shall sentence him to imprisonment
(2) Judge *F* finds the defendant *G* guilty of theft
(3) Thus: Judge *F* shall sentence *G* to imprisonment.

In example (d'), then, judge *F* stands in the normative relation (is in the legal position) vis-à-vis *G* that *F* shall sentence *G* to imprisonment.

[7] For a thorough analysis of legal positions, see L. Lindahl, *Position and Change* (1977).

[8] Cf. H.L.A. Hart, "Definition and Theory in Jurisprudence" (70 *Law Quarterly Review*, 1954).

The main component of a legal organisation is public *authorities* of different kinds. An authority is, as I see it, a system of legal positions (juridico-normative relations)—just as the relationship between a seller and a buyer or a husband and his wife (i.e., a marriage) are systems of legal positions. In the case of authorities, the position-holders are that special kind of individual we call *officials*. *A legal organisation* is (or, at least, includes) an ordered set of official legal positions.

I regard norms as a kind of abstract entities (ideas, or thought-contents). Legal positions, including authorities, have the same ontological quality as norms, deductively derived, as they are, from legal norms.

Two important features concerning authorities shall be pointed out already here.

1. Authorities are not the only products of legal systems. There are others, e.g., limited companies and marriages. I am well aware of the fact that, in practice, it is not difficult to distinguish the marriage between Mr. and Mrs. Jones from the local sanitary authority—but how shall we draw the line between authorities and other products of a legal system as a matter of principle?

As far as I can see, the difference lies in the fact that authorities are *obligatory* according to a given legal system. There are norms in the system stating, or at least presupposing, that certain bodies shall exist—e.g., the Stockholm Court of Appeal, the Swedish Government or Uppsala University, according to the Swedish legal system—while, on the other hand, this is not the case with respect to limited companies and marriages. The legal system does not state, or presuppose, that such entities *shall* in fact exist. It only states that if persons want to create them, this must be done according to rules in the legal system.

2. Authorities are, as a rule, *institutions*. By an institution I mean, roughly, an organisation such that individuals can be replaced by other individuals as position-holders in it without any change in the identity of the organisation.[9]

So, when we say that norms of *N* constitute *O*, we mean that the legal positions which together form *O* are deduced from norms in *N*. On the other hand, position-holders in *O*—people of flesh and blood—create, remove, change, interpret and administer norms in *N*, or give advice to persons on how to act given the existence of *N*—in short, they *all handle norms of N* (in that way *maintaining the legal order*). In more developed legal orders we can discern different kinds of position-holders, with corresponding separate professional roles. This fact is of utmost importance from the viewpoint of realising the values of the law-state ideology.

The clauses (iii)–(v) in our characterisation of the concept "legal order" are justified by the following considerations.

Clause (iii), which states that legal systems have, as it were, general social ambitions—their norms, taken together, regulate social life as a whole and constitute a kind of framework for it—has the function of excluding from the class of legal orders, on the one hand moral systems, and on the other social orders such as trade unions, religious communions (churches) or the Mafia. Certain difficult borderline cases may appear, but that gives us no reason to despair: we can never draw sharp lines of demarcation around social concepts of such a high degree of abstraction as, e.g., "legal order".

[9] It should be obvious that my concept "institution" is something completely different from the concept named by the same term in N. MacCormick and O. Weinberger, *An Institutional Theory of Law. New Approaches to Legal Positivism* (1986).

Clause (iv) makes the existence of courts of law (or bodies with essentially the same functions) a necessary component of legal orders. Surely, one can imagine social orders satisfying clause (iii) but not clause (iv); such orders would be a kind of legislative-administrative orders, and in societies organised by such orders the rule of law may well be applicable to a large degree. But one might argue that, for a social order to be a genuine *legal* order, some kind of institution trying disputes and alleged non-compliance with the social norms, which institution is distinct from, and independent of, other, purely administrative authorities, must be a necessary ingredient of a legal order. On the other hand, clause (iv) cannot be a sufficient condition for a social order to be a legal order; also the Mafia may have its special "courts of law" (cf. the medieval *Feme*-courts).

A social order lacking a mechanism of sanctions (clause (v)) is little more than institutionalised morality. As a last resource legal orders resort to force and violence, and that is a characteristic feature of them. It also seems strange to imagine the existence of courts of law without a mechanism of sanctions attached to them.

Clauses (i) and (ii) can be said to define a concept of "social order", while clauses (iii)–(v) state the additional conditions necessary for distinguishing legal orders from other social orders.

The reason why it is justifiable to lay down both (iii) and (iv) as necessary conditions for something to be a legal order is of a historical nature. Legal orders, such as they have developed in the Occidental world, are a joining of two, somewhat different social functions: *adjudication*, aimed at "solving" individual cases, and *legislation*, aimed at regulating society in its entirety, ideally without any adjudicative interference at all. In former times, these two functions were not separated from each other but pursued, both of them, by bodies like the Germanic *Thing*. Later in the development of the legal organisation the two functions are to a large extent—though to a greater or lesser degree in different countries—separated from each other and pursued by different bodies within the legal organisation. But whether or not this separation has taken place, there is a genuine difference between the two functions and they might even conflict. This built-in tension within legal orders is of a special interest from the viewpoint of law-state thinking.

Conceived in this way, legal orders are abstract objects: intersubjective systems of ideas, structured normative thought-contents (or meaning-contents) and as such artefacts, products of human culture, usually constructed and amended by a collective effort often ranging over a very long period of time.

A legal order, so defined, can function (be at work) in a society, *S*, at a given time, *t*, and thus be the valid law of *S* at *t*; or a legal order may have been valid law during some past period of time but is no longer valid, e.g., classical Roman law, whose rules are no longer applied and whose authorities, e.g., the praetor, no longer function; or legal orders can be programmes, projects for the future, drafted by official legislators or, why not, by yourself in your study, and thus no valid legal orders now (or ever). Not all legal orders are valid legal orders. Hence, the existence and the validity of legal orders are two different things. Existence is a matter of ontology, validity a matter of praxeology.

2.3 Some Praxeological and Teleological Points of View

Legal orders are not ends in themselves. They are, ultimately, means for ends outside the legal orders themselves. They are instruments pure and simple, and their handling is a kind of technique. In stating this I join those who have an *instrumental* (teleological, finalistic) view on legal orders.[10] For a legal theorist with this standpoint, it is an urgent task to analyse, on a general level, the ways in which this instrument is handled and functions, and to evaluate its fitness as an instrument for achieving the goals which it is supposed to achieve.

Legal orders are designed for certain functions. But one thing is to have a function, another to be actually functioning. Valid legal orders are tools at work, legal orders as such mere tools—just as the hammer in the cupboard has a function but the hammer in the hand of the carpenter in addition to that also functions.

Like other instruments, legal orders can be misused. In order to avoid this, some juridico-ethical restrictions must be laid down with respect to the handling of a legal order by its functionaries. Law-state thinking puts forward some such restrictions. Its principles are, logically, situated on a meta-level in relation to the law—or, if they are incorporated in the legal system, to the rest of the law. By regarding legal orders as instruments which can be dangerous, sometimes deadly dangerous, weapons in the wrong hands, the importance of law-state thinking stands out all the more clearly. The existence of a valid legal order in a society is not at all in itself a guarantee for the protection of individual freedom or security in that society.

When we regard legal orders in their relations to social reality, i.e., how they are *handled* in differerent respects, we lay *a praxeological aspect* on them; those relations are *praxeological relations* and the concepts we use to characterise them are *praxeological concepts*.

In order to articulate ideas concerning praxeological matters, four concepts seem to be necessary and, hence, basic praxeological concepts:[11]

(1) A legal order, *LO*, *is expedient* in relation to a set of goals, *G*, if and only if it is suitable as a means for achieving *G*
(2) *LO is realised* if and only if it is on the whole observed (followed) by the public
(3) *LO is efficacious* if and only if it is (i) expedient, and (ii) realised
(4) *LO is valid* if and only if it is on the whole observed by its functionaries (judges, prosecutors, lawyers, policemen, legislators etc.), when brought to the fore.

Legal orders function as instruments mainly by directing human behaviour. A legal order is an action-oriented idea system. To any legal order, *LO*, corresponds a set of human actions, A_{LO}, such that A_{LO} *is the realisation of LO* (A_{LO} is the set of adequate

[10] I have found ideas concerning the ontology and instrumental character of law very similar to my own in P. Amselek, "Le droit dans les esprits", in *Controverses autour de l'ontologie du droit*, ed. P. Amselek and C. Grzegorczyk (1989), pp. 27–49.

[11] Cf. Å. Frändberg, "Some Aspects on Rationality in Legislation", in *Juristische Logik, Rationalität und Irrationalität im Recht*, eds. A.-J. Arnaud, R. Hilpinen, J. Wróblewski, *Rechtstheorie*, Beiheft 8 (1985), pp. 123–137, at pp. 129–134.

actions by which *LO* "is fulfilled"). "Law in action" is idea-guided behaviour of legal functionaries and the public. The study of normatively determined actions within the legal sphere, and the interrelations between such actions and the legal order, belongs to the praxeology of legal orders.

A tacitly implied presupposition (or ideal) is that if *LO* is realized by A_{LO}, the social goals (purposes) of *LO*—or, rather, the social state of affairs, G_{LO}, such that these goals are fulfilled in them—will be achieved as well; either because A_{LO} is identical with, or includes, G_{LO} or because some state of affairs which includes A_{LO} causes some other state of affairs which includes G_{LO}. Of course a legal order can exist even if it is not realised (to any degree).

But this tacitly implied ideal might surely turn out to be false (not achieved). It might well be, as a matter of empirical fact, that some rules of *LO*—$r_1, \ldots, r_n$—are realized by actions $a_1, \ldots, a_n$ but their goals, $g_1, \ldots, g_n$, are not achieved. In such a case, *LO* cannot be said to be effective as an instrument. Nor is *LO* effective, however expedient it is, if it is not on the whole observed by the public subject to it.

Legal orders function as an instrument to a high degree through linguistic behaviour. Legally adequate action consists very often, not to say usually, in the use of (oral or written) language. Disputes are settled legally by words, not by violence. In a law-state violence is monopolised by the state (with a few exceptions, such as self-defence) and is used only as a last resort and in forms stipulated in advance. Apart from that, legal orders preserve peace in society mainly by the help of linguistic behaviour. And many socially important legal positions—contractual relationships, marriages, private and public institutions—are created, changed and, to a certain degree, also extinguished, not by muscular activites or natural events, like death, but by performative utterances. Performatives play a crucial role in legal behaviour and "law in action" cannot, in fact, be properly understood without a thorough analysis of performative legal language.

A necessary condition, in practice, for a legal order to be realised is that it is valid. For if its functionaries do not do their job, it is highly unlikely, at least in the long run, that the public, on its part, will adhere to law. This puts the legal functionaries at the centre of the legal endeavour and gives them a decisive role there.

Legal orders can be more or less "juridicalised". A legal order is juridicalised when its organisation is manned by professional functionaries, especially when they are academically educated and trained in law faculties, law schools and the like. The "juridicalisation" of legal orders in Europe had a break-through with the revival of the *Corpus Juris* and the scholarly study of it in the twelfth century and onwards. The classical Roman legal order was to a high degree a juridicalised one, while the legal order of ancient Athens was not. There the borderline between politics and legal activity was not yet marked out in a more thorough way. In a juridicalised legal order, more or less elaborated juridical techniques (principles and methods of interpretation and other kinds of argumentation) were developed in the course of time. In theory, a completely non-juridicalised legal order—a functioning legal order without professional lawyers—is perfectly possible. But the development in the Occidental world has been towards an increasing division of labour and professional specialisation within its legal orders—that is, towards a greater juridicalisation. Diverse, specified legal roles have crystallised: the role of the judge, the advocate, the prosecutor, the draftsman of statutes, the jurist (legal dogmatist), etc.

A valid legal order is composed of a very close relation between the four phenomena *legal norm, legal position, legal role* and *legal argument*. This relationship can, indeed, be seen as the main characterisation of any valid legal order. Legal norms create legal positions, some of which, viz. the authorities, are manned by professionals with certain functions within the legal order. Such functions contribute to the development of certain professional traditions, or roles. These roles, on their part, influence the style of argumentation among the functionaries acting in them. And, to close the circle, through legal argumentation legal norms are created, changed, repealed, interpreted, used analogically, and so on. The argumentative intercourse with the law is considerable; the law allows itself freely to be influenced by argumentation.[12] And this is perfectly in line with the fundamental peace-keeping function of legal orders: ideally, arguments, not stones, are what counts.

What is, then, in general terms, the relation between legal orders and judicial processes of thought?

"Valid law" may mean two different things:

(i) It might be used as an elliptic expression referring to certain people's acting according to a system of normative ideas.
(ii) It might refer to such an actually functioning system of normative ideas itself.

(iii) is a more abstract notion and the one I refer to in this essay by the term "valid legal order". A valid legal order is "an objectification of" a set of normative ideas guiding juridical behaviour. This objectification brings about a certain order among the disparate legal phenomena and *provides us with a general framework of legal thought*, which in practice is a necessary condition for interpersonal legal communication over space and time.

Legal orders—or, more precisely, the thought-content of legal orders (*the law*)—are integral parts of legal thinking. That is apparent in two respects:

(a) Legal orders are products of collective legal thinking.
(b) Portions of legal orders are components of individual processes of legal thinking.

A legal order is a latent mass of normative ideas from which portions can be mobilised and incorporated in the thought process of some judicial functionary. Pieces of a legal order may be the starting-point of a certain process of thought, but such pieces may also enter into the course of such a process. They may also be a result of a legal thought process. In that case, the result may involve a change of the legal order in question. The analogy between a hammer and a valid legal order as an instrument breaks down, as we see: the valid legal order is not a thing, separate from its use, but an entity created by abstraction from the behaviour of "the users". The concept "legal order" *simpliciter* (i.e., valid or non-valid legal orders) is, in its turn,

---

[12] For a painstaking discussion of the arguable character of law and its relation to the rule of law see N. MacCormick, *Rhetoric and the Rule of Law* (2005).

an abstraction from the concept "valid legal order". Legal life is idea-guided behaviour, and a legal order *simpliciter* is a set of normative ideas such that it is logically qualified to become a valid legal order. Legal orders *simpliciter* are legal phenomena which "transcend" the behaviour of individual human beings—their existence is independent of particular human beings and their actions.

One important consequence of the juridicalisation of legal orders is that legal thinking (legal argumentation) itself has been a subject of debate and normative regulation. Already in the medieval law schools methodological programmes were formulated and discussed and that medieval tradition, by way of, e.g., Savigny's *canones*, still continues. The scientific study of such programmes may be regarded as a meta-discipline of the praxeology of legal orders, viz. *the methodology of legal orders*. This discipline is of utmost importance from the viewpoint of law-state thinking since that thinking has distinct requirements when it comes to the methodological programmes.

If we have an instrumental view of legal orders, a highly important task for general jurisprudence is, of course, to discern and classify the goals which legal orders, typically, are designed for. The branch of general jurisprudence which deals with this task I refer to as *the teleology of legal orders*.[13,14]

Now, it might seem to be a totally impossible task to give an account of all the various uses men make, and have made over the centuries, of the legal instrument. Legal orders are, indeed, both powerful and highly flexible instruments—with respect both to their intended and their unintended consequences—and in these qualities are embedded its greatest advantages as well as its most perilous disadvantages. Legal orders can be used to maintain peace among members of society, organise men in the task of cultivating land, developing industry and taking care of children and old people. They can also be used, and have indeed been used, to keep people in misery and slavery, harass individuals, limit freedom of speech and hold witch-trials and legal proceedings against pigs, hens, dogs and oxen, before sentencing them to capital punishment.[15] Legal orders surely are chameleon-like phenomena.

However, I find it justified to distinguish between *perpetual* and *variable functions of legal orders*. The latter are those functions for which legislators and others from time to time choose to use the legal orders at hand. The perpetual function, on the other hand, is a function more closely connected with legal orders as such. Since my view on the perpetual function of legal orders has some bearing upon my view on law-state thinking, some words about it might be appropriate.

---

[13] Cf. J. Raz, "The Functions of Law", in J. Raz, *The Authority of Law* (1979), Ch. 9 (first published in A.W.B. Simpson (ed.), *Oxford Essays in Jurisprudence*, 2nd series (1973)).

[14] When reading literature within the field of general analytical jurisprudence, or philosophy of law, or listening to speakers lecturing in this field, I have developed a habit of diagnosing what is discussed by means of the following 7-piece typology of problems—(i) ontological, (ii) morphological, (iii) teleological, (iv) praxeological, (v) methodological, (vi) ideological (evaluative) and (vii) epistemological problems—which, I have noticed, helps a bit. While methodology has a meta-character in relation to praxeology, ideology has a meta-character in relation to both praxeology and methodology. The present essay is, on the whole, a study in the ideology of legal orders. Epistemology has, by its very nature, a meta-character in relation to each of (i)—(vi).

[15] See E.P. Evans, *The Criminal Prosecution and Capital Punishment of Animals* (1906).

Legal orders have emerged as an attempt to set bounds to the use of unhampered violence among men. The ways of achieving this goal have been to regulate and, later in legal history, monopolise violence, and to provide society with peaceful means for settling disputes, keeping order and organising cooperation, as an alternative to violent means. The peace-keeping function is the constant, perpetual function of legal orders. In more developed legal orders, the decrease of violence gives pride of place to reason and argument. In their design for maintaining peace and order, and doing so *by peaceful means*, lies the main civilising value of legal orders. This shows itself, *inter alia*, in the following four respects.

(1) Monopoly of violence—which, indeed, can be a fatal threat against individuals—can, however, also be a motive for, and a means of *controlling violence*, i.e., controlling the state's own use of violence. This can be achieved by statutory regulations stating the conditions under which violence is allowed to be used and by sanctions directed towards transgressors of these regulations. Most important in this respect—at least in times of peace—is the regulation of state violence exercised as *punishment*. The state's monopoly of punishment is contained in its monopoly of violence as a whole.

The justification of punishment and the justification of a state monopoly of punishment are, as I see it, inseparable issues.

The often intense hatred and desire for revenge on the part of the victim of an assault, fraud or theft, would inevitably lead to an escalation of violence in society, if given free rein. Punishment through state organs supplies society with the means to replace private vengeance by "organised revenge". Take away criminal sanctions, decided and executed exclusively by the state, and people and groups of people would inevitably begin to take the law into their own hands. Violence would become severe and out of control.

To base a justification of punishment on this fact does not imply adherence to a primitive retributivism. Mental states of the kind just mentioned, when not driven to extremes, are neither anti-social nor "bad". Such mental dispositions may even be in our genes. Members of society, who are not themselves victims of crime, but are informed of crimes by mass media or otherwise, are also widely captured by such feelings out of compassion with the victims. Closely akin to such a vicarious desire for revenge is the deeply rooted idea among men that no one shall profit from his own wrong. And if people, on a large scale, actually were to profit from criminal deeds, the morality (or social discipline) in society would be in serious danger and the law of the jungle close at hand. To *punish* criminals in order to *improve* them is, on the whole, a futile business. Totally different means, indeed, are needed for that task. In fact punitive measures often, not to say regularly, conflict with measures aimed at improving the culprit, and have to be balanced against them. The only reason for punishing criminals is, in my opinion, that in so doing we uphold the morals of the law-abiding citizens by preventing profit from one's own wrongdoing—or, which amounts to about the same thing, by revenge. Seeing others get away with, and profit from, criminal deeds on a large scale would sooner or later erode the willingness of the ordinary member of society to adhere to the law himself, and would increase the temptation, on his part, to break the law for his own gain. This, in turn, would make society more exposed to violence.

To the extent that punishment has such a deterrent effect, it is a device for preserving peace by peaceful means.

With this conception of the rationale of punishment, the state monopoly of punishment can be justified by the following considerations. By means of punishment through state organs, unhampered blood-shed might be stemmed. By means of official punishment, humanitarian values and rational considerations concerning, e.g., different degrees of criminal seriousness, the culprit's youth or state of mind, and (general or individual) prevention can be balanced against claims for revenge. In short: By channelling revenge through official punishment, violence might be reduced and submitted to humanitarian values and rational argumentation. Even a very rude *lex talionis* (e.g., *Lev*. xxiv. 20) performed in its time this peace-keeping function by restraining the unhampered use of blood-feud.

But let us, on the other hand, never forget that the misuse of the administration of criminal justice (sanctions and other coercive measures) is one of the most efficient means of terrorising individuals in the hands of the ill-disposed powers that be (of which more will be said in Chap. 8).

(2) The invention of the judicial process (civil as well as criminal), no doubt one of the most valuable social inventions ever made, is a big step forward in the direction of replacement of violence by argument. Ideally, access to an examination of what has happened by an impartial judge, where each party has his say, and opportunity to argue in one's own cause, all before a court of law, with the observance of dignified forms, and in front of the public—and the menace to be subject to such a procedure—all this is likely to reduce the temptation to resort to violent means. Arguments, not stones…

(3) More developed legal orders have built-in devices for changes, based on argumentation, *of the legal orders themselves*. In the institutional forms of legislation and adjudication, legal rules may be submitted to expert advice and rational discussion *ex ante* (especially with respect to legal orders based on statutory law), and to rational critical exposure *ex post*. Inhuman or irrational rules can be modified or repealed altogether, and the system of rules as a whole can be subject to rational control. In this way society can adjust itself to changing economic and social conditions by peaceful means.

(4) In order to survive, men have to rely upon each other, especially in modern, multi-cultural mass societies where people are daily involved in transactions with complete strangers. Two reasons for the belief that legal orders are universally passable are that they can be constructed in a relatively culture-neutral manner and that they are workable on a minimal level of ethical standard. A working legal order designed to diminish private use of violence, but which itself uses coercive means against law-breakers and contract-breakers as a last resource, is a prominent factor in creating conditions for *mutual confidence* among people in their dealings with each other. There is an obvious connection between mutual confidence and peace in society. In the same way as pun-

ishment, civil sanctions are peace-preserving, and are so largely by peaceful means. A working legal order upholds a law-abiding morality in society at large.

In my opinion, then, legal orders—with all their imperfections—are the hitherto best-known instrument for upholding peace and order in (national or international) multi-cultural mass societies. However, there are alternatives—each of them with its own particular advantages and drawbacks. Modern legal orders have, in fact, emerged, or borrowed a great deal, from some of them. The most important of these alternatives are

(i) interpersonal control, which is workable only in very small communities;
(ii) religious orders, of which no one is universally adhered to;
(iii) terror, which is too high a price for peace;
(iv) military regimes, which have the sword but lack the balance;
(v) mandarin justice, i.e., justice administered ad hoc by sages—who are, perhaps, not always that wise, unbiased or consistent;
(vi) negotiations, which often lack both the balance (the stronger never loses) and the sword;
(vii) mental influence, by education, propaganda or social therapy—as we all know, a sometimes very dangerous instrument in the hand of the fanatic, the unscrupulous or the merely naive.

The close connection between this view on the perpetual function of a legal order and the basic idea of law-state thinking is obvious, and no one has formulated it better than John Locke. If the perpetual function of legal orders is to restrain and control the use of violence, so much the worse for the citizens if *the state itself*, having a monopoly of such use, indulges in violent deeds under no restrictions and control. To think that men would wish such a state of affairs, Locke says, "is to think that Men are so foolish that they take care to avoid what Mischiefs may be done them by *Pole-Cats*, or *Foxes*, but are content, nay think it Safety, to be devoured by *Lions*".[16] *The perpetual function of legal orders cannot be properly fulfilled unless the fundamental law-state principle is strictly adhered to.*

In Western societies, legal orders have been the traditional instrument for preserving peace and order within *a community; a community governed by law* has been the ideal community. In such a society, the state (or whatever we call supreme social power) plays the role of guarantor of peace. But we cannot trust that guarantor without reservations. A state claiming monopoly of violence can be deadly dangerous in its own use of violence against the disarmed. In addition to a community governed by law, we urgently need *a state governed by law*, a law-state. Peace is, indeed, the most basic of social values, but far better than the kind of peace reigning in a penitentiary house is a peace compatible with a life of human dignity. Therefore, we are justified in assessing that the two (highly interrelated) main tasks of legal orders are peace and power restriction.

[16] J. Locke, *Two Treatises of Government*. The Second Treatise (93), (1689).

Chapter 3
Prolegomena to the Clarification of Law-State Thinking

3.1 Introduction

The answer, then, to the question about the nature of the relationship between law-state thinking on the one hand, and the legal order and its handling on the other, can be formulated in a general manner as follows.

Law-state thinking is in a way a political "ideology", viz., an "ideology" for those in public power—politicians and officials. But without the participation of professional lawyers in exercising authority and in the process of legislation, the realisation of the law-state values probably comes to very little. Hence, law-state thinking is, in the first place, a concern for lawyers; it is *a juridical ideology*, making claims on how lawyers shall carry on their technical-juridical activities. Lawyers shall see to it that the law-state values are realised when they handle the legal orders they are set to handle. On the other hand, law-state thinking has no direct claims on private citizens, the public.

So the touchstone of whether the law-state values are realised or not in a given society is ultimately the legal order itself and the handling of it. By examining the legal rules—statutory or such embedded in precedents—and the relationship between the legal rules and the actual exercise of authority, we ascertain whether the law-state values are realised or not. In other words, the law-state principles form together a kind of *standard* by which we judge the legal order and the handling of it by the legal functionaries.

Law-state thinking is a product of Western culture, just as secular, "juridicalised" legal orders themselves are products of Western culture. However, it is of the utmost importance when dealing with some doctrine (a scientific theory, a philosophical system, a normative ideology) to distinguish between, on the one hand, the doctrine as such, and on the other, the historical circumstances which cause the appearance of the doctrine in question. The tenability of a scientific theory is, of course, completely independent of the history of its origin, and in the same way the universal applicability of an ethical doctrine is independent of its historical background. The very point of a *moral* attitude towards certain values, to which one adheres, is, indeed, that one regard those values as universal, i.e., applicable to all human beings. The assertion that, e.g., the burning of widows or the circumcision of women

Å. Frändberg, *From Rechtsstaat to Universal Law-State,* Law and Philosophy Library 109, DOI 10.1007/978-3-319-06784-1_3, © Springer International Publishing Switzerland 2014

is something morally evil means that such things are evil wherever they are found. Thus, the objection raised by the platitudinous "cultural tolerance" to the effect that such a morality is no more than a manifestation of a parochial Western idea, and that you are guilty of "cultural imperialism" if you do not take into consideration, say, Indian or African cultural tradition in the sphere of life in question, is from the viewpoint of ethics completely irrelevant and lacking in all value as an ethical argument. (After all, every existing idea must have come into existence somewhere). Would anybody regard as particularly intelligent an argument given by, say, an educated Chinese in the 1930s, addressed to some fellow-citizens of his, to the effect that they were culturally intolerant when criticising European Nazism? Exactly the same is the case with law-state thinking. Although in origin a Western idea, it has universal ambitions and assigns to its values a universal validity. Torture in Bagdad, Damascus or Pyongyang is no less repugnant than it is in New York, Paris or Stockholm. A consequence of these universal claims is that law-state thinking may conflict with other normative doctrines also having universal claims.

A variation of "the cultural imperialism" argument is the following. "European history" itself, the argument goes, has deprived Europeans (and Occidentals on the whole) of the very right to advocate universal moral values. Not only have Europeans committed utterly cruel atrocities against people of other continents and organised the most barbaric kinds of slavery. Also on their own continent, in the twentieth century, Europeans are guilty of crimes unknown earlier in human history: the deliberately organised extermination of millions of human beings perpetrated by Nazis and communists such as the Holocaust and Gulag. Nor is outrage on a large scale an unfamiliar phenomenon earlier in European history: the number of people killed or tortured under the auspices of the Catholic Church up to the end of the seventeenth century and those up to the present day who have been the victims of child abuse can, all told, probably be counted in the millions. So for Europeans to preach morals to the world is nothing but shameless hypocrisy. In reality, it has been said, the so-called European humanitarian, democratic and liberal values have only one function: to legitimate imperialistic ambitions.

This picture of European history is tragically true. Unwavering orthodox religious zeal, ruthless capitalistic exploitation, colonial policy, stony fascism, Nazism and communism are indeed part of Western cultural tradition. But so is humanism, democracy, liberalism and human rights. That reference to humanitarian values has sometimes served the purpose of covering up a naked lust for power does not conceal the irrefutable fact that there is a strong, genuine humanistic tradition in the Occidental culture—the upholders of which have at times displayed great courage and suffered heavy sacrifices in their struggle for humanistic values. Furthermore, there is nothing whatsoever in, e.g., Japanese, Chinese, Indian, Arab, Jewish, Turkish and African history that gives us the slightest ground to believe that these peoples are in any respect more peaceful and less disposed to violence and abuse of power than are Occidentals. It belongs indeed to the tragic predicament of mankind that such phenomena can be found anywhere on earth.

Far from being deprived by "history" of asserting law-state values, Europeans, *precisely because of their monstrous experiences of the past*, are in the position of being able to propagate law-state values without hypocrisy. Also this predicament is, in fact, universal. The law-state ideas have their roots in a mould of shared bitter human experiences.

A normative doctrine may be independent of its origin also in another sense. It may well be the case that you embrace the normative part of the doctrine although you do not accept the original justification of it. You might, e.g., without any inconsistency perfectly well be an ardent democrat without accepting the (often not particularly convincing) arguments for democracy put forward by its classical theorists, e.g., Rousseau.[1] Law-state thinking in its classical form justified the law-state values by natural law arguments—or, at least, articulated them in the framework of natural law concepts. Concluding from this that every formulation of a law-state doctrine would be a natural law doctrine—or that an adherent of the law-state values inevitably must be an adherent of natural law as well (if his convictions are consistent)—is of course a false conclusion. It is perfectly possible to embrace wholeheartedly the law-state values and, at the same time, decidedly reject every natural law theory without rendering oneself guilty of any inconsistency. In other words, there might be justifications, other than those of the natural law doctrine, for these values. A justification of that kind will be articulated later in this book.

3.2 Some Methodological and Conceptual Remarks

3.2.1 Clarification

Modern philosophy can to no small extent be characterised as thinking about thinking. Conceived in this way, legal philosophy (or analytical jurisprudence) is thinking about legal thinking. Legal thinking, then, is taken in its widest possible sense, including thinking within the framework of legislation and administration of law as well as legal dogmatic thinking or evaluative thinking from a point of view external to some legal order or orders, etc. The data subject to investigation in legal philosophy are thoughts (ideas, concepts, statements, conceptions, notions—whatever the difference between them might be), not least ideas such as norms, values and evaluations within the realm of legal thinking.

What unites philosophers of the analytical creed is the view that the aim of philosophical thinking about thinking is that the former shall clarify the latter—whether this activity is called conceptual analysis, logical analysis, rational reconstruction, explication[2], or simply clarification.

I regard *clarification* as covering a wider range of intellectual activities than *analysis*. Furthermore, I prefer the term "clarification" to "analysis", since the for-

[1] J.-J. Rousseau, *Du contrat social* (1762).

[2] About the methodological program of explication, see R. Carnap, *Logical Foundations of Probability* (1951), p. 3–4.

mer also indicates the very purpose of this kind of philosophical activity, namely to *make* something clearer. But the essence of clarification undoubtedly consists in analysis. And the essence of analysis, in its turn, of some thought (concept) T consists in an interaction between making *distinctions* among different kinds, or different meanings, of T—T_1, T_2,..., T_n—and investigating the mutual *connections* among these different kinds or meanings and between them and other concepts standing in some relevant relations to them. The new, unexpected and fruitful distinction is no doubt one of the most telling and clarifying of philosophical achievements. But in order to sharpen our awareness of T it is equally important to clarify relationships of the kind just mentioned between concepts. Most concepts naturally belong to some *family of concepts*, and in order to clarify any one of its members it is important to clarify the relations between that member and the other ones. A classic example of an excellent piece of distinguishing and connecting in jurisprudence is W. N. Hohfeld's investigation of the family of concepts called "jural relations" (right (claim)—duty, privilege—no-right, power—liability, immunity—disability).[3]

Let me elaborate a little on clarification. Clarification goes beyond analysis. We find an excellent characterisation of the kind of conceptual investigation I have in mind in G.H. von Wright's *The Varieties of Goodness*.[4] Let me quote from it.

> An urge to do conceptual investigations… is *bewilderment* concerning the meaning of words. With the words in question we are usually familiar. We know on the whole, how and when to use them. But sometimes we are at a loss as to whether a thing should be called by some word '*x*'. We are at a loss, *not* because we are ignorant as to whether this thing has some feature *y*, which would be a ground for or against calling it '*x*'. We hesitate because we do not know which features of this thing *are* grounds for calling it '*x*'.
>
> Reflexion on the grounds for calling things by words is a *type* of conceptual investigation. How is such investigation conducted? Here a warning is in place. The aim of the type of investigation, of which I am speaking *is not to 'uncover' the existing meaning… of some word or expression* [my italics], veiled as it were behind the bewildering complexities of common usage. The idea of the philosopher as a searcher of meanings should not be coupled with an idea or postulate that the searched entities actually *are there*—avaiting the vision of the philosopher. If this picture of the philosopher's pursuit were accurate, then a conceptual investigation would, for all I can see, be an *empirical* inquiry into the actual use of language or the meaning of expressions.
>
> Philosophic reflexion on the grounds for calling a thing '*x*' is challenged in situations, when the grounds have not been fixed, when there is no settled opinion as to what the grounds are. The concept still remains to be *moulded* and therewith its logical connexions with other concepts to be *established.* The words and expressions, the use of which bewilder the philosopher, are so to speak *in search of a meaning.*

Clarification is the moulding of concepts. It comes closer to concept formation than to pure conceptual analysis. It assumes a weak connection between a linguistic expression (term, word) and its "corresponding" concept. Clarification is to investigate a whole sphere of thought connected with some term. Terms "cover"

---

[3] W.N. Hohfeld, *Fundamental Legal Conceptions as Applied in Judicial Reasoning* (1923).

[4] G.H. von Wright, *The Varieties of Goodness* (1963) pp. 4–6. Cf. G.H. von Wright, *Norm and Action* (1963), p. 48: "In ordinary language, it seems, the words 'act' and 'action' are used pretty much as synonyms. The philosopher is free to give to the two words different meanings for the purpose of marking some conceptual distinction which he thinks important". See also p. 113.

an often wide range of thoughts. A modest example of clarification is my pursuit in the present monograph to investigate, to the best of my ability, the sphere of thought connected with terms such as "the law-state", "the *Rechtsstaat*" and "the Rule of Law".

Philosophical analysis is not linguistic analysis—and hence, a *fortiori*, neither is clarification. The tremendous as well as eternal question of the import of language on thinking lurks alarmingly in the background here. Contemporary thinkers have gone very far in the direction of calling into question the possibility of thinking without language (not to mention the coining of slogans like "everything is in the language" and "there is no reality outside language"). This question is, as far as I can see, in the first place not a philosophical but an empirical one. Perhaps language in recent times has been given more than its due. After all, animals without language without a doubt think (*modus ponens* is, for instance, my dog's speciality; whether she masters the more sophisticated *modus tollens* is more doubtful) and also our pre-language ancestors must have done likewise. Language appears in fact at a very late stage in our evolution. And what about the problem-solving we do unconsciously, as in our sleep—why presume that this kind of thinking is of a linguistic nature? Is it wise then to rule out the possibility that language is secondary in relation to our capacity for thinking? Could it be that it is not language that begets thought but thought that begets language? Maybe it is not in the first place our language that directs our capacity for thinking but our capacity for thinking that directs our language? We think thoughts, don't we, not words and sentences ("thoughts" of course not taken in the psychological sense but in the sense of "thought contents".) Logical relations hold, or so it seems, between thoughts, not between linguistic entities. And we know that often there is no isomorphy between language and thought—often enough the structure of language does not mirror the structure of thinking. When we speak of concepts, conceptions, notions, ideas, etc. we speak, in all probability, of thoughts. Is not language merely the vehicle of our thoughts? Maybe language is nothing more than the surface of something much more profound, through which our thoughts surface (sometimes with some difficulty) and ooze out—and which we have to pierce in order to catch the thoughts of others. Through language we, however defectively, *share thoughts*. Perhaps it is time to demolish the myth of language as a cage from which no escape is possible.

Let us make two distinctions, the one between the concepts "thought" (in the singular without an article) and "thoughts" (in the plural, or in the singular with an article), and the other between "thoughts" and "concepts". Thought can be seen as a mental process in which thoughts (as non-mental entities) are produced. We think thoughts. We know little, so far, about what thought really is. We reach it only indirectly, from two directions—from perceivable occurrences in our brain studied by neurophysiologists on the one hand, and the thoughts themselves, produced by thought and getting a perceiveable expression in speech and writing on the other. Thought, one might say, is a mysterious relationship between occurrences in our brain and manifest thoughts. "Thinking" is, of course, often used synonymously with "thought" but in this essay I use the term—also a common manner—as designating a cluster of interrelated thoughts, like in "law-state thinking".

Concepts can be regarded as a subset of thoughts. We can *conceptualise* our thoughts. Concepts are a more or less fixed kind of thoughts. They are, as it were, isolations or abridgments of more loose thoughts, functioning as something for our thought to hold on to. They are more objective, de-personified thoughts—fixed in intersubjective communication and fixed just for facilitating such communication (lat. *communicare* = making common). They are also more intellectualised than "ordinary" thoughts. Without concepts, what could be called "the convergence effect of communication on thought" would hardly be possible.

To sum up, the aim of clarification of some concept or family of concepts, C, is to present *a better version of C, C**, which, if successful, (i) faithfully represents the essential intentions of *C* (adequacy) and (ii) is formulated in a more exact, illuminating and fruitful way (not least by taking concepts related to *C* into consideration), than is *C* itself (relevance).

How do we know that a clarification *C** of a thought (idea, concept) *C* is successful? The answer to this question is by its nature subjective. *C** is successful for some person, if she can say to herself after having acquainted herself with it: *C** has given me a clearer view of *C*. Successful clarifications are no small contribution to the improvement of human intersubjective understanding.

The present essay has a predominantly philosophical character. However, it also contains elements of a more juridico-technical nature. For that reason I have chosen to call it an essay in philosophical jurisprudence.

Since law-state thinking basically is a cluster of valuations and normative ideas, I find it appropriate to offer some special comments on the clarification of ideas having a valuational or normative character (which will be done in Sects. 3.2.2–3.2.4 below). But let me first say something about the concept of "value" itself.

This concept is not unproblematic. G. H. von Wright makes a sharp distinction between "values" and "things valued", which, according to him, is "of paramount importance" in this matter.[5] He deplores the widespread habit of using the term "value" for things valued. For instance, democracy is said to be a value but is in fact a thing valued (a good). Values themselves, if they exist at all, are not a kind of entity but "linguistic fictions".[6]

I cannot follow von Wright here. Like von Wright, I regard as inescapable some kind of emotive theory of value. If men were deprived of any emotional mental life, the term "value" would be meaningless. Hence, valuations are by nature also subjective and relative. The only alternative as an apprehensible candidate, qualified for being called "values", would then be certain—utterly varied, often fluctuating and highly inaccessible—emotional states of affairs. (Even pain could be a component of such a state of affairs, e.g., fear of losing something valued.) But would it not be even more strange to call phenomena of this kind "values"? An object (thing, state of affairs) is not valued from the point of view of a value, it is valued because someone has a certain kind of feeling for the object. In this sense there are no freely

[5] G. H. von Wright, "Valuations—or How to Say the Unsayable" (*Ratio Juris*, vol. 13, 2000, p. 348 f.).

[6] Ibid. p. 357.

floating values, ready to be attached to some object. Rather, it is objects that arouse value-generating emotions. With von Wright we can use the (somewhat bloodless) expression "approving attitudes" as an umbrella term for value-generating emotions of this kind. We can say that *to value* is to have an approving attitude to some object, a value.

There are also "negative values", i.e., things we dislike. Then the absence of such states of affairs can be regarded as values. In this mode of speech the absence of the use of torture, for instance, is a value.

In this connection, I would like to make a distinction between evaluation and valuation. Valuation as an activity (or, perhaps better, process) is to value something. Evaluation I regard as a wider activity than valuation. Evaluation is to evaluate something. Evaluation as an activity comprises not only valuation but in addition to that all deliberation preceding and leading to a valuation. I, for one, value law-states, and that valuation is based on an evaluation, viz., the deliberations presented in this book, in the first place with respect to the way I justify the basic law-state values (in Sect. 3.6.).

There are good reasons, I think, for calling objects valued "values". For one thing, it is in line with the common use of language. More important, though, is this. Conceptually to think of values in terms of valuable things provides us with a concept more appropriate to moral, legal, aesthetic and political reasoning. After all, such reasoning revolves mainly round things valued, such as whether a certain state of affairs should be regarded as valuable and why it should be so regarded (Sect. 3.2.4), how it should be realised (Sect. 3.2.3) and how to deal with conflicts arising when valuable states of affairs compete to be realised (Sect. 3.2.2).

Ontologically speaking, the approving attitude to some object is not a property of that object. Just as looking at the moon through a telescope is not a property of the moon, values are not properties of the object valued. The moon is the same whether we look at it or not and the valued object is the same whether valued or not. Valuations take place exclusively in the mind of the valuating subject.

Finally, something must be said about the special kind of values that we refer to as *general values*. General values are often ideas (value-ideas). For instance, democracy, individual freedom and legal security are values as well as ideas. Are such ideas states of affairs or is there some other ontological phenomenon different from states of affairs (and physical things), capable of being valued objects? The question is relevant, since the values dealt with in this essay are in fact ideas.

Let us make two distinctions that might be of some help here. We can differentiate between (i) individual and (ii) common (shared) values, and between (i') particular and (ii') general values. For instance, my memory of when I first met the woman who would become my wife is an individual value, a value for me. (Fortunately, it seems that *her* memory of the occasion is an individual value for her as well.) Watching football is a common value, shared by many. That person A has access to courts of law when claiming the right R against person B is a particular value (which, logically, could be a common value too). That everybody has access to a court of law when claiming legal rights is a general value. This last value is a general value even if only a single person were to cherish it (the value being an individual value), since its range of application is the whole of mankind.

A particular value is a state of affairs. A general value can be regarded as a set of particular values. The general value termed legal accessibility is the set of particular values of the type “that *x* has access to a court of law when claiming a right *y* against *z*”. Value-ideas are a kind of general values. Hence, value-ideas are sets of valued states of affairs. The values discussed in this essay are general as well as common.

3.2.2 Value Relations. Conflicts

Of particular importance, not least from a practical point of view, is that the clarification of law-state thinking clearly exhibits the way in which the law-state values and principles can *conflict* with each other when they are to be considered simultaneously, e.g., in a concrete legislative or adjudicative situation—or how they might come into conflict with values or principles outside law-state thinking itself, e.g., the value of efficiently protecting people from crimes.

This aspect of our clarification is particularly important for the following reason. Terms expressing value-concepts with a heavy positive charge always live perilously, risking, as they do, exploitation for different, not always laudable, purposes. Suppose there is something which some people regard as valuable, but other people do not, say *V*. Then the former often, consciously or unconsciously, try to subordinate *V* to a term, *t*, which does not refer to *V* at all but to certain other values, *V'*, which are commonly embraced. That device entails that the positive emotions which *t* generally disposes people to experience with regard to *V'* are transferred also to *V*. Often such changes of meaning are facilitated and accelerated by the use of reinforcing expressions like “pure (real, genuine) *t* is *V*” (e.g., “real democracy means a socialised economy”). Definitions of this kind have been called *persuasive definitions*.[7] This trend is strongly developed not least in politics and there it prevails now and then rather unhindered by intellectual or other scruples. Demands for, e.g., closing down nuclear power stations or building more day-nurseries are often presented as “democratic claims” although they have nothing at all to do with democracy, democracy being a special form for conferring public power and for public decision-making, irrespective of whether those in power allow hundreds or no nuclear power stations. Often such shifts of meaning are small and hardly noticeable, but there are also examples of grandiose persuasive definitions where the meaning of a term has changed into its exact opposite. “Democracy” means, roughly, “government by the people”, but in the post-war communist dictatorships in Eastern and Central Europe this term has been used—sometimes in the (etymologically horrid) reinforced form of “people’s democracy”—for designating their own, blatantly undemocratic political systems.

[7] By C.L. Stevenson, *Ethics and Language* (1944), where the mechanisms directing the use of them are brilliantly analysed.

There are considerable dangers in such extensions of the meaning of essential political, legal or other value-terms. One such danger is that the reading into terms like "culture", "democracy" or "rule of law" everything you have positive feelings towards will sooner or later inflate these terms to the point where they cease to be interesting—they become rhetorical balloons, the sight of which eventually fills people with indifference and weariness. And this consequence is particularly disastrous in a society which pays respect to, e.g., democracy and the rule of law. In such a society, on the contrary, it is of vital necessity that the concepts expressed by terms of this kind are kept fresh and alive. Characteristic of dictatorships of different shades is, sure enough, the development of a double language: in official rhetoric an empty, rattling, choking and, as time passes, increasingly surrealistic language, while everything essential is expressed in an obscure crypto-language, or left in silence.

Another danger in such a watering-down of language, which is of particular interest in our context, is the tendency towards the idyll—that, too, a not unknown phenomenon in political discourse. This tendency manifests itself mainly in the smoothing over of tensions and conflicts between different values or principles. By including two or more different values or principles in one and the same concept, expressed by a common term, one hides the fact that they might be potentially contradictory, i.e., that in certain situations they might conflict. Everything co-operates smoothly towards simple, clear-cut goals. If, e.g., "equality before the law" is taken to express both equal treatment of the parties in a court trial and distributive justice in their legal relationship, the fact that these two values can conflict in certain situations (the realisation of one of them obstructs the realisation of the other) is easily obscured.

An important task for our explication of law-state thinking, then, must be to uncover, and even to counteract, such tendencies to inflate and idealise. Hence, it is a desideratum that the values attributed to that ideology are defined as narrowly as is possible without deviating too much from everyday language. By doing so, it also becomes easier to discern typical potential conflicts between the different law-state values. The main component of *minimal law-state thinking* (a concept that will be further clarified below) is found in a few narrowly defined values clustering about what we in Chap. 1 referred to as the nucleus idea of the law-state thinking.[8]

Hence, a clarification of law-state thinking must expose conflicts between law-state principles among themselves and between such principles and other noteworthy principles. In recent legal theory, fruitful analyses of the concept of "principle" and the uses of principles have been made.[9] As I see it, there are two, diametrically

[8] Compare the critical attitude with regard to definitions in this inflating fashion of the term "the rule of law" in J. Raz, "The Rule of Law and its Virtue", in Raz, *The Authority of Law* ,1979, Chap. 11. In R. Summers, "The Ideal Socio-Legal Order. Its 'Rule of Law' Dimension", *Ratio Juris*, Vol. 1, 1988. pp. 154–161, esp. at pp. 154–155 and 160–161 is advocated, in the same vein, a "deflated" concept "the rule of law" as "one way of rehabilitating this ideal". For the methodological difficulties connected with definitions of value-loaded concepts see also D.N. MacCormick, "Der Rechtsstaat und die rule of law", *cit. supra* n. 11, pp. 66–67.

[9] See, e.g., R. Alexy, *Theorie der Grundrechte*, 1985, and R. Dworkin, *Taking Rights Seriously* and *A Matter of Principles*, 1985.

opposed ways to deal with principles. One is the attitude of orthodox consistency. A principle shall be observed whatever the consequences. A principle is "holy". For people with this attitude "firmness of principle" is a virtue; weighing *pro et contra* a sign of weakness and confusion. This attitude is, in my opinion, not only stupid, it is fatal.

There is a passage in Dorothy L. Sayers' *Gaudy Night* (1935) where Lord Peter Wimsey eloquently expresses the dangers of dogmatic handling of principles. (The setting is a dinner at the High Table of the—imaginary—Shrewsbury College in Oxford, and the following is a fragment of a conversation between Lord Peter and the Warden, Dr. Margaret Baring.)

> [says Lord P.]… But now that you have the age of national self-realisation, the age of colonial expansion, the age of the barbarian invasions and the age of the decline and fall, all jammed cheek by jowl in time and space, all armed alike with poison-gas and going through the outward motions of an advanced civilisation, *principles have become more dangerous than passions. It's getting uncommonly easy to kill people in large numbers, and the first thing a principle does—if it really is a principle—is to kill somebody.* [my italics]
>
> – The real tragedy is not the conflict of good with evil but of good with good'; that means a problem with no solution.
>
> – Yes. Afflicting, of course, to the tidy mind. One may either hulloo on the inevitable, and be called a bloodthirsty progressive; or one may try to gain time and be called a bloodthirsty reactionary. But when blood is their argument, all argument is apt to be—merely bloody.
>
> The Warden passed the adjective at its face-value.
>
> – I sometimes wonder whether we gain anything by gaining time.
>
> – Well—if one leaves letters unanswered long enough, some of them answer themselves. Nobody can prevent the Fall of Troy, but a dull, careful person may manage to smuggle out the Lares and Penates—even at the risk of having the epithet *pius* tacked to his name.
>
> – The Universities are always being urged to march in the van of progress.
>
> – But epic actions are all fought by the rearguard—at Roncevaux and Thermopylae.
>
> – "Very well," said the Warden, laughing, "let us die in our tracks, having accomplished nothing but an epic."

The other way to deal with principles is rather the opposite of the orthodoxy of the dogmatist. The function of principles, with that attitude, is to weigh and balance *pros* and *cons* when solving difficult problems (e.g., hard cases in Dworkin's sense, or the balancing of interests in legislation) by formulating more general principles behind these *pros* and *cons*, and with the help of such principles constructing "systems of coordinates" where the optimum is "the point" where "the bearings" of the principles meet. This is to use principles with consideration –not with rigidity and orthodoxy—and is, in my opinion, superior both to starchy dogmatism and petty, unprincipled pragmatism.[10]

---

[10] It has been argued that "use of principles with consideration" is very much the same as St Thomas Aquinas' concept of *determinatio*; see J.M. Finnis, "On 'The Critical Legal Studies Movement'" (1985) 30 *American Journal of Jurisprudence*, pp. 21–42, esp. at 23–5, and N. MacCormick, "Reconstruction after Deconstruction: A Response to CLS", (1990) 10 *Oxford Journal of Legal Studies*, pp. 539–558, esp at 548–551.

It seems obvious, then, that the study of possible conflicts between values (principles) is crucial.

The law-state values are general values. Between values of any kind there exist certain relations, let us call them *value relations*. Some, but not all, value relations are *value conflicts*.

Let me present two classifications of value relations. I take a value relation to be a relation between two (or more) values *V* and *V'*, ($V \neq V'$). The first one can be called a formal classification, since it is based on the logically possible ways in which two values, *V* and *V'*, can be related with respect to their simultaneous realisation. I have already characterised a value as a valuated thing or state of affairs. Let us say that a state of affairs that is a value (a state of affairs appreciated by someone), *V, is realised*, if *V* is a fact. The value of my owning a copy of Kelsen's *Reine Rechtslehre* is realised if I am actually the owner of a copy of that work. From the point of view of causality, the term realisation has two connotations: (i) *V* is realised by actions performed by a valuing subject (strong realisation) and (ii) *V* is realised independently of any valuing subject (weak realisation). An example of (i) is my buying a copy of *Reine Rechtslehre*. If owning a copy of *Reine Rechtslehre* is a value for me at time *t* and I already own such a copy at *t*, or a copy is falling down from the skies into my hands at *t*, this value is realised in the weak sense at *t*. We must also distinguish between "realisation" as an action (realising) and as a result of an action. From the point of view of realisation as result we can further distinguish between complete and partial realisation.

Now to the first classification. Let **V** stand for a realised value *V* and **V′** for *V'*. For two separate values, *V* and *V'*, there are the following possible combinations of realised values **V** and **V′** ("~" is read "not"): (i) **V & V′**, (ii) **V & ~V′**, (iii) **~V & V′** and (iv) **~V & ~V′**.

I. **V** and **V'** are *mutually independent* of each other. By that I mean that it is possible simultaneously to realise (i)–(iv). Example: The value of equality before the law and the value of moderation with respect to alcohol consumption. (Of course it is always possible to construct strained counter-examples but let us restrict ourselves to what is reasonable.)
II. **V** is *one-way independent* of **V′**. That means that **V** is independent of **V′** but **V′** is not independent of **V**. It is possible simultaneously to realise (i), (ii) and (iv) but not possible simultaneously to realise (iii). Example: With respect to legality and legal accessibility, it is possible to realise legality without realising legal accessibility, but not the other way round. Legality is one-way independent of legal accessibility.
III. **V** is *one-way dependent* on **V′**. It is possible simultaneously to realise (i), (iii) and (iv) but not possible simultaneously to realise (ii). III is the converse relation of the relation one-way independence. In II, **V′** is one-way dependent on **V**. Legal accessibility is one-way dependent on legality.
IV. **V** and **V′** are *positively mutually dependent* on each other. That means that it is possible simultaneously to realise (i) and (iv) but not possible simultaneously to realise (ii) and (iii). This relation is, I think, unusual. When it exists, it holds

between values so close as to constitute virtually one single value. One example might be the value of the right to life and the value of not having the death penalty. It could be said that two mutually dependent values live in symbiosis with each other. Only both or none of them can be realised.

V. **V** and **V′** are *negatively mutually dependent* on each other (they *collide* with each other). It is possible simultaneously to realise (ii), (iii) and (iv) but not possible simultaneously to realise (i). Example: The value of direct democracy collides with the value of representative democracy. When **V** and **V′** are highly important values from a humanistic point of view, it might be said that a collision between them is a tragic state of affairs—there is no way of realising both. Only one of them or neither of them can be realised.

The second classification can be called a material classification, since it is based on the societal effects of joint realisation of values *V* and *V′*. We say that a value *V* is harmed by a person or collective of persons, *a*, if *a* performs an action which renders the realisation of *V* more difficult or forbears from performing an action which would be of use for the realisation of *V*. In this connection the harming of *V* lies in the realisation or harming of another value, *V′*. General values can, of course, be more or less realised or harmed.

Let us differentiate between four situations:

1. *Negative counteraction*: *V* is harmed by realising *V′*
2. *Reinforcement*: *V* is realised by realising *V′*
3. *Depreciation*: *V* is harmed by harming *V′*
4. *Positive counteraction*: *V* is realised by harming *V′*.

Examples: (1) Let *V* be the value of legal security. That includes—it might for good reasons be argued (which will be done in Chap. 8)—the value of not having capital punishment. Let *V′* be the value of democracy, including the value of the politicians respecting the will of the people. Suppose that a legislative assembly inaugurates capital punishment, thereby following the will of the people. Then *V* is harmed by the realising of *V′*. There is a negative counteraction between *V* and *V′* with respect to the harmed value *V*. (2) If there is equality in the law, *V′*, the value of equality before the law, *V*, is reinforced (legal equality is dealt with in Chap. 5). For when this is the case, to respect the value (principle) of equality before the law warrants to a higher degree that the litigants' life of human dignity is respected. The value of equality before the law is reinforced by the realisation of equality in the law. (3) If the value *V′* of legality is harmed, the value *V* of legal accessibility is harmed as well. For in order to achieve a satisfactory amount of legal accessibility in society, the procedural rules regulating legal accessibility must be strictly complied with. *V* is depreciated by the harming of *V′*. (4) The value *V* of not having capital punishment is realised by harming the value *V′* of democracy, when the value of the politicians' respecting the will of the people is included therein and the people want capital punishment. There is a positive counteraction between *V* and *V′* with respect to the realised value *V*.

Is (4) simply the converse of (1)? To be sure, empirically it is very often the case that if *V* is harmed by realising *V′*, *V′* is also realised by harming *V*. But, as far as I can see, it is not necessarily (logically) so. Nor are reinforcement and depreciation converse relations, although they often are empirically connected. None of the four relations is symmetrical.

A very special, and indeed important, kind of value relation is *betrayal* of a value by violation of another value. This is a kind of depreciation of values. *V* can in fact be depreciated by *V'* in two different ways: (i) The realisation of *V* is harmed by the violation of *V'*, and (ii) *V* is realised, even to the full extent, although *V'* is harmed, but by violating *V'*, *V loses its very quality as a value*—*V* is betrayed by the violation of *V'*. Example: In the Third Reich the Jews had a certain amount of legal certainty (predictability based on information of the content of the law). But due to the outrageous violations of legal security, the value of legal certainty was betrayed. For what was legal certainty worth for a Jew in Nazi Germany? Nothing but the victims' certainty of imminent suffering and the oppressors' certainty that they could pursue their trade with impunity. At best, this legal certainty had the value that potential victims could get out of harm's way by escaping from the law—surely not what we usually regard as constituting the value of legal certainty. (More about betrayal of values in Chap. 6.)

What is typical for conflicts on the whole is that something, *x*, which is not necessarily absurd, illogical, unrealisable, difficult to carry out, evil or wrong by itself, becomes so in combination with another something, *y*, which, *y* too, by itself is not necessarily absurd etc. If the realisation of a value, however strong, is driven to an extreme, it inevitably harms some other, perhaps equally strong or even stronger, value. In this sense there are no holy values.

Conflicts need solutions. But what is a solution to a conflict of values? "Ontologically", solutions are realisations. To solve a value conflict between *V* and *V'* is to choose some realisation from among the logically possible realisations **V&V'**, **V&~V'**, **~V&V'** and **~V&~V'**. In addition, it is often possible to mitigate the negative effect of the yielding of one of the conflicting values by some additional measures, for instance, time limits or economic compensation.

As guidelines for solving value conflicts certain arguments (principles) can be formulated. In the sequel (*passim*) I shall present some such principles which I regard as proper components of law-state thinking.

3.2.3 Juridical Technique

In one respect our concept "law-state thinking" must be somewhat expanded. One thing is the law-state values as such, another is how these values are to be realised with the help of practical juridical technique—or, in other words, what claims does this thinking have on juridical methods and on legal organisation itself? Such claims are directed towards legislation as well as adjudication. The law-state values stand a bad chance if there are no established methods for realising them in the practical juridical handling of valid legal orders. For that reason I include such technical principles and methods in law-state thinking and, hence, our clarification of it will also include them—a proper task, indeed, for philosophical jurisprudence. In Chap. 9 we shall investigate the no less important claims that law-state thinking makes on the bodies of a legal organisation.

3.2.4 Justification and the Contrast-Method

Rational justification of values always reaches a point where no further rational justification is possible. *Ultimately, we have to choose our values.*[11] This predicament is felt by some as a frightening threat against their sense of security—the security that lies in being subject to authority—and felt by others as if everything were equally valuable, as if everything were permitted. It can also, however, be regarded as the hallmark of an adult, a free and responsible man or woman.

We have to choose, and in so doing it is important to make clear to ourselves what the choice is about.

For that purpose I recommend a very simple device, which I shall make use of when discussing the justification of the law-state values. Let us call it *the contrast-method*. The purpose of the contrast-method is to justify a given value *by showing the consequences of that value's being violated.*

In Sect. 3.6 it is argued that the law-state values can best be justified by showing that their realisation contributes to the realisation of a life of human dignity for individuals. Violations of the basic law-state values—legal equality, certainty, accessibility and security—are inevitably a violation of a life of human dignity. By means of the contrast-method we justify the law-state values by exposing, in an ostensive manner, the true colours of legal inequality, uncertainty, inaccessibility and insecurity and by confronting those colours with the value of a life of human dignity.

In societies where law-state values are violated, such violations—unless they are flatly denied—are often justified by the assertion that they, however deplorable, are necessary for achieving some common good—which good will surely be achieved in some remote future. It is of vital importance to disclose the hollowness of expectations of this kind. Is it, for instance, probable that torture, false accusations or labour camps, where the prisoners live a life of near-starvation, promote higher salaries or better teaching in schools or better medical services for the people as a whole, or a never-before-seen life in solidarity and harmony in two centuries' time or so?

3.2.5 Legal Protection and the Law-State Paradox

The basic function of legal orders is to achieve, and maintain, peace. By that I mean, roughly, that members of society refrain from attacking one another, and that disputes among them are settled without the use of violence. It could be said that a legal order is aimed at peace by guaranteeing the members of the society in which

[11] An insight I owe to Professor Ingemar Hedenius, Uppsala.

it operates—and also guests and strangers—*legal protection* in different respects and forms.

For our analysis of law-state thinking, the point of departure is a concept "legal protection".

The term "protection" refers to a relation, P, which, for our purposes, must be regarded as (at least) 6-ary:

(P) x is protected by y by means of $m(y)$ against z:s threatening $o(x)$ by means of $m(z)$

where

(i) x designates *a protection subject*: the one who is protected
(ii) y designates *a protector*: the one who protects
(iii) $m(y)$ designates *a means of protection* in the hands of y: that by which y protects x
(iv) z designates *a threat subject*: the one x is protected against
(v) $o(x)$ designates *a protection object* connected with x: that which is protected in the interest of x
(vi) $m(z)$ designates *a means of threat* in the hands of z: that by which z threatens $o(x)$.

Example: Person N.N. (protection subject) is protected by the functionaries of the Swedish legal order (protector) with the help of activities according to the criminal and procedural rules in the legal system (means of protection) against person P.P's (threat subject) threatening of N.N.'s possession of his silver cup (protection object) by P.P.'s stealing it (means of threat).

We stipulate that protection subjects, protectors and threat subjects are always human beings (acting either individually or collectively). Since what is in the focus of our interest here is the guarantee of legal protection through legal orders, we let protectors always be functionaries in the organs of the legal order. Thus, when in the following, for the purpose of abbreviation, we now and then talk about "the state", what is usually intended is official functionaries in their exercising of public power, i.e., a certain class of individual human beings.

The nucleus idea of law-state thinking points to a special category of threat subjects against which the individual shall have legal protection. So let us start by listing different kinds of threat subjects, against which a legal order can offer protection. From the point of view of the individual we can discern

1. his protection against himself
2. his protection against other private individuals (including private organisations of individuals)
3. his protection against the state, in the forms of
    a. his protection against a foreign state (i.e., a state of which he is not a citizen) on the territory of his own state
    b. his protection against a foreign state on the territory of a foreign state
    c. his protection against his own state on the territory of a foreign state
    d. his protection against his own state on the territory of his own state.

The individual has legal protection against himself (whether he wants it or not) for example when the legal system makes attempted suicide a criminal offence or when it makes possible taking care of mentally deranged persons who are dangerous for themselves.

With regard to the individual's legal protection against his fellow human beings, the whole civil law and considerable parts of criminal law and administrative law stand out boldly in a grandiose legal panorama: the law of contracts, breach of contracts and torts, the protection of children's rights, traffic regulations, the protection given by criminal law to life, limb and property, and so on and so forth. Of particular interest in this connexion is the vital question in modern democracies concerning the protection of the individual against big and powerful private organisations, e.g., enterprises and trade unions (whether he is a member or an outsider).

The individual's legal protection against state power can take many different forms. The protection against a foreign state on the territory of one's own state can, for example, be manifested in a prohibition against extraditing a citizen of the state to another state, where he has committed a crime. The protection against a foreign state on the territory of a foreign state has—due to the trivial fact that there are more than two states on earth—two forms:

(i) citizens of state *S* have legal protection against state *T* on *T:s* territory, and
(ii) citizens of state *S* have legal protection against state *T* on state *U:s* territory.

Situation (i) is related to the question whether, and to what extent, a state should extend the protection it guarantees its own citizens to foreigners. With regard to situation (ii)—as well as, of course, to the individual's protection against his own state on the territory of a foreign state—the right of asylum is very much in focus. It is a depressing sign of the present state of the world that one of the most necessary ingredients of legal relations among states is the right to asylum. Finally, the individual's protection against his own state on the territory of his own state—about which we will have much to say in the following—mobilises important parts of constitutional, procedural and administrative law, but also the law of torts and criminal law, viz., those parts of these that deal with the tort liability and criminal liability of officials.

It is out of the question to look upon law-state thinking as a doctrine which deals with all these variations of legal protection, i.e., in fact the whole legal order. From a historical point of view, the development of this thinking is to a large extent connected with the growth, consolidation and concentration of public power in the European nation-states, and it cannot be properly understood as anything but a reaction against certain consequences thereof. As has already been stated, a first clarification of the ideology, then, is to confine it to legal protection against the exercise of state power, i.e., the concern expressed in point 3 above.

This, however, is not always taken for granted. In the current debate we often hear the opinion that a main task for the Government is to "uphold the law-state" by protecting the public—or even the state—against crime, or against misuse of power by powerful private organisations.

But this is an extension which is not warranted by the classical law-state doctrine, and it also has the drawback that it cloaks important potential value conflicts.

The ambition to protect effectively private citizens against crime might conflict with the demand for protection of personal integrity against the powers that be, not least the demand for satisfactory guarantees of a fair criminal procedure with respect to arrested or detained persons, and defendants (the last-mentioned is undoubtedly a law-state value). And when the state itself is a subject of protection, its ambition to safeguard its rights might conflict with the principle of equality before the law (which is undoubtedly a law-state value). Finally, the protection of the individual against powerful private organisations is, in my opinion, most urgent in modern societies. But from the point of view of principle this kind of protection is not different in character from, e.g., the protection of the individual against crime.

This restriction on the law-state ideology certainly does not imply that the protection of private individuals against other private individuals or organisations would be of less importance in society than their protection against state power. What I am saying is only that the former is of no concern from the special viewpoint of law-state thinking.

It is clear from what has been said so far, that I regard situation 3d and also 3b (i), as being of main concern for law-state thinking. But what about situations 3a, 3b (ii) and 3c in this respect?

Of course there is nothing to prevent us from letting the sphere in which law-state thinking is relevant include all situations where the individual's protection against state power is at stake—whether it is a question of protection against the individual's own state or another state, and regardless of whether he resides in his own territory or on foreign soil. In this essay, however, we shall not deal particularly with the law-state thinking in its transnational aspects.

Let me just add a small comment on the subject before we proceed. Several forms of transnational protection against state power which are available to individuals by national or international law are, as a matter of principle, no doubt often less anchored in classical law-state ideas than in another powerful idea in Western legal and political history of ideas: the notion that princes or states have *sovereignty* (an idea developed by, among others, the French jurist Jean Bodin in the sixteenth century[12]). This idea has about as long a history as law-state thinking. Its relationship to the law-state ideas is complicated both from the viewpoint of the history of ideas and of logic: in their application both ideas might at times cooperate towards a common result, at times, on the contrary, lead to incompatible results. In, e.g., allowing asylum, the asylum-giving state not only grants a person legal protection against another state, but also manifests its own independence of that state, i.e., its sovereignty. But, unfortunately, sovereignty is also a very handy tool for mobilising a defence and counter-attack when it has been proven that a state has committed atrocities against its own people. When such excesses are openly exposed by the media of the surrounding world, the well-known old waltz is trumpeted through state news agencies: "This is an interference with our internal affairs!". We remember that outburst of perverted indignation launched from Peking after the massacre in Tiananmen Square in June 1989. It is, no doubt, a very high price to pay for the guarantee of peace which is implied in the maintenance of the national sovereignty

[12] J. Bodin, *Les six livres sur la république* (1576).

of states. Sovereignty, and the closely related idea of immunity, can, indeed, also function as a means to discharge political gangsters from liability. The recent establishment of the International Criminal Court (ICC) in The Hague is a hopeful sign of improvement in this respect.

Finally, there must be a further clarification of the range of application of the law-state ideology. This range cannot reasonably be taken to include every action those in power perform with negative consequences for individuals. Usually, changes in, for example, civil law legislation lead to the result that some people enjoy an expansion of their rights whereas others see their rights restricted or their duties expanded. Consumer protection legislation, e.g., strengthens the rights of the buyer at the expense of the seller. Such limitations of rights, or expansions of duties, are, of course, not *per se* infringements on the law-state ideology. Allocation of rights and duties—which is indeed the very point of legal orders—always leads to the result that some people find their range of action more or less limited by the law. The kind of legal protection against the state which law-state thinking claims is directed towards certain more qualified measures against individuals on the part of the state, viz. such measures which are *violations of the four basic law-state values* (to be dealt with in the next section of this chapter).

But it is certainly an obvious fact that we cannot delimit the range of application of a doctrine of this kind by drawing fixed and sharp boundaries around it. The law-state thinking has developed in the course of many centuries, and during this space of time it has taken somewhat different shapes in different countries, and has also been subject to an extensive intellectual discussion. It therefore necessarily appears with vague boundaries. Efforts at drawing sharp boundaries around the range of application of law-state thinking constitute a merely stipulative activity, the intellectual and moral value of which I doubt. A far better way to proceed, when analysing law-state thinking, it seems to me, is to limit its range to the sphere where this kind of thinking is applicable without any doubt—i.e., such as it appears in its classical works as well as in the modern, more serious literature in the field. For that reason too, we are, in this book, explicating *minimal law-state thinking* (cf. p. 38 above).

It follows from our demarcation of the law-state values that those values are not identical with the values embedded in the so-called human rights. "The law-state rights" are only a proper subset of the human rights (i.e., all "law-state rights" are human rights but there are *human rights* which are not *per se* "law-state rights", e.g., the right to marry and to raise a family or the so-called economic, social and cultural human rights). It goes without saying that this does not imply that we regard "the law-state rights" as necessarily having a higher value than other human rights. What gives the former their distinctive character is that they are related to the very handling of legal orders. Incidentally, let me draw our attention to the fact that the concepts "human rights" and "law-state rights" might seem to be somewhat abstract ones. But let us keep in mind that infringements of human rights are always infringements of human beings.

Let us conclude this section with some words about the relation between law state-thinking and the idea of legal protection, by reference to our 6-ary protection relation.

a. The subjects of protection according to law-state thinking are always individuals.
b. The objects of protection according to law-state thinking, i.e., that which is protected in the interest of individuals, are at least the following (with respect to which the risk of manipulation by the state, as we know from historical experience, is particularly high; see below under e):

   (i) that important social states of affairs, in which individuals may find themselves, and potential, typical disputes among individuals concerning such states of affairs, are regulated legally—and in a clear, distinct and non-contradictory way.
   (ii) that individuals without any great difficulty can get information about the law-content
   (iii) that individuals can rely on legal rules actually being applied in compliance with their content when brought to the fore
   (iv) that every individual is treated by the state in the same way as other individuals with regard to the application of the law
   (v) that every individual has the same access as other individuals to courts of law and other authorities and that if he is a party in a trial he is on an equal basis with the opposite party
   (vi) that the individual in his relation to the state can live in safety as regards his life, his physical and mental states, his personal integrity, and his property
   (vii) that the individual can apply to courts of law and other authorities if he finds himself in a dispute or is accused of violations of legal rules, and that those organs are easy to access.

It must be stressed that the demand of legal protection, in this connection, means not only that the state shall maintain these objects of protection, but also that the state, when necessary, shall create them—that is, provide the public with those protection objects, e.g., by seeing to it that there are clear rules and easily accessible courts of law.

c. Threat subject, according to law-state thinking, is always public power (the state, the Government).
d. Protector, according to law-state thinking, is always public power (the state, the Government).

It follows from c and d that, according to the law-state ideology, the state shall protect the individual against the state itself. In this predicament—let us call it *the law-state paradox*—lies the most serious and most difficult problem of law-state thinking. This paradox was perfectly clear already to such an early proponent of law-state thinking as John Locke.

The traditional recipe for solving the law-state paradox is separation of public power. For this purpose Locke and Montesquieu developed their well-known separation of powers doctrines. "Mais c'est une expérience éternelle", says the latter, "que tout homme qui a du pouvoir est porté à en abuser, il va jusqu'à ce qu'il trouve des limites", and he adds: "Pour qu'on ne puisse abuser du pouvoir, il faut que, par la disposition des choses, le pouvoir arrête le pouvoir".[13]

Locke's separation of power doctrine advocates, roughly, a separation of power between king and parliament, while Montesquieu, under the influence of Locke, separates the power of legislation, execution and jurisdiction. Both doctrines deal with supreme power. In Chap. 9 I shall argue that law-state thinking demands a more far-reaching separation of power than that: it claims separation of power also on the lower level of various judicial authorities.

e. The means of threat, according to law-state thinking, mirrors the protection objects (see *supra* under b), for instance

   (i) that the state omits legal regulation or makes the legal rules obscure or conflicting in different respects
   (ii) that the state makes the sources of information about the rules in force difficult to access, or even secret
   (iii) that the state does not follow its own rules, or that it violates private individuals' rights by means of surprising changes of the rules or retroactive legislation
   (iv) that the state discriminates unduly against certain individuals compared with others when administering the law
   (v) that the state obstructs access to courts of law and other authorities for certain individuals and does not grant them the guarantees of procedure that it grants to other individuals
   (vi) that the state uses, e.g., legislation in the field of criminal law and criminal procedure as a means of harassing individuals by the use of physical or mental violence
   (vii) that the state fails to provide legal means ("law-ways") which enable individuals to realise their rights or refute legal claims against them, or that these means are made difficult to access.

f. That the state provides means which secure the protection of the individual against the state itself is, of course, a fundamental component of law-state thinking, and has been so since the Enlightenment. This task is, to a large extent, a matter of legal technique concerning, e.g., statutory drafting, legal informatics, interpretation of statutes and precedents etc., and the organising of judicial authorities. For that reason, lawyers of different kinds have a special responsibility for the maintenance of the law-state. Law-state thinking is, as has already been emphasised, to a large extent an ideology for lawyers.

---

[13] C.L. de Montesquieu, *De l'ésprit des lois* (1748), livre XI, Chap. IV: "But it is a perennial experience that every man who has power is apt to abuse it. He goes as far as he can until he meets with limits… So that one shall not be able to abuse power, it is in the nature of things that *power must check power*" (my trans. and italics).

3.2.6 The Four Basic Law-State Values. Legality. Nomocracy

We have formulated (in Chap. 1) the core idea of law-state thinking in the following manner: that the individual enjoys legal protection against violations caused by the exercise of power on the part of the state (the Government, the public power). Such violations may, of course, take different forms and vary in degree. It is, to be sure, a deeply tragic fact that violations are made possible by the existence of a legal order, or would even be impossible without such an order. History shows that there are some standard devices at hand for functionaries of legal orders, the use of which is likely to bring about violations of private individuals through the legal order itself. For the deliberately acting abuser of the legal order these devices are powerful tools; for the functionary taking the law-state values seriously they involve a constant risk. Those devices are, generally speaking:

a. to discriminate between individuals in the same kind of situations (legal inequality, undue discrimination)
b. to keep the law obscure or unreliable (legal uncertainty)
c. to make legal remedies difficult, or even impossible, to have access to (legal inaccessibility, lawlessness)
d. to use physical or mental violence against individuals "in the name of the law" (legal insecurity).

Against these four standard means of violation, law-state thinking claims, articulates, and justifies the following *four basic law-state values*:

1. legal equality
2. legal certainty
3. legal accessibility
4. legal security.

In the following, each of those values will be dealt with in a chapter of its own. Here a few general remarks may suffice.

I. Violating the individual, on the part of the state, is to expose him to *undue discrimination* in legal matters by comparison with other individuals. This is the case when certain people are "above the law" and are given advantages not allowed by the law, or spared duties or sanctions imposed on them by law—or when certain people are outlawed and not able to benefit from rights allowed to them by the law, or subjected to duties or sanctions not imposed on them by the law. It is also undue discrimination when there is unequal access to justice and unequal treatment of parties in legal proceedings. Against undue discrimination, law-state thinking defends *legal equality* (equality before and in the law) as a fundamental value. Legal equality is dealt with in Chap. 5.

II. Violating the individual, on the part of the state, is to expose him to *arbitrariness* in legal matters. Such arbitrariness has its special conditions and forms. Room for arbitrariness might be brought about by a *lack of law*, i.e., absence of legal regulation, in some social area or another, or by legal rules being *vague* or *conflicting* with each other. A serious kind of arbitrariness is *perversion of law*—there are rules but the powers that be do not pay attention to them, or do so only when it suits them. Another kind of arbitrariness is the *manipulation of law*—capricious and surprising changes of the legal rules. In all these ways the public is held in a state of legal uncertainty. Law-state thinking opposes *legal uncertainty* by defending legal certainty as a fundamental value. Legal certainty is dealt with in Chap. 6.

III. Violating the individual, on the part of the state, is to deprive him of access to legal means for obtaining his right, or to make these means difficult to find—in short, *lawlessness*. Lawlessness prevails when the state does not place judicial organs at the disposal of the citizens, i.e., organs which in an impartial manner try, and authoritatively decide, disputes between individuals or between individuals and the state—or when the state obstructs access to such organs. Lawlessness also reigns, when such a trial is denied to persons accused of non-compliance with legal rules. Lawlessness exists when there are no means for appeal against, and re-trial of, disputes and alleged non-compliance with rules. Lawlessness, finally, exists when external circumstances (lack of legal aid, geographic distance) put obstacles in the way of individuals to realise their rights. A central idea in law-state thinking is that a legal order that does not provide the public with accessible "law-ways" is not acceptable. *Legal accessibility* is a third fundamental law-state value. Additional reinforcement of legal accessibility is enhanced by creating a control function over public organs with respect to their rule-making and rule-applying functions, e.g., judicial review-organs and Parliamentary *Ombudsmen*. Legal accessibility is dealt with in Chap. 7.

IV. Violating the individual, on the part of the state, is to expose him to *violence* and *outrage*—legal, illegal or extra-legal. This is the case when the state attacks individuals' life or limb, health, property, freedom of movement or personal integrity. Both history and our own age give us an abundance of standard examples: torture, police assault, confinement of mentally healthy citizens in mental hospitals, breaking down people with the aid of drugs, telephone terror, threats and pestering, arrest and detention for indefinite periods, terror-like searches of premises, arbitrary confiscation of property, bodily searches, sexual assault, telephone tapping, violation of the secrecy of correspondence, shadowing and spreading of rumours—in short, *legal insecurity*. To law-state thinking all this is obnoxious. It claims *legal security* as a fundamental law-state value, which means that violent measures on the part of state organs are permitted only if there are very strong social or humanitarian reasons for them, that certain kinds of violence are not permitted at all and, no less important, that the conditions and forms for using violent measures are regulated in a precise manner in statutory provisions and, in addition to that, exposed to severe and close examination and control, including means of holding officials responsible for violations of the rules. Legal security is dealt with in Chap. 8.

A necessary background condition, in practice, for the realisation of the four fundamental law-state values is *legality* (lawfulness; *the rule of law* in Anglo-American countries), i.e., that law-applying organs, and public power as a whole, comply with the legal rules in force. *Legalism* is "the ideology of legality", i.e., an "ideology" the central content of which is that legality is a good thing, a positive value, and hence ought to be pursued.

In what way is legality, in practice, a necessary condition for the realisation of the basic law-state values?

If legality is not upheld, you cannot rely upon the legal rules, however clear and easily available they may be, and, hence, legal certainty is in jeopardy. If legality is not upheld, the field is open to undue discrimination, and legal equality is in jeopardy. To discriminate is very much the same as making exceptions from legal rules. If legality is not upheld, regulation of judicial means (procedures, "law-ways") is likewise of little use and, thus, legal accessibility is in jeopardy. Finally, if legality is not upheld, regulation and control of state violence will be undermined and, thus, legal security is in jeopardy.

From the viewpoint of law-state thinking exclusively (i.e., regardless of, e.g., the importance of legality for the efficiency of the legal order) legality has, as far as I can see, no independent value apart from being a condition for the realisation of the basic law-state values. For this reason I do not include legality among these values, although, in a certain respect, it is more basic than those values, being a condition for their realisation. This being the case, legalism is, however, an important component of law-state thinking (and accordingly, a chapter will be devoted to legality in this monograph, Chap. 4).

But, as we have hinted here and there, law-state thinking has also more far-reaching claims upon the use of legal orders than this demand for legality, or lawfulness. It also demands *subordination* of certain areas of the exercise of legal power under legal rules, e.g., the subjection of supreme power to a (written) constitution, or the use of sanctions or coercive measures by the police or other authorities in accordance with statutory provisions. (Also legal subordination will be dealt with in Chap. 4.)

The close connection between legalism and the idea of subordination is manifested in an old idea in Western legal culture of a more general nature than the law-state thinking—let us refer to it as the idea of *nomocracy*—to the effect that the organisation of society shall be accomplished by means of a legal order, based upon legislation. This means subordination of vital areas of human social life to legal regulation, and the attendant idea that this regulation shall be strictly adhered to (legalism). Organising society through legislation was an idea held in great reverence by the ancient Greeks early in their history, and that idea is no less prominent in classical Greek thinking, expressed, e.g., in the famous formulation: *nómos basileús* (the law is the king). In the medieval Nordic provincial codes we often find manifestos like "Land shall be maintained by the law and not by violent deeds". Nomocracy was a prominent feature of the Enlightenment. Montesquieu, Beccaria and, above all, Bentham argued for large-scale codifications, which, when in force, should be strictly complied with. Included in the idea of nomocracy is *constitutionalism*, i.e., the idea that even *supreme* official power shall be subjected to law, which law is to be followed loyally by those exercising that power.

3.3 Law-State Thinking, Democracy, Judicial Review and the Idea of Restrictions on Power

It seems to me appropriate to say something in these Prolegomena about the relationship between law-state thinking and another, closely related ideology, viz. democracy. Suppose we painted, on a map of the world, those countries which are democracies with a certain colour and, in so doing, gave the colour a deeper tint the more democracy is realised in the country in question. Suppose, further, that, on another map of the world, we did the same thing, with the same colour, with regard to countries which "are law-states". It is highly probable that these two maps would be quite similar, and the causes of that are not particularly difficult to discern. There are good reasons to unite the two ideologies under the general, and commonly used, designation "the democratic law-state". (Unfortunately, the two maps would also reveal that democracy and law-state protection is something that a considerable part of mankind is deprived of.) In an effective democracy, those in supreme power are probably less apt (although sometimes apt enough) than their colleagues in dictatorships to violate, or let public authorities violate, individuals by misuse of the legal order, knowing that a collective of such individuals might well deprive them of their power in the next election.

But this state of things cannot always be trusted. The relation between democracy and law-state thinking also involves certain complications. A democracy driven to extremes might lead to violations of law-state protection, for it is always possible, by democratic majority rule, to tamper with legal certainty, discriminate against minorities, expose groups of individuals to physical abuse, replace court trial of individual rights by majority rule, etc. This complication was already observed by the early classics of the democratic law-state ideologies. In fact, it brings the law-state paradox to a head. This potential incompatibility is of a special interest when it comes to questions such as how to legislate in constitutional matters and whether to confer on courts of law the power of judicial review.

The mere existence of a constitution places restrictions upon an unhampered exercise of democracy (the drawbacks of which were known already in ancient Athens). The need for a constitution is seldom questioned even by the most ardent democrat. This, however, is not the case with judicial review, which has often been considered incompatible with democracy. "The democratic argument" against judicial review is well known. As John Ely states it: "The central problem of judicial review is: a body that is not elected or otherwise politically responsible in any significant way is telling the people's elected representatives that they cannot govern as they'd like".[14]

When taking a stand for or against judicial review one must take into consideration the fact that there are different grades of this phenomenon. Generally speaking, judicial review means that (i) a certain body (or bodies of a certain kind) (ii) under certain circumstances (iii) has a competence (iv) after comparison with provi-

[14] J. Ely, *Democracy and Distrust* (1980), pp. 4–5.

sions of the constitution and a certain legal action (legislative, executive or administrative) (v) to declare unconstitutional (vi) that action.

Judicial review may vary in design and strength in each of these six respects. As for (i), the competence of judicial review may be conferred on a special constitutional court (as in Germany), or on the ordinary courts of law (as in the US and Sweden) or, among these, exclusively on a supreme court. As for (ii), judicial review may be formal (i.e., consist in ascertaining whether the constitutional forms of legislation have been adhered to or not), or material (i.e., consist in ascertaining whether the content of a given statute conflicts with constitutional restrictions on statutory content or not). A court may be competent to exercise judicial review only in connection with an ordinary civil or criminal action or *in abstracto* and *ex officio* (as in Germany). Other restrictions are also possible. According to, e.g., the Swedish constitution, statutory provisions issued by the Parliament (*Riksdag*) or the Government may be set aside only if the discrepancy between the provision in question and the constitution is "manifest".[15] As for (iii), the competence of judicial review may be given in the constitution or be developed in judicial practice (as in the US). As for (iv), the strength of judicial review may vary according to the number of constitutional provisions and, more important, which rights are expressed by them. As for (v), a declaration that a statute is unconstitutional may have the result that that statute is generally invalid (from the date of its coming into force or from the date of the decision) or that it is invalid (formally) only with respect to the case under trial or situations of the same kind as that case. It might also have the consequence that the legislature is under an obligation to repeal or change the statute declared unconstitutional. As for (vi), finally, the scope of judicial review might vary depending upon which branches of the state are subject to it (the legislature, the Government—even the head of the State, as in the US—or the administration).

Is it possible for a democrat consistently to be in favour of judicial review? I think it is. In defence of this standpoint two different lines of argument are possible:

(1) To argue that judicial review is in fact a democratic institution. One way to do so is to differentiate between a procedural and a material concept (or justification) of democracy and to base a justification of judicial review on the material one.
(2) To argue that the scope of democracy—and, for that matter, the scope of any (positive) value—has its limits when confronted with other, equally strong or stronger values. Judicial review might be a means to give such values their due and to draw a reasonable limit between them and democracy.

In this book there is no need to discuss the relationship between democracy and judicial review in all its important aspects. I shall confine myself to a few remarks on judicial review in situations where the fundamental law-state values come into conflict with (the exercise of) democracy. From this starting-point it is natural to argue along line (2).

[15] This prerequisite has been removed as from January 1, 2011.

Let me first make a remark of a more pragmatic kind, concerning the background conditions for constitutionalism and judicial review. In societies in deep decay, disorganisation and brutalisation, delicate legal devices like judicial review provide, of course, precious little protection to the individual. Judicial review is, in fact, rather for the usually law-abiding democratic legislator who has respect for law-state values, but who now and then feels the temptation to strenghten the efficiency of law by tampering a bit with those values. Examples of legislators yielding to such temptations can be found also in the most successful democracies.

An important principle of law-state thinking with respect to its relation to democracy is, in my opinion, that the exercise of democracy must halt at the border, the crossing of which means a violation of the basic law-state values.

If this principle is accepted, it is, of course, easy to justify judicial review, as far as the basic law-state values are concerned, as a social device contributing to the defence of these values against democratic excesses.

How, then, can this principle be justified? I do not think that this issue can be decided by rational arguments only. We have to choose. In the choice, let us make use of the contrast-method.

A democratically elected body of legislators issues a criminal code where the crimes are so vaguely formulated that the public lives in constant fear of being prosecuted for having committed them. A democratically elected body of legislators issues a statute which strongly discriminates against coloured people, refugees, Jews or women. A democratically elected body of legislators issues a statute permitting the police to keep suspects in custody for an indefinite period of time (*sine die*), or a statute allowing the taxation authorities to search private premises, without notice but with use of force if needed, or to violate the privacy of correspondence. A democratically elected body of legislators issues a statute allowing the courts of law to withhold the prosecutor's evidence from defendants charged with crimes against the security of the state.

Is there any quality of democracy that makes things like these acceptable? As far as I can see: No.

It might perhaps be answered that, e.g., giving tax authorities the right to search private homes is necessary for securing taxation, or that giving terrorists access to evidence against them threatens the security of the state. But such answers will not do. They do not pertain to the conflict between law-state thinking and democracy, but to the conflict between law-state thinking and the efficiency of the legal order for attaining certain goals. Answers of this kind have nothing to do with democracy and are equally valid, or invalid, in a non-democratic society.

Democracy itself does not insure against wrongs of the above-mentioned kind. This task lies with the law-state mechanisms. If, in situations of the kind exemplified, democracy gives in—i.e., if democratic legislators, with or without help from the courts of law, impose a certain degree of self-restraint on themselves—democracy loses little or nothing, but individual security and safety gain a lot. Maintenance of the law-state values is a necessary condition for civilised social life. As a student of mine once wrote: "To live in a state with a balance between law-state ideals and democratic ideals is probably the most wholesome".

The idea of democracy and the law-state idea are both, as I see it, parts of a superior and more comprehensive idea, viz. *the idea of power restriction*. With this view, the boundary between law-state values and democracy loses some of its sharpness. A third component of this idea is the idea of the separation of powers. This idea is neither identical to nor included in the idea of democracy. In many respects the separation of powers is closer to the law-state idea than is democracy.

The anarchist idea of a society where no man exercises power over another is a naive utopian dream, totally divorced from reality. (The spontaneous social life that some anarchists dream of would, no doubt, in practice be the rule of the stronger). Social life necessarily requires that people be equipped with power on every level of society. Equally naive is the socialist idea that, in an accomplished socialist society, the power-holders exercise their power for the benefit of society as a whole and, hence, abuse of power ceases to be a problem.

Power is a necessary element in social life. A legal order is, to a large extent, a mechanism for restricting human rampaging by obligations and prohibitions, and for distributing power with the aid of norms conferring competence in different fields on legal (public or private) and natural persons. Such a legal competence may well confer power on official organs to use force. In fact, a legal order without recourse to force is a toothless tiger.

Power, in contrast to competence, is not a legal concept (a right). Power is factual domination—whether or not allowed by the legal system—of one man or a collective of men over another man or collective of men. Power includes a rich variety of forms, ranging from terror and threats to paternal benevolence, mild influence and objective authority.

Lust for power is a quality deeply rooted in the human condition. Without it, mankind would probably stand a lesser chance of surviving. With it, mankind is in constant danger of catastrophe. The psychology of power is a complicated branch of psychology. The German psychiatrist Alfred Adler analyses lust for power, at least in extreme forms, as an expression of a superiority complex, being a negative response to feelings of inferiority.[16]

Also, reactions to power have a wide range, from violent opposition or reluctant passivity to merry acceptance, admiration or servile, cringing submission. The psychology of obedience is no less complicated, and has perversions of its own.

A famous passage in Hobbes' *Leviathan* is the following:[17]

> So that in the first place, I put for a generall inclination of all mankind, a perpetuall and restlesse desire of Power after power, that ceaseth onely in Death. And the cause of this, is not alwayes that a man hopes for a more intensive delight, than he has already attained to; or that he cannot be content with a moderate power: but because he cannot assure the power and means to live well, which he hath present, without the acquisition of more. And from hence it is, that Kings, whose power is greatest, turn their endeavours to the assuring it at home by Lawes, or abroad by Wars; and when that is done, there succeedeth a new desire; in some, of Fame from new Conquest; in others, of ease and sensuall pleasure; in others, of admiration, or being flattered for excellence in some art, or other ability of the mind.

[16] A. Adler, *Über den nervösen Character* (1912).

[17] Th. Hobbes, *Leviathan* (1651), Part I, Ch. XI.

It is a time-honoured and established fact that power is necessary but dangerous. The ideology of power restriction emerges early in Western legal and political thinking. Its basic idea is simple: No man or group of men shall have unlimited and uncontrolled power. Every power-holder shall be held responsible for his use of power.

The idea of power restriction (including democracy, separation of powers, and law-state thinking) is no utopian ideology. It does not promise any special kind of society. It just sets the rules of the game. It has to do with the means of power, not with the ends of power.

In a democracy one power-holder can be replaced by another from one day to the next. This gives to democracy an almost anarchist touch: A political party in power, with a utopian, blue-print plan for society, cannot feel assured that it can realise this plan without interruption, or even at all. For non-democratic utopians democracy is therefore a cumbersome obstacle, for democratic utopians a problem. For the anti-utopian (like myself), this quality of democracy is one of its further advantages.

Democracies also seem, as a matter of empirical fact, to be more peace-preserving than non-democratic societies. It is often pointed out that no two developed democracies have up to now fought each other in war. But this is of course not a matter of natural necessity.

Power restriction is, as I see it, the most important purpose of a constitution. In order to realise the idea of power restriction in a constitution, at least the following decisions must be made.

(1) Which power spheres there shall be.
(2) How the scope of the different power spheres shall be confined.
(3) To what kind of person or persons shall power be attributed (within each different power sphere).
(4) How power shall be assigned and, not least, deprived. (The very point of democracy is, in my opinion, that it is in practice the only way, legally and peacefully, of getting rid of people with supreme power, instead of killing them, performing a coup d'état or waiting until they die or become senile. This is, to be sure, no small value.)
(5) For which period of time a person shall be in power.
(6) How power shall be controlled. (The classic device being to create a doctrine of the separation of powers and let the different spheres control each other.)
(7) How power-holders shall be held responsible for their exercise of power. (The main mechanisms are constitutional, criminal and civil responsibility.)
(8) Under what conditions it is allowed that power be exercised in individual cases. (This is usually regulated in so-called power-conferring norms, or competence norms, through which power, as it were, is channelled. To have competence is to have a right, conferred by the legal system, to exercise power.)

Mankind must never forget the lessons learned from Hitler, Mao and Stalin. People of their kind will always appear, and some of them will strive for power. However important it is for science to understand the psychic mechanisms involved, more important is the establishment of legal mechanisms for power restriction and power control that is sufficiently effective to stop in good time the rampant self-realisation of psychopaths and scoundrels. The career of Hitler and the state of things in the Weimar Republic are particularly instructive in this respect.[18] Telling is Hitler's taking every opportunity to advance his positions, never taking the slightest step backwards, let alone compromising, unless really forced to. At an early stage, during the years before the seizure of power, he could at certain moments have been disposed of without too much trouble, had the political and judicial state organs been free of corruption and efficient. After the seizure of power it was too late, the point of no return was passed. The power was now his, and he exercised it without any restrictions or scruples whatsoever. To oppose him now was not a matter of ordinary peaceful and decent competition for power in a civilized society, but to risk one's life and the lives of one's family. Opposition was now a matter of extreme individual courage, fundamentally tragic as standing a very slim chance of success. With respect to Hitler's warfare, the same lesson can be learnt. German aggression could have been stopped with much less suffering and bloodshed, had the Western democracies reacted more forcefully at earlier stages of German expansion. The longer they waited, the more devastating the consequences. It is a striking observation that, at those moments at which Hitler really met forceful opposition, and only then, he in fact retreated, sometimes surprisingly quickly. The lesson is simple: The rampage of the lethally dangerous among us must be contained at an early stage—long before the point of no return—by efficient state organs free of corruption, which are equipped with power sufficient for the purpose.

And let us not forget the simple-minded flocking round the evil, often as a result of ideological aberrations or romantic day-dreaming among otherwise intelligent people—those who readily take leave of their capacity for reason in favour of the glorification of (societies ruled by) men like Hitler, Stalin and Mao. Included here are people who in all seriousness disregarded the murders of millions while praising German *Autobahnen,* Soviet local state theatres, or Chinese day nurseries.

A feature highly characteristic of mankind by comparison with other animal species—to judge from its history—is its strongly developed destructive inclinations towards other specimens of the same species. Ours is the species which is its own most dangerous enemy. (Consider the murders and the devastating wars!) Another feature, also highly characteristic of mankind compared to other animal species, is its capacity, within its species, for both profound and enduring mutual sympathy, care and love. (Consider husband and wife in a long and happy marriage or people's help to victims of natural disasters in another part of the world!)

This predicament of mankind is the conditioning factor of law-state thinking—and its hope. The struggle for the law-state values is doomed to continue for as long as mankind itself exists.

To conclude. Nomocracy has as components the idea of legal subordination and legalism. Constitutionalism is included in nomocracy. Nomocracy is, in practice, a necessary condition for the realisation of the basic law-state values. Power restriction is a main justificatory reason for nomocracy. Democracy can be conceived of as

[18] For excellent accounts, see A. Bullock, *Hitler. A Study in Tyranny*, rev. ed. (1962), and I. Kershaw, *Hitler. 1889-1936 Hubris* (1998), and *Hitler. 1936–1945 Nemesis* (2000).

a means among others to realise the idea of power restriction, pertaining mainly to points (4) and (5) above. Democracy is to a high degree a *legal* idea, closely related to the idea of legal subordination: official power shall be assigned (for a certain period of time) and withdrawn through popular intervention in forms regulated by the law. The ideas of democracy, the separation of powers and the law-state are, all of them, components of the idea of power restriction.

3.4 Are the Basic Law-State Values Justifiable?

Can the basic law-state values (the law-state protection of the individual) be justified by reference to something even more fundamental than these values themselves? Is there something which is not identical with the basic law-state values and without which these values would mean nothing?

In my opinion there is.

What I have in mind are two highly intertwined ideas, deeply rooted in classical antiquity, which since the late Middle Ages in a radical way—during certain periods of history even revolutionary—have marked the life of Western man: *individualism* and *humanism*.

Individualism, regarded as a value-based idea, opposed to collectivism[19], includes two closely connected, basic ideas:

(1) That individual freedom, individual success, individual welfare, and individual security is something good—and, hence, that violations thereof is something evil.
(2) That social values are not attached to impersonal collectives of persons as independent entities, abstractions standing by themselves and not regarded as reducible to values pertaining to individual human beings—a family, a people, a race, a church, a guild, a nation, a party, a class, a corporation, a gender, a "culture"—but are exclusively attached to individual human beings: nothing, for instance, is good for a nation which is not good for individual persons.

Seen historically, Western individualism as a value-based idea has its background in the process of individualisation taking place in the cosmopolitan Hellenistic Period, informed by Epicureanism, Stoicism and Skepticism, and later in European societies from the late Middle Ages and onwards, and whose essential origin is found in middle class life in the medieval independent commercial towns and in the city cultures of northern Italy during the Renaissance.

Individualism provides the basis for humanism. In Chap. 2, I presented what I called a humanistic view of legal orders. By that I meant that legal orders are created by men, that they are products of human culture (and nothing inherent in human or non-human "nature", or given by gods). "Humanism", as I use the term, is something totally different, viz. the name of a fundamental value.

[19] K. R. Popper, *The Open Society and Its Enemies*, Vol. 1, The Spell of Plato, 5th ed., 1966, pp. 99–106.

Humanism in this sense is a kind of picture of ideal human life. Let us call it "*a life of human dignity*". This ideal is based on individualism in the respect that it necessarily pertains to individual human beings. What matters is the individual's life of human dignity.

What, then, does it mean that a person leads a life of human dignity, and why is that valuable?

These two questions cannot, as I see it, be answered separately and the reason is that the idea of a life of human dignity is based upon what I am tempted to call an aesthetic conception of man: the picture of a human being living a life of human dignity is something beautiful in itself.

This image is a multifarious phenomenon. It displays a human being who meets others without submissiveness and obsequiousness on the one hand, and without oppression of others and pomposity on the other—the independent, self-respecting (but not self-sufficient), free, adult human being, not slaving under the yoke of gods or human oppressors. It is the beauty, if one can see it, of that image that renders it an ideal. The realisation of that ideal is, to my mind, something desirable.

It must be strongly emphasised that this is a "normative" ("valuative") picture—the picture of an ideal. Human dignity is nothing you "have", like dark hair. It manifests itself in your way of living, in the way you respond to others. It is a matter of how you live—hence "a life of human dignity" as the name of this fundamental value. Of course there are people who do not find it in the least revolting that other people are humiliated (history is full of them), and some even enjoy it. (If things were otherwise this monograph need never have been written.) Neither is there any lack of people yielding to humiliation, some even deriving a perverse pleasure from it. But measured by the picture of a life of human dignity, all this is something evil.

This humanistic ideal of a life of human dignity I regard as the most precious part of our heritage from the ancient Greeks, where it shines forth here and there in drama, philosophy, poetry, and art—but, needless to say, less often in real life. We find it in *The Iliad*, in the sublime meeting in Book 24 of the ageing King Priam with Achilles, who has killed the king's son, Hector, or in Helen's upright and proud attitude to goddess Aphrodite in the third Book (even taken into consideration that Helen was a demigoddess herself). We find it in the poet Archilochus' famous Fragment 67 (trans. R. Lattimore):

> Heart, my heart, so battered with misfortune far beyond your strength,
> up, and face the men who hate us. Bare your chest to the assault
> of the enemy, and fight them off. Stand fast among the beamlike spears.
> Give no ground; and if you beat them, do not brag in open show,
> Nor, if they beat you, run home and lie down on your bed and cry.
> Keep some measure in the joy you take in luck, and the degree you
> give way to sorrow. All your life is up-and-down like this.

Moderation was a revered virtue in ancient . We find it also in the pathetic grave epigrams[20] as well as on the noble Athenian grave-reliefs of the late fifth century BCE, showing husbands bidding farewell to wives, or children to parents. We find it

[20] Of which we find striking examples in M. Wolfe (trans.), *Cut These Words into My Stone. Ancient Greek Epitaphs* (2013).

in Sophocles' tragedy *Antigone*, in Antigone's defiance of King Creon's proscribing that her brother Polyneices receive a proper burial. Pomposity and sentimentality are totally absent here. What a life of human dignity is shines forth everywhere.

It might be objected that since humanism in a way is an older idea than individualism (the idea of individualism was not thoroughly articulated in Pre-Hellenistic Greece), how could individualism provide the basis for humanism? The simple answer to that is, of course, that here I am not dealing with the history of ideas. The relationship between individualism and humanism I regard as a conceptual one, since humanism necessarily pertains to individuals.

Of course I do not claim that humanism is a unique Western, let alone Greek, idea. We see it manifested in the literature of other, even older, cultures as well (e.g., in the *Gilgamesh Epic*). The reason for my representing it with the aid of Greek expressions of it is simply that I am more familiar with Western classical antiquity.

Humanism is a universal idea. It takes as a fact that the human condition is basically the same for all mankind, that there is a common ground of shared human experience. We all know that we live in a difficult, perilous, ever-changing, and unpredictable world. We all know what our basic needs are: food, drink, shelter, rest, sex, love, friendship, and the respect of others. We all know what vice is: brutality, meanness, greed, deceitfulness. These things are ugly everywhere. For that reason humanism has a universal dimension.

If humanism in this sense is not embraced, I find it hard to see how the law-state values can be justified at all. But if humanism is adhered to, the realisation of the law-state values stands out as a necessary condition for the realisation of the fundamental humanistic value and, hence, the latter justifies the former.

It is, indeed, a sheer triviality to call attention to the fact that in societies where ideologies hostile to individualism have been successful, humanism has always been scoffed at and the law-state values have always been violated.

Violations of the law-state values inevitably lead to violations of a life of human dignity. Such violations have corrupting and humiliating effects on human beings. To lead a corrupt life or a life in humiliation is contrary to a life of human dignity. A person thus affected is prone to idolisation of either herself or others, or to disdain for either others or herself. A life of humiliation or idolisation is the contrasting picture to a life of human dignity.

This idea will be developed further in later chapters of this monograph. Let me, however, elaborate a little on it already here.

To live a life of human dignity is to live a life in moderation of mind. Violating a person's life of human dignity is degradation. How, then, shall we characterise the relationship between moderation and degradation?

Moderation (*σωφροσύνη*, *sôphrosúnê*) is a state of mind characterised by the absence of four vicious, or ugly, things: (1) Overestimating oneself in relation to oneself: *hubris*, (2) overestimating oneself in relation to others: deprecation of others, (3) underestimating oneself in relation to oneself: self-deprecation, and (4) underestimating oneself in relation to others: idolisation. The beautiful state of mind that is free from these extremes could also be called "self-respect". In Aristotelian terms, self-respect is the the golden mean between *hubris* and self-deprecation and between the deprecation of others and idolisation. The connection between *hubris* and the deprecation of others—of special interest with respect to the justification of the law-state values—is that they, although not identical, are psychologically closely tied to each other. The same is the case with self-deprecation and idolisation.

To be degraded is to be exposed to another person's deprecation of others (which, in its turn, usually is an expression of that person's *hubris*). One is also degraded when exposed to self-deprecation (and idolisation). And since the value idea, or virtue, of self-respect is directed against both forms of deprecation, it is also directed against degradation. Self-respect is to have a certain amount of appreciation of oneself and others—but in neither case *in extremis*. The virtue of self-respect can be so characterised: By having self-respect one also has respect for others, and shows consideration for them. In Kantian terms, respecting other people's life of human dignity is a duty to oneself. The inescapable connection between my own life of human dignity and that of others creates an indissoluble moral bond between human beings.

Of course, what we are talking about here is a matter of differences in degree. The deprecation of others embraces a vast field, from extreme, sadistic humiliation to irony, banter and hurting someone's feelings. Different steps on this scale can roughly be characterised by words such as "cruelty", "ruthlessness", "inconsiderateness", "indifference", "thoughtlessness" and "flippancy". There is a limit here, though, where claiming violation of one's life of human dignity is out of place, or even ridiculous. In a free society there are, and should be, things that we must endure, e.g., when our religious beliefs or political opinions are made fun of or scoffed at, or when someone's dignity as a woman is compromised when facing scantily clad ladies on posters. In such situations it is beneath one's dignity to complain that one's own or someone else's life of human dignity has been violated. It is too presumptuous to claim a right to go through life with one's feelings completely intact. It is, in fact, a token of lack of moderation in two respects to appeal in such situations: "Beloved Big Brother, look what they do to poor little me (self-deprecation)—so be hard on them (*hubris*)!"

From the viewpoint of law-state thinking, the task of legal orders is to contribute to the humanisation of social life. For achieving this, adherence to the law-state values is necessary.

The value I refer to as "a life of human dignity" must not be confounded with the conditions for its existence (just as freedom of expression is not a component of democracy but, besides being an intrinsic value, is a condition for the effectiveness of democracy). A life of human dignity is not the same as a life fit for human beings. The latter pertains to our standard of living. It goes without saying that living in great misery and want makes it hard to lead a life of human dignity in the sense of self-respect and respect of others. But even persons living in the most miserable circumstances can give proof of great dignity and integrity (there are examples even from concentration camps), whereas persons living in the lap of exuberant (and vulgar) luxury (such as Ceaucescu and the Ukrainian president Viktor Yanukovych) and having great power can lead a most repugnant life of human ruthlessness.

Can humanism, on its part, be justified by reference to some, even more basic idea? It follows from what I have said that I do not think so. On this level one has to choose. Then it is important to make clear to oneself what this choice really comes to. For that purpose I have recommended the contrast-method.

3.5 The Law-State

So far, I have left the term *law-state* itself unanalysed. Let me conclude these Prologomena by briefly indicating what I mean by that term.

The set of all conceivable law-states is a proper subset of the set of all conceivable states (i.e., all law-states are states but there is at least one conceivable state that is not a law-state).

The set of states is a proper subset of the set of human organisations. An organisation I regard as an order for human co-operation constituted by norms. (In that respect, e.g., General Motors, the Trades Union Congress, Arsenal FC and the state of Denmark are organisations.)

A state is an organisation (or a set of organisations) which, explicitly or implicitly, is obligatory according to the rules of a given legal system. Which qualifications a legal organisation shall satisfy in order to be "a state" shall not be discussed here. *Law-state thinking pertains to any supreme official power, state or not.*[21] Let us roughly define "state" in the following way: A state is (ideal-typically) an organisation that has a supreme, heteronomous, and general legal competence to rule over a certain class of human beings (the subjects, or citizens) within a certain geographic space (the state territory). ("Heteronomous competence" is here taken in the Kelsenian sense of competence to issue norms where the issuer and the addressee are two different subjects.) In addition to this, states usually have a limited, heteronomous competence to rule over non-citizens (aliens) within the state territory and over citizens outside that territory.

As soon as there is a state in a society, that state can be regarded as identical to the legal organisation, in a wider sense of that term (cf. Sect. 2.2, above and p. 176, below), of that society—or, in other words, the state is the totality of all organisations (organs, bodies, authorities) which are obligatory according to the legal system of that society. A state belongs to the legal order in the respect that it is constituted and regulated by the legal system and, hence, is a legal organisation. On the other hand, a legal organisation in the wider sense can exist without being or including a state. All states are legal organisations, but not all legal organisations are states. As examples, one can mention modern supranational organisations that are parasitic upon nation-states, such as the organisations of the U.N. and the European

[21] See further Å. Frändberg, "On the Relation between Law and State", in *Recht, Gerechtigkeit und der Staat.* Rechtstheorie, Beiheft 15 (Berlin, 1993), pp. 37–44. Reprinted in Å. Frändberg, *Rättsordningens idé* [The Idea of a Legal Order] (2005), pp. 151–158. See further N. MacCormick, *Questioning Sovereignty* (1999), *passim.*

Union. When in the course of history a legal organisation develops into a state cannot, of course, be stated in a clear formula. (In order to conceive all states as being legal organisations we might be compelled to weaken to some extent clauses (iv) and (v) in our (ideal-typical) characterisation of "legal order" (p. 11 f. above).)

A state in this sense has a complicated internal structure consisting of a variety of different organs. Characteristic of a state is that it claims supremacy (sovereignty) in different respects over private persons and organisations outside itself; that it produces general social norms which are applied by its organs; that it levies taxes; that it keeps armed forces; that it claims a monopoly of certain enterprises; that its sovereignty is geographically confined to "a territory"; that it stands in certain relationships to other states, etc.

It might seem that this use of the term "state" is incompatible with the use of the term in certain contexts, for instance, when it is asserted that a given person is a citizen of the state of Sweden. But that is to disregard the fact that such assertions are highly elliptical and rather a kind of abbreviation for much more complicated assertions. Thus the statement

(i) person *p* is a citizen of the state *s*

is equivalent to (with respect to the legal consequences of having become and not ceased to be a citizen of *s*)

(i') *p* stands in relations $r_1,\ldots r_n$ to *s*

where $r_1,\ldots,r_n$ is a set of relations between *p* and *s*, e.g., that *p* has a liability to pay taxes to *s*, that *p* is obligated to do military service in the armed forces of *s*, that *p* has a right towards *s* to social benefits, or that *p* has an obligation to behave in certain ways towards other private persons according to rules enacted by *s*, etc.

In the same manner the statement

(ii) *p* visits the state *s*

is equivalent to

(ii') *p* stands in relation *R* to *s*

where *R* is a relation between *p* and *s* such that (a) there is a place, *g*, visited by *p*, and (b) *g* is situated in that part of the world which, according to the legal system constituting *s*, is the territory of *s*.

A law-state is a state giving individuals law-state protection within its territory.

Since a state can provide law-state protection in different ways, and in different degrees, it is proper to formulate an ideal-type definition (in the Weberian sense) of the concept 'law-state'.[22]

[22] About the use of ideal-type definitions in legal science, see Å. Frändberg, "An Essay on Legal Concept Formation", in J.C. Hage & D. von der Pfordten (eds.), *Concepts in Law*, (2009) p. 6 f. As for the logical aspects of ideal-type definitions, see C. Hempel & P. Oppenheim, *Der Typusbegriff im Lichte der neuen Logik* (1936).

As dimensions of this ideal-type definition we choose the four basic law-state values (and, hence, get a four-dimensional ideal-type definition).

Thus, the ideal law-state (in a non-normative sense) is the imagined state where each of the four fundamental law-state values are maximally realised. The more a given state approximates the ideal type along a given dimension (i.e., the closer the real type is to the ideal type), the more that state is a law-state (on that particular dimension). It might well be the case that a certain state has, e.g., a high degree of legal certainty but a low degree of legal security. The ideal-type technique permits us to talk about such variations in a more nuanced manner and also to make more detailed comparisons between different states with respect to their quality as law-states. We could do with a term designating the society (state) where the law-state values are more realised than less. A most proper such term is "law-state".

Chapter 4
Legality and Legal Subordination

4.1 What is Legality?

Legality (lawfulness, the rule of law) prevails in a society to the extent that the legal system of that society is complied with by the official functionaries to whom the rules of the system are addressed (thus, "legality" is an ideal-type concept).

Legalism is a normative idea according to which legality shall prevail (in a certain society or in any society). The normative idea that legality shall prevail—that is, that legality shall be aimed at by every law-applier and, in a more mediate way, every legislator—we call *the basic principle of legalism*. This basic principle can be stated in a more exact manner if it is split up into several more precise principles. To the idea of legalism also belong justificatory arguments for the basic principle and thereto connected conceptions of social reality.[1]

Legalism is the cornerstone of the law-state ideology.

Four distinct (and not altogether mutually coherent) normative ideas of legalism can be stated in the form of the following *legality principles* :

(L1) A legal rule shall always be followed (applied) by the law-applying functionaries to whom the rule is addressed when adequate operative facts are present.

(L2) A legal rule shall never be followed (applied) by the law-applying functionaries to whom the rule is addressed when adequate operative facts are not present.

(L3) A legal rule shall always be followed (applied) adequately with respect to its norm theme by the law-applying functionaries to whom the rule is addressed.

(L4) For the law-applying functionary to comply with the legal system when deciding an individual case, he must consider the legal system in its totality as well as its underlying value basis (its teleology, or axiology). He shall be loyal to "the spirit of the law".

[1] For a similar view on legalism, see N. MacCormick, "The Ethics of Legalism", 2 *Ratio Juris*, 1989, pp. 184–193, esp. p. 184, and "Reconstruction after Deconstruction: A Response to CLS", 10 *Oxford Journal of Legal Studies*, 1990, pp. 539–558, esp. p. 541.

Å. Frändberg, *From Rechtsstaat to Universal Law-State,* Law and Philosophy Library 109, DOI 10.1007/978-3-319-06784-1_4, © Springer International Publishing Switzerland 2014

L1 says that a legal rule shall be applied to *all* cases where the prerequisites of the rule are fulfilled, i.e., it expresses a prohibition of a so-called reduction of the rule (see below, Sect. 4.2)—it is forbidden for the law-applier to make, on his own authority, exceptions from the rule in question. Let us call L1 "the principle of positive legality". The maxim *Nullum crimen sine poena* in criminal law is an instance of the principle of positive legality.

L2 says that a legal rule shall be applied *only* to such cases where the prerequisites of the rule are fulfilled. It expresses a prohibition of so-called extensive interpretation, and, even more, of analogical use of the rule (see below, Sect. 4.2)—it is forbidden for the law-applier to expand, on his own authority, the scope of application of the rule in question. Or, in other words, it is obligatory for the law-applier to make a restrictive interpretation of the rule, or to use it *e contrario* (see below, Sect. 4.2). Let us call L2 "the principle of negative legality". The maxim *Nullum crimen sine lege* in criminal law is an instance of the principle of negative legality.

L3 is concerned, not with the adequacy of operative facts relative to the prerequisites of a norm, but with the adequacy of norm-realising actions relative to the norm theme of a norm.

By "the norm theme" of a given norm, *n*, I mean the generic state of affairs (usually a set of actions) that is obligatory, permitted or forbidden by *n*. (In the language of deontic logic: formulas like *Op* and *Pq* consist of two components—the normative modality, or operator, *O* and *P*, and the norm themes *p* and *q*.) For instance, the legal rule

(*r*) When driving a car, it is forbidden for the driver to exceed the speed limits

has the norm theme

(*t*) The driver exceeds the speed limits

which, according to the normative modality of *r*, is forbidden.

L3 demands lawfulness with respect to norm themes. It is forbidden for law-applying functionaries to manipulate them. (In the language of deontic logic: The law-applier must never create a norm *Op* or *Pp* with the aid of another norm *Oq* or *Pq*, where $p \neq q$, however similar *q* is to *p*.)

If, e.g., the norm theme of a given rule is imprisonment for at least 2 years and at most 5 years, L3 forbids the judge to sentence offenders, by virtue of that rule, to imprisonment for 1 year or for 6 years; or if the norm theme is fines, it is forbidden for the judge to sentence offenders to undertake work that is advantageous to society instead, even if the salary amounts to the same sum as that of the fines.

Let us call L3 "the principle of normative adequacy". The maxim *Nulla poena sine lege* in criminal law is an instance of the principle of normative adequacy.

But is not L3 implied by L1 and L2? Well, that depends on what we mean by the terms "follow" or "apply". If these terms are taken in the strong sense of what I have called "follow adequately", then L3 follows from L1 and L2. But sometimes "follow" and "apply" can be used in a looser sense, permitting smaller deviations from the norm theme. Then L3 is not implied by L1 and L2. Example: A family agreement to the effect that X shall prepare the family's dinner on Sundays is followed by X in a weak sense even if X instead takes the family out for dinner once a month or so. In any case, L3 draws attention to the fact that legality is directed, not only to prerequisites and operative facts, but also to norm themes and norm-realising actions.

We can, of course, also formulate a legality principle *L3**, corresponding to, and generalising, Feuerbach's maxim *Nulla poena sine crimine*. The idea behind that maxim can be interpreted in the following manner: (i) It is possible for a law-applier to impose punishment on a person without even relating the evil thereby inflicted upon her to some criminal act of hers in the past, and (ii) this kind of behaviour on the part of law-appliers must not be accepted.

However, it is, as far as I know, unusual for law-appliers to behave like that, even in the most unscrupulous circles. Even the regimes of Hitler and Stalin made certain efforts, however far-fetched, to present circumstances as adequate operative facts for the legal consequences they desired. It is far more usual to tamper with the operative facts or sanctions (legal consequences) as such, which brings us back to principles L1—L3.

L4 is brought to the fore mainly in four standard problematic situations:

(a) When it is difficult to ascertain, with respect to a given rule, *r*, and a given situation (case), *s*, whether *r* is applicable to *s* or not
(b) When there is no rule at all in the system applicable to *s*.
(c) When *r* undoubtedly is applicable to *s* but there are good reasons not to apply *r* to *s* (i.e., good reasons for making a reduction of *r* with respect to *s*).
(d) When two (or more) rules, r_1, and r_2, ($r_1 \neq r_2$), are both (all) applicable to *s*.

According to L4, the law-applier, in situations of these kinds, shall use the whole of the legal system in a mediate way. He shall pay attention to (i) the consistency and coherence of the legal system, (ii) "the legislator's" intentions concerning the legal field in question, and (iii) the value basis of the whole legal system. When a law-applier of the legal system *L*, in some situation, *s*, belonging to one of the kinds (a)–(d), creates and applies a rule, *r**, to *s*, then, according to L4, *r** shall be created in the spirit of *L*. The legality prescribed by L4 is a more diluted kind of legality than that of L1–L3. In relation to L1–L3, L4 has a "supplementary" function (see further Sect. 4.3.2. below). We call L4 "the principle of loyalty" .

The principles of positive and negative legality may conflict in one certain respect: when the prerequisites of a rule under interpretation are vague and, hence, the law-applier has to choose between an extensive interpretation (which to a certain extent violates L2) and a restrictive interpretation (which to a certain extent violates L1; see below under 4.2). On the other hand, L1 and the principle of normative adequacy (L3), as well as L2 and L3, are mutually independent in the respect that it is possible without any inconsistency to adhere to one of them and reject the other or adhere to, or reject, both.

The principle of loyalty (L4), for its part, may conflict with any one of the others. A mediate use of the legal system may result in an analogy from an existing rule in it, which violates the principle of negative legality. It may result in a reduction of an existing rule in it—a rule peculiar in the respect that the rule itself is contrary to the spirit of the system as a whole—in which case the principle of positive legality is violated. Or it may urge a judge to manipulate the norm theme of a rule in order to adapt it to the general outfit of legal consequences (e.g., the system of civil sanctions), and thus to violate the principle of normative adequacy.

For the sake of clarity, L1–L4 are stated in their strongest possible form. As such they must, of course, be weighed against other noteworthy principles in concrete decision-situations.

How shall one characterise the social state of affairs that is the opposite of the one where legality, the rule of law, prevails—or, in other words, where the foundations of the law-state are not present?

The law-state can be contrasted with the naked power-state. To be sure, also in societies governed by a naked power-state, the exercise of power is restricted. It is restricted by things like the amount of pure collective physical strength of those in power, the degree of concord among them, their ability to control the territory over which they rule, and their sensitivity to external disapproval. It might also be restricted by fear or by certain ideological or religious scruples in the minds of those holding power. Within these natural and cultural boundaries, however, their exercise of power is unlimited. If there exists a legal order in such a society, that order is not a power-restricting element in society but merely a strategic alternative at the disposal of those holding power, ready to be used by them when, but only when, it suits them.

To uphold legality is to provide the public with protection against the abuse of the legal order that lies in the strategic use of it by those holding power. *It guarantees that those holding power do not tamper with the legal order itself*, by using it *ad hoc* when they find that suitable and by not using it when that is to their advantage.

The basic principle of legality can be justified by the following six reasons (included in legalism).

(1) Legality is a necessary background condition for legal equality in the administration of law (equality before the law). For if the principles of positive and negative legality and normative adequacy are not strictly adhered to, people are placed "above" or "outside" the law.
(2) Legality is a necessary background condition for legal certainty. For if the law-applying organs do not constantly follow the legal rules, but apply them only occasionally, and that for more or less irrelevant and arbitrary reasons, the possibility for the public to predict what will happen legally in given circumstances is severely reduced. It is true that knowledge about such reasons, if available, to a certain extent can facilitate predictability. But the ideal of legal certainty, as a component of law-state thinking, means *certainty based on (knowledge of) the law*.
(3) Legality is a necessary background condition for legal accessibility. With respect to legal accessibility too, legality presupposes legal subordination. For if there are no established "law-ways" to the benefit of individuals seeking justice, or such law-ways are stated in a fuzzy way, and, furthermore, if the rules regulating these things are not strictly adhered to, legal accessibility certainly comes to very little.
(4) Legality is a necessary background condition for legal security. In order to achieve legal security two things are needed (and for that reason these two things are both important parts of law-state thinking):

(i) that there are restrictive statutory regulations of the authorities'use of physical and mental violations of individuals' integrity (i.e., a claim of legal subordination)
(ii) that these regulations are strictly adhered to (i.e., a demand for legality)

If these two necessary background conditions are not fulfilled, legal security is constantly at risk.

I am not claiming that legality is a sufficient background condition for legal equality, certainty, accessibility, and security respectively. Legal subordination, too, might be a necessary background condition for them (see further Sect. 4.5 below).

(5) Legality makes possible the control of those officals holding power. Through the claim of legality, those holding power can be made legally responsible for their actions, since liability for breach of duty can be connected with, and measured after, a deviation from a lawful exercise of power.

(1)–(5) state the importance of legality for the realisation of the four basic law-state values. A further argument for the basic principle of legality, independent of law-state thinking, is the following:

(6) A necessary background condition for the efficiency of the legal rules is that the citizens follow the rules addressed to them, and do so in a uniform manner (another necessary condition for their efficiency is the expediency of the rules). Lawful (legalistic) handling of the rules by the authorities, in turn, is no doubt a necessary background condition for the citizens' following the rules addressed to them.[2]

The rest of this chapter has four parts. In order to get a better understanding of the idea of legality we must gain a clearer conception of what it means to comply with legal rules. This will be dealt with in Sect. 4.2. In Sect. 4.3 some technical aspects of the realisation of legality are considered. Since the basic principle of legalism often must be weighed against other principles, something has to be said about the limits of legality. This is done in Sect. 4.4. In Sect. 4.5, finally, we pass from legality to legal subordination and discuss the demands of law-state thinking for the creation and subjection under legal rules of certain practices. Of special interest in this connection is the subordination of supreme power under the law, i.e. constitutionalism.

4.2 Compliance with the Law

In this section we shall examine a bit more closely the crucial concept of legality: the relation *compliance with* (as used in phrases like "Judges shall comply with the law").

The concept "comply with" belongs to the family of jurisprudential concepts which I have called "praxeological concepts". A legal order is an abstract product

[2] Cf. J. Raz, *op. cit.* (note 17), pp. 224–226.

of human culture, and it has a normative character. As such it is an entity related in many and various respects to human behaviour. It causes mental and physical actions (including strategies for action). Legal orders are handled intellectually by their functionaries. Indeed, the very point of legal orders is their action-causing quality, since the desired social states of affairs, the achievement of which a legal order is the means, ultimately consist of certain actions or omissions caused, directly or indirectly, by that legal order. Praxeological concepts are, e.g., the following (*a* is a person, *r* a legal rule and *S* a legal system):

(i) *a* follows (observes, obeys, adheres to, complies with, conforms to) *r*
(ii) *a* breaks (violates) *r*
(iii) *a* applies (administers) *r*
(iv) *a* interprets (constructs, uses) *r* (literally, analogically, restrictively, *e contrario*)

and also

(v) *r* is a valid rule in *S*

since (in Chap. 2) we have defined validity in terms of the officials' following the legal rules in their jurisdiction.

In our analysis we choose the term "comply with" to name the key-concept of legality. (In such an analysis the close affinity between morphological, praxeological and ideological concepts becomes apparent.)

It seems reasonable to assume that for a judge, e.g., to comply with the law with respect to a given situation, he must apply some general rule which "covers" that situation; that general rule must in some sense be proven to "belong to", or at least "be in accordance with", the legal system in question (in order to ascertain that, we must state the legal rule in question in an "independent" way, i.e., it must be formulated in a way that does not presuppose that it already belongs to the legal system, which would be to beg the question); and, in addition to that, the judge's very application of this rule to the situation must itself be "legal", or "legally valid". For if any one of these conditions is not fulfilled, it cannot be said that the judge has complied with the law. Our definition of the compliance relation is based on this assumption.

We define the relation "compliance with" (CW for short) in the following manner.

(DEF.CW)

1. Let

   (a) *S* be a given legal system
   (b) *a* be a person
   (c) *r* be a legal rule
   (d) *s* be an "individual" state of affairs (a situation, a case).

2. *a* complies with *S* when deciding *s*=def.

   (i) *r* is system-independent relative to (the rules of) *S*
   (ii) *a* applies *r* to *s*
   (iii) *r* is in accordance with *S*

(iv) *a's* application of *r* to *s* is legally valid according to *S*.

A closer analysis of CW, then, consists in making the four relations more precise:

(1) … is system-independent relative to …
(2) … applies … to …
(3) … is in accordance with …
(4) … is legally valid according to …

A. r is system independent relative to S

Let us clarify this notion in two steps.

Step 1. With regard to a given situation (case), *s*, it might be doubtful whether a given rule is applicable to *s* or not, and there might exist two or more rules acting as possible candidates for application to *s*.

By the term "system-independent case-description" I mean a description (a statement or conjunction of statements) of a case, which description is independent of any rule or rules which are candidates for being applicable to *s* and which belong to the legal system in question.

Suppose that the following two provisions (legal rules) are included in the penal code of a certain country:

(r_1) Anyone who steals something, the value of which is minor, shall be sentenced for larceny to a fine

and

(r_2) Anyone who, without being guilty of another crime in this code, illicitly takes, uses or otherwise appropriates something, shall be sentenced for arbitrary conduct to a fine.

Suppose, further, that person X has taken person Y's cheque-book out of her handbag in an unguarded moment without Y's consent. We say that the description of this case

(cd) X has without Y's consent and knowledge taken Y's cheque-book when it was in Y's possession

is system-independent relative to r_1 and r_2, which are both candidates for application to this case.

A case-description, *d*, describing a case, *c*, is system-independent relative to any rule, *r*, in a given system if and only if it is inadmissible to draw an inference from *r* in conjunction with *d* alone resulting in a conclusion that attaches the legal consequences of *r* to *c*. Hence, e.g., the inference from r_1 and cd to the conclusion

(cr) X shall be sentenced for larceny to a fine

is logically invalid. What is needed in order to get a logically valid inference is an additional premise

(p) To take a cheque-book without the possessor's consent and knowledge is to steal something, the value of which is minor.

But by stating p, we have qualified cd in accordance with r_1 (i.e., we have made an interpretation of r_1 to the effect that r_1 is applicable to the case described by cd). But whether we add p or not, cd alone is still independent of r_1.

An example of a non-system-independent (i.e., a system-dependent) case-description is, on the other hand

(cd′) X has stolen Y's cheque-book, the value of which is minor.

Step 2. On the basis of a system-independent case-description, a legal rule can be formulated such that the operative facts described by the prerequisites of that rule are such states of affairs which are described by that case-description. In other words, that case-description itself—with irrelevant indices (names of persons and the like) generalised—becomes the prerequisites of the rule. The legal consequences attached to these prerequisites, however, can be chosen ad lib. We call such a rule *a system-independent rule* relative to a given legal system. To that category belongs, e.g.,

(cdr) If anyone takes another person's cheque-book which is in that person's possession without her consent and knowledge, the perpetrator shall be sentenced for arbitrary conduct to a fine.

The criterion of whether the prerequisites of a given rule, *r*, are an adequate generalisation of a given case-description, *d* (or, in other words, whether *r* is a system-independent rule with respect to *d*) is that it shall be possible to make a valid inference attaching the legal consequences of *r* to the case described by *d* without adding any further legal qualification as a premise. This is, e.g., the case with respect to cdr and cd.

As we pointed out, the legal consequences of *r* has nothing to do with the system-(in)dependence of *r*. Whether they are taken from some rule in the system (as is the case with respect to cdr) or not, *r* is still system independent, if its prerequisites are a system-independent case-description.

Since legality consists in something's being in *accordance with the rules* of a given legal system, it is reasonable to assume that what is to be tested with respect to its legality is itself a rule. The test consists in ascertaining whether or not the rule actually applied is in accordance with some rule in the system. The former rule must therefore be formulated in a way that does not presuppose that it already belongs to the system. *Hence, what shall be tested with respect to its legality—its accordance with law—must be a rule that is system-independent.*

Since it is the official law-appliers' conformity with law that is to be tested, it is, further, appropriate to formulate system-independent rules as addressed to them.

B. a applies r to s

We can use the term "apply" within the field of legal reasoning in two senses, a weaker and a stronger, where the stronger includes the weaker.

What is applied is, strictly speaking, always system-independent rules. They are *per definitionem* immediately applicable, i.e., applicable without any further qualifying premise added.

a applies r to s in the weak sense when *a* draws a conclusion about the legal consequences of *s* from *r* and a (system-independent) case-description, *d*, describing *s*. An example of an application in the weak sense is the inference from cdr and cd to

(cr′) X shall be sentenced for arbitrary conduct to a fine.

We call a system-independent rule used in application of law *a subsumption rule*. The conclusion of such an inference (e.g., cr′) we call, with Kelsen, *an individual legal norm*.

We can, then, specify our statement above about what is to be tested with respect to its accordance with law by saying that it is a system-independent rule when it functions as a subsumption rule.

a applies r to s in the strong sense of the word when *a* actually slavishly follows the individual norm addressed to him which is the result of an application in the weak sense. Thus, e.g., *a* applies cdr strongly when *a* pronounces *a judgment sentence* (the term "sentence" of course used in its linguistic, not its judicial, sense), such as

(j_1) X is sentenced for arbitrary conduct to a fine of 1,000 Swedish kronor

or

(j_2) X is sentenced for arbitrary conduct to ten day-fines at 200 Swedish kronor each.

In clause (ii) of our definition of CW we use the term "apply" in its strong sense. The reason for that is the following.

Suppose (a) that there is an individual legal norm, *n*, derived by *a* from a system-independent legal rule, *r*, (i.e., *a* applies *r* in the weak sense), (b) that *r* is in accordance with law and (c) that *a* has the competence to apply *r* (in the strong sense) to the given case. Then, even if these conditions are fulfilled, it may still be the case that *a* does not comply with the law, since *a* may pronounce a judgement sentence which goes beyond *n*, i.e., *a* does not follow *n* slavishly. And that would be to violate the principle of normative adequacy (L3; see Sect. 4.1 above). Therefore, a necessary condition for compliance with the law is application of legal rules in the strong sense of the term.

Hence, e.g., the inferring of cr′ and the pronouncement of j_1 or j_2 on the basis of cdr and cd is an application in the strong sense. On the other hand, to pronounce the following judgment sentences on the basis of cdr, cd and cr′ is to violate L3:

(j_3) X is sentenced for arbitrary conduct to one year's imprisonment

or

(j_4) X is acquitted of the charge of arbitrary conduct.

If *a* pronounces j_3 or j_4 under the given conditions, *a* is, consequently, not complying with the law.

C. r is in accordance with S

The crucial point of "CW-tests" is to ascertain whether a given subsumption rule is in accordance with the law or not. To be tested is to determine whether relations of a certain kind exist between a given subsumption rule and (the rules of) a given legal system. The core of legalism consists in certain claims upon the qualification of given states of affairs as falling under legal rules or not (i.e., the labelling of states of affairs in the light of the prerequisites of legal rules). In this connection, the legality principles L1, L2 and L4 are in focus.

Let us assume, for a given subsumption rule, *sr*, to be in accordance with law, that *sr* must stand in some set-theoretical relation to a legal rule which belongs to the legal system in question (an assumption that will be subjected to some modification below). Let us call such a rule, belonging to the system, *a basic rule* (relative to a given subsumption rule).

In order, then, to establish these relations, we have to establish all possible set-theoretical relations which can hold between a subsumption rule and a basic rule within a certain set-theoretical framework.

Suppose that we have a statutory legal rule, *br*. To *br* corresponds a set, *M*, of situations (cases) which are covered by "the purely linguistic" (literal) meaning of *br*. *M* will be graphically represented in the schema below by double circles. The cases within the inner circle are such cases which, without any doubt whatsoever, are covered by the wording of *br*, while, with regard to the cases which lie within the outer circle but outside the inner one, it is uncertain whether they are covered by the wording of *br* or not, due to the general vagueness of natural language.

To *br* also corresponds another set, *A*, of all cases to which *br* are actually applied by the law-applying authorities of the given legal order when a case of that kind is presented to them. Of course, *M* and *A* are, in real legal life, not necessarily identical sets (although such an identity in fact is what the legality principles L1 and L2 taken together demand).

Finally, we can also form the set *I* (represented by the rectangle) of all cases where it makes sense at all to consider the use of *br* (the influence sphere of *br*). *M* and *A* are subsets of *I*.

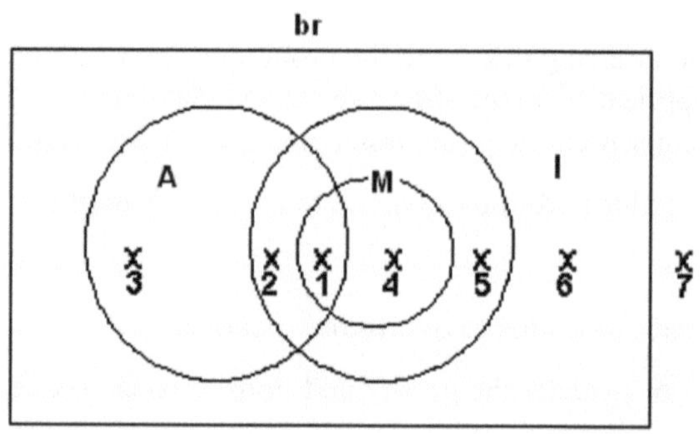

Example:

Suppose that there is a sign at a park entrance with the text "Large dogs not allowed". Beside the sign there sits, on a little folding chair, an elderly park-keeper, who in his youth followed an introductory university course in law. Now he is confronted in turn by cases of the kind represented in the schema with numbers 1–7.

(1) First comes a lady with a Great Dane. The dog is not allowed to enter the park. The park-keeper simply *applies* the rule of the sign. From the basic rule "Large dogs not allowed" (*b* for short) he constructs the subsumption rule

(s_1) Great Danes not allowed.

"Simply applies" means in this case (i) that the prerequisite set of s_1 (the set of Great Danes) is a proper subset of "the core set" of *b* (the set of all undoubtedly large dogs) represented by the inner *M*-circle and (ii) that the prerequisite set of s_1 is a proper subset of *A*.

(2) Then comes a boy with a cocker spaniel. Now the park-keeper hesitates, owing to the vagueness of the wording which expresses the rule of the sign. Cocker spaniels, it is true, are normally rather small dogs but, he says to himself, this one is an unusually large specimen. It is not allowed to enter the park. The park-keeper makes *an extensive interpretation* of the rule by constructing the subsumption rule

(s_2) Large cocker spaniels not allowed.

"Extensive interpretation" means in this case (i) that the prerequisite set of s_2 (the set of large cocker spaniels) is a proper subset of "the uncertainty set" (the set of dogs such that it is uncertain whether they are "large dogs" or not) of *b* and (ii) that the prerequisite set of s_2 is a proper subset of *A*.

(3) Now an old man with a chimpanzee appears. Obviously, a chimpanzee is not a large dog, or even a dog at all. But, argues the park-keeper, the reasons behind the rule, viz., not to frighten the small children on the play-ground nearby, are just as valid with respect to chimpanzees. The ape is not allowed to enter the park. The park-keeper uses the rule of the sign *analogically* by constructing the subsumption rule

(s_3) Chimpanzees not allowed.

"Analogy" means in this case (i) that the intersection of the prerequisite set of s_3 (the set of chimpanzees) and *M* is empty, (ii) that the prerequisite set of s_3 is a proper subset of I (the set of cases about which it makes sense at all to consider *b*) and (iii) that the prerequisite set of s_3 is a proper subset of *A*.

(4) After this a blind man turns up with an enormous Alsatian as a guide dog. It is without any doubt a large dog. But in this case, the park-keeper argues, strong counterbalancing reasons are at hand for allowing entrance to the park. The dog is allowed to enter the park. The park-keeper has made *a reduction* (to use a nowadays common German term for the phenomenon) of *b* by constructing the subsumption rule

(s_4) Large dogs that serve as guide dogs are allowed.

"Reduction" means in this case (i) that the prerequisite set of s_4 (the set of large dogs which are guide dogs) is a proper subset of the core set of *b* and (ii) that the intersection of the prerequisite set of s_4 and *A* is empty.

(5) Then a little girl with an Alsatian puppy stands before the old park-keeper. "Well", he says, and hesitates for a moment because of the vagueness of the rule, "Alsatians are normally large dogs, but this one is, after all, a small rascal". It is allowed to enter the park. The park-keeper makes *a restrictive interpretation* of *b* by constructing the subsumption rule

(s_5) Alsatian puppies allowed.

"Restrictive interpretation" means in this case (i) that the prerequisite set of s_5 (the set of Alsatian puppies) is a proper subset of the uncertainty set of *b* and (ii) that the intersection of the prerequisite set of s_5 and *A* is empty.

(6) There enters a gentleman with a frightful cat on the leash. It is neither large, nor a dog, so it is allowed to enter the park. But before the park-keeper decides this, he considers whether the kind of reasoning he performed in case 3 would not also be appropriate in this case, i.e., he considers the possibility of an analogy. In this respect the rule of the sign has a certain relevance also in this case. But he rejects that idea. The park-keeper uses the rule of the sign *e contrario* by constructing the subsumption rule

(s_6) Frightful cats allowed.

"*E contrario*" means in this case (i) that the intersection of the prerequisite set of s_6 (the set of frightful cats) and *M* is empty, (ii) that the prerequisite set of s_6 is a proper subset of *I* and (iii) that the intersection of the prerequisite set of s_6 and *A* is empty.

(7) A married couple makes its appearance. The park-keeper, who as an old man has become a misogynist, feels a strong temptation to send away the wife by appealing to the sign, but he realises that in doing so, he would be far off the mark. The rule of the sign is irrelevant in this case—it is *beyond the scope of the influence sphere* of that rule.

(8) Autumn is here, with cold and whirling leaves. The old park-keeper is freezing and takes resort to the bottle. Boxers, Alsatians, collies, bulldogs, and St. Bernards come streaming in, but he does not care. The rule of the sign has *fallen into desuetude* (become obsolete). "Desuetude" means that the intersection of *M* and *A* is empty, or—stronger—that *A* is empty. After a while we get a new, unwritten rule

(s_7) Large dogs are allowed.

As we see, the rule-relations "(simple) application", "extensive interpretation" and "analogy" together make a family: extension is a marginal case between simple application and analogy; i.e., to say that we are making an extension of a given rule is the same as saying that we do not know whether we are just applying that rule or using it analogically. In the same way, restriction is a marginal case between reduction and *e contrario*; we do not know whether we use the rule *e contrario* (by contrast) or make a reduction from it.

The terms presented in (1)–(8) are not names of principles (methods) of statutory interpretation but names of the result of the use of such principles (the use of, e.g., a teleological or an intentional method can result in an analogy).

As we have already pointed out, subsumption rules are conceived of as addressed to law-applying organs directly. But of the basic rules corresponding to them, that are found in statutes, only some are so addressed, while others are addressed to the public (as sellers and buyers, employers and employees, etc.). But every rule of the latter kind can always be transformed into adequate counterparts addressed to law-appliers.[3] When in the following we talk about basic rules, we take them as rules addressed to law-appliers (directly or after transformation).

The set of rule-relations now presented will serve as a framework for our analysis of CW. We shall begin by submitting them to the test of the legality principles L1 and L2 (the principles of positive and negative legality).

1. "Simple" application
This rule-relation is ideal from the point of view of legality. L1 is strictly adhered to and L2 does not need to be mobilised.

2. Extensive interpretation
This rule-relation is doubtful as far as L2 is concerned—the field of application is expanded into the uncertainty sphere.

In situations of this kind some *supplementary legality principles* can be mobilised (*in dubio*-rules). In criminal law one such supplementary principle is formulated in the classical form of *in dubio mitius* (in situations of uncertainty: choose the interpretation which is most favourable to the defendant!). Since an extensive interpretation of penal provisions always is to the defendant's disadvantage, this maxim prescribes a general use of restrictive interpretation in criminal law.

The same point of view is applicable to administrative law (including taxation law), when burdens and impositions are laid upon private citizens: *(in dubio) odia sunt restringenda* (in situations of uncertainty: choose the interpretation which is most favourable to the one exposed!). As for private law, however, such a general benefit-rule in favour of the defendant or the plaintiff would not, indeed, be possible since in private law what is to the benefit of the one usually is to the disadvantage of the other. All the same, one could argue that legal certainty requires a general use of restrictive interpretation also in private law. But such a general principle is, as far as I know, not accepted in any private law system.

Another *in dubio*-principle is the classical one that, in situations of uncertainty, rules that provide exceptions shall be interpreted restrictively—for the reason, no doubt, that otherwise the corresponding principal rule would be watered down and thus lose some of its force just as a principal rule.

3. Analogy
This rule-relation is even more doubtful as far as L2 is concerned than is extension—here the field of application is expanded outside even the most uncertain (though possible) literal interpretation of the rule in question. In fact, L2, in the strong formulation given above, simply rejects any analogical use of legal rules. And the reasons against extension within different spheres of law are, or so it seems, valid *a fortiori* as regards analogy.

[3] In Å. Frändberg, "The Legal Philosophical Addressee Problem" in *Logic, Law, Morality. Thirteen essays in honour of Lennart Åqvist*. K. Segerberg, R. Sliwinski (eds.) Uppsala Philosophical Studies 51., Department of Philosophy (2003), pp. 99–109 I have formulated some such "transformation rules".

I know of no legal order where the principle of negative legality is adhered to in an orthodox fashion. But in many standard works in criminal law a prohibition against an analogical use of penal provisions to the disadvantage of the defendant is advocated and conceived of as, at least, a corollary of L2. The same opinion seems to prevail within taxation law with respect to expansion of tax liability (a Swedish scholar, Seve Ljungman, has coined the maxim *Nullum tributum sine lege*—No taxation without law).

With respect to analogy, the conflict between L2 and L4 is obvious. While L2 rejects any analogical use of legal rules, L4, on the contrary, favours it to the benefit of the evaluative coherence within the legal system as a whole.

4. Reduction
Since this rule-relation can be seen as the opposite of simple application, which is the ideal one from the point of view of L1, it must be rejected by that principle. If the law-applier on his own authority makes exceptions to a completely clear provision, then, of course, this provision is not applied to all cases described by the prerequisites of it. L2, on the other hand, is irrelevant in the case of reduction.

From one point of view, reduction can be regarded as a more radical interference than analogy in the sphere of legislation on the part of the law-applier—it seems to be a more serious thing to correct the legislator by reduction than to expand his regulations by analogy to unregulated situations. Behind this contention lies, of course, the idea of the supremacy of the legislator (an idea justified, e.g., by democratic arguments), which supremacy would be violated by reduction. On the other hand, it might seem less objectionable to make a reduction from a penal provision than to expand criminalisation outside its literal scope—at least when there are substantial reasons of criminal policy for a reduction and the principle of equality before the law does not have a strong restrictive influence in the particular situation.

With respect to reduction, the incoherence between L1 and L4 stands out clearly. While L1 rejects any reduction of legal rules, L4, under certain circumstances, might favour reduction, viz. when the coherence of the legal system as a whole demands it—which can be the case when the given provision, due perhaps to negligence in the legislative work, is a means to ends contrary to the general value basis of the system.

5. Restrictive interpretation
This rule-relation is favoured by L2 and its supplementary *in dubio*-principles. On the other hand, one could say that it to a certain extent violates L1. But my guess is that most lawyers would regard L2 as more important than L1—which, significantly enough, does not have any *in dubio*-principles connected with it—with respect to cases in the uncertainty sphere. The antithetical thinking, favouring *e contrario* and restriction, seems to be deeply rooted in legal discourse, which, of course, is a consequence of the importance of legalism in such discourse.

6. E contrario
This rule-relation, like 1, stands out as ideal from the point of view of legality. L2 is strictly adhered to and L1 does not need to be mobilised. However, the more diluted

kind of legality claimed by L4 may prefer analogy to *e contrario* under certain circumstances.

7. This situation contains no rule-relation at all
The scope of the influence sphere delimits the sphere where analogical and *e contrario* uses of a legal rule can be taken up at all. Admittedly, influence spheres can be expanded quite a bit. But sooner or later an unhampered expansion will end in absurdity.

8. Desuetude
This is not a rule-relation of its own but a marginal case of reduction—it is the maximal reduction possible. The whole of the *M*-set ("literal meaning-set") is reduced, and what is left is only an empty shell in the shape of a linguistic formulation in a statutory provision. For the law-applier to regard a statutory provision still in force as obsolete is, of course, a considerable intervention in the legislator's competence but happens, as we all know, now and then (especially with regard to very old and out-of-date rules).

While L1–L3 ties their guarantees for legality to the literal meaning of individual legal rules, L4 relates legality to the legal system as a whole. In the first case, we can talk about *rule-legality* and in the latter of *system-legality* and, as we have seen, rule-legality and system-legality may conflict in individual situations. (Correspondingly, we can use the terms "rule-legalism" and "system-legalism".)

It is obvious that the degree of legality is conditioned by the quality in certain respects of the legal source material used by the law-applier.

We say that *a perfect legality setting* exists relative to a given legal system, *S*, and a given set of individual cases, *C*, when the following four *legality conditions* are fulfilled:

(1) That there are rules in *S* regulating *C*
(2) That the rules of *S* are clear with respect to *C*, i.e., that it is possible to decide without doubt that they are applicable or not applicable to *C*
(3) That the rules of *S* applicable to *C* do not conflict
(4) That the rules of S applicable to C are, each of them and together, teleologically adequate (expedient), i.e., that, if applied to elements of *C*, they lead to the goals they are intended for.

In a state of affairs where perfect legality prevails, there is no need for L4 from the point of view of legalism, and L1–L3 are easily applicable.

When there are deficiencies in the fulfilment of (1)–(4)—and in real life there always are, more or less—an imperfect legality setting is at hand. L4 is made for this predicament. Its task is to defend *a second front legality*.

Condition (1) contains a claim for legal subordination. It is the most fundamental of legality conditions, for if there are no rules for a given case, it is meaningless to talk about legality with respect to that case.

Deficiencies related to condition (2)—the legal rule being vague, obscure or ambiguous—threatens legality by making it hard, or even impossible, to decide whether or not a given rule is applicable to a given case, when the decision is meant to be built on an understanding of the relevant source material, based exclusively on the linguistic expression (wording) of that material.

But why should legal decisions be based upon "the wording" of a piece of source material at all? Should not "interpretation" be based on as rich a context as possible in order to achieve the best decision available?

Of course, law-appliers regard it as appropriate, and sometimes even compulsory, to take into consideration a broad context. This approach, however, may conflict with an important law-state principle: It must be easy, for the layman as well as the lawyer, to get relevant legal information. Otherwise, legal certainty is in jeopardy.

In order to live up to this principle, certain methodological and technical devices have been developed by the legal profession. Some of these have to do with statutory language. The ideal of legal certainty requires compartmentalisation; each article of a statute shall be as self-contained as possible: there shall be a minimum of references to other statutory provisions and it shall be as rich in content and as clearly formulated as to make a broadening of the interpretative context and a mobilisation of metaprinciples of interpretation unnecessary. Statutes shall be written in a way that allows, to a high degree, an acontextual interpretation of their provisions.[4]

Equally important from the point of view of legal certainty is to write statutes in a way that avoids deficiencies related to condition (3). For if two or more rules conflict, we are in a state of uncertainty about which of the conflicting rules we ought to rely upon.

Condition (4)—apart from its obvious relevance for the efficiency of the legal order—is important from the point of view of legality in the following way. If a given statutory provision is not teleologically adequate, the law-applier can be tempted, or even forced, to tamper with it, and to give to it an interpretation that differs from a literal, acontextual interpretation in order to adjust it to his goals. And again we are placed in a state of uncertainty that threatens legal certainty: which of the two competing interpretations shall we rely upon?

Faced with deficiencies of the kind described above, are there any means at the law-applier's disposal, that enable him to uphold a second front legality that is strong enough to guarantee the maintenance of the basic law-state values?

The core of legalism is *conformity*: legality shall be upheld by *all* legal functionaries "in a law-state". A society where some functionaries adhere to legalism while others do not might even be in a worse position from the law-state point of view than a society where legality is not respected at all, especially with regard to legal equality and certainty.

Clear, non-conflicting and expedient rules lead to interpretations of them conforming to the law within the group of people entrusted with their application. Is there, then, anything at the law-applier's disposal besides clear, non-conflicting and expedient rules, capable of securing conformity precisely in those situations where rules are not clear, non-conflicting or expedient, or where there are no rules at all?

---

[4] Cf. R. Dworkin, *Law's Empire* (1986), p. 17, where Dworkin talks about the "acontextual meaning" of the words of a statute, "that is, the meaning we would assign them if we had no special information about the context of their use or the intentions of their author".

The answer to that question is to a large extent a matter of legal technique. Therefore, technical devices in the service of legality will be dealt with later in this book (Sect. 4.3, below).

We conclude the analysis of "is in accordance with" with the following definitions:

(DSA) A system-independent rule, *r*, is in *strict accordance* with a given legal system, *S*, if and only if

(i) there is a rule, *r**, in *S* such that *r** is a basic rule relative to *r* (i.e., *r* is a subsumption rule relative to *r**)
(ii) the relation between *r* and *r** does not violate L1–L3.

(DLA) A system-independent rule, *r*, is in *loose accordance* with *S* if and only if *r* is based on *S* in a way that satisfies the demands of L4.

Very often, to claim strict accordance is to claim too much of law-appliers. In order to give due respect to noteworthy values other than legality, the law-applier often has to rest content with that kind of second front legality which lies in loose accordance.

D. a's application of r to s is legally valid according to S

The fact that a applies *a* rule which is in accordance with the legal system in question does not by itself mean that *a's* application is in compliance with law. The very act of application must also be warranted by legal rules in the system. *a* must *be competent to* apply the rule which he applies to the case. Otherwise his act of application is *invalid*. An act which is invalid according to a given legal system can never be an act which is in compliance with that system.

4.3 The Technique of Legality

4.3.1 Introduction

In legal life, ideology and technique are inseparably intertwined. The techniques for approximating a perfect legality setting as well as those aimed at a second front legality lie in the hands of both legislators and law-appliers. The task of the legislator, from our point of view, is to approximate a perfect legality setting. Often, however, the legislator cannot aspire to more than a second front legality. The law-applier, on his part, can never aspire to more than that.

When a perfect legality setting is too remote, law-appliers as well as legislators, aiming at legality, are reduced to the use of certain *substitutional legality-warrants*.

These insights, if correct, provide us with a scheme for our presentation of various legal-technical devices aiming at legality. First, we shall investigate which substitutional legality-warrants there are in the hands of the law-applier, when there are deficiencies with respect to the four legality conditions mentioned in the previous Sect. (4.2. above). Secondly, we shall examine techniques that can be used by the legislator striving for a perfect legality setting, and also substitutional legality-warrants at his disposal when such a state of affairs for some reason or other is not available.

When reading this section, the reader must bear in mind that we are here interested exclusively in legality as a guarantor of the four basic law-state values.

4.3.2 Technical Devices in the Hands of the Law-Applier

As stated earlier in this monograph, in a state of affairs where a perfect legality setting obtains, there is no need for L4 from the point of view of legalism, and LI–L3 are easily applicable. But, as we all know, this state of affairs never obtains in real life. Which logically possible, not totally unreasonable, options are open to law-appliers in that predicament?

The following five, it seems to me.

I. To dismiss the case in question without even trying it (the lack of clear, unequivocal law being a kind of procedural hindrance).

In Western legal orders, this alternative is usually not available to the law-applier. The prohibition of *déni de justice*, denial of justice, (or, with another common term, the prohibition of *non liquet*) is a, mostly unwritten—though in French law codified (Article 4 of the *Code Civil*)—basic principle in Western legal orders. The law-applier must "interprete" the law, or even create new legal rules, when confronted with a hard case (i.e., a case which is difficult to decide due to deficiencies with respect to the four legality conditions). This will be dealt with a bit more thoroughly in Chap. 6.

II. To ask the legislator how to decide the case *(référé législatif)*. *Référé législatif* is the historical predecessor to the prohibition of *déni de justice* and was, in most countries, replaced by the latter during the eighteenth and nineteenth centuries.
III. To decide the case by observing strict (radical) legalism. The law-applier acts according to strict legalism when he adheres exclusively and slavishly to principles LI–L3 (with connected *in dubio*-principles) in hard cases.

The consequences of strict legalism are (i) that the legal rules are always applied to clear cases (i.e., cases beyond any doubt covered by the wording of some rule), however strange the social consequences thereof may be, and (ii) that the legal rules are never applied to cases such that it is either unclear whether they are covered by the wording or not, or it is clear that they are not covered by it—again however strange the consequences thereof may be.

It must be stressed that strict legalism is unable to solve genuine rule-conflicts (i.e., conflicts where one and the same action is permitted or obligatory according to one rule in the system and forbidden by another). If a given case, *c*, is undoubtedly covered by two rules, r_1 and r_2, which conflict in this way, then, according to L1, both r_1 and r_2 shall be applied. It is, of course, perfectly possible to do so; it is not impossible to *pronounce* a contradiction. But if a person sentenced that way chooses to perform an action both forbidden and permitted (or obligatory), she inevitably violates the prohibition, and if she chooses not to perform an action both forbidden and obligatory, she inevitably violates the obligation.

Such a harsh legalism is, I think, seldom advocated even by very devoted legalists, at least outside the field of criminal law.

As we see, deciding a case by observing strict legalism is perfectly compatible with the prohibition of a denial of justice. A radical use of L2 by the law-applier, finding that a rule *r* is not literally applicable to case *c*, leads to a dismissal on the merits of *c* with respect to the claim based on *r*—which, in fact, is to apply a rule *r'* created *e contrario* from *r*, (e.g., when a prosecutor invoking *r* gets his claim rejected and the defendant is acquitted, in pursuance of the maxim "*in dubio* or *in silentio* to the benefit of the defendant"). The prohibition of denial of justice is not violated since the case has actually been tried (tested against existing legal rules) and a judgment has been given.

One of the main principles of statutory interpretation is that the law-applier shall apply a given provision in its literal, or acontextual, meaning (a principle referred to as "literal interpretation", "linguistic interpretation", "logical-grammatical interpretation" etc.). Paradoxically enough, this principle is useless precisely in situations where principles of interpretation are needed, viz. when provisions are uncertain with respect to their interpretation—the very characteristic of such situations being that there is no "literal meaning" to cling to. The cause of the interpretative problem is the obscurity of the wording of the provision with respect to the case, and this very state of affairs shall guide the law-applier in his interpretation of that wording with respect to the case, which is absurd. However, what one has in mind, I think, when talking about literal interpretation, is a radical use of L2, i.e., a consequent restrictive or *e contrario* use of statutory provisions and a rejection of analogies and extensions.

IV. To use free (unbound) discretion when making subsumption rules.

Nor is this alternative considered among lawyers as available to the law-applier, obviously repugnant, as it is, to even a rudimentary form of law-state thinking.

V. To use bound discretion.

Here we find the most important substitutional legality-warrants used by law-appliers.

A law-applier's discretion is *bound* when certain *restrictions* are laid upon his freedom to make any subsumption rule he likes for the case in question.

Such restrictions are sometimes articulated in statutory provisions, but mostly they consist of a kind of unwritten principles belonging to an international juridical culture (with local variations, of course, as to the general and relative importance of such restrictions). Let us refer to such principles by the term *restrictive principles*. Such principles function as substitutional legality-warrants in legal argumentation.

Restrictive principles can be classified into two main groups: (i) restrictive principles directly pertaining to the legal system, and (ii) restrictive principles indirectly pertaining to the legal system. The underlying idea behind this is an assumption (for which, in my opinion, there is strong empirical evidence), that, when a legal deficiency (i.e., a divergence from some legality condition) obtains, the law-applier is apt to take refuge in the legal system as a whole, either by just adapting the intended subsumption rule to the rules of the existing legal system, or by using phenomena in some way or another related to the system. L4—the principle of loyalty—expresses this idea in a concentrated form.

The four basic law-state values can be sufficiently guaranteed in a substantial way only by statutory provisions. Hence, in this essay we regard "legal sources" other than statutes, e.g., precedents, *travaux préparatoires* (legislative material), custom and the doctrine, as auxiliary "legal sources".

A. Restrictive principles directly pertaining to the legal system Of course, the actually existing legal system exerts a mighty influence as a barrier to potential intruders in the form of newly created subsumption rules. A clumsy interference by an unsuspecting law-applier can do much harm to people's law-state protection, however good his intentions are.

Existing law provides the basis for *systemic restrictive principles* such as

(RP1) A term occurring in normative sentences expressing the law shall have the same meaning wherever it occurs (in a given statute, in every statute belonging to a certain field of law or in every statute on which the legal system is based.) (*The principle of unequivocality.*)

(RP2) There must not be any logical inconsistencies between rules in the legal system. (*The principle of consistency.*)

From RP1 follows that if a term *t* occurs in an intended subsumption rule *s* and *t* has a fixed meaning *m* in existing rules in the system, then *t* shall mean *m* in *s*.

From RP2 follows that an intended subsumption rule *s* must not be applied, if the incorporation of *s* in the legal system would lead to a logical inconsistency between *s* and some rule in the system.

Suppose, however, that there is already a built-in inconsistency in the legal system before any intended subsumption rule has been ventured. The classical means to be mobilised in that predicament are the following principles (usually expressed as maxims in a fixed Latin form):

(RP2a) If the law-applier has to choose between a subsumption rule *s* based on a basic rule *r*, belonging to the system, and another subsumption rule *s′* based on a basic rule *r′* also belonging to the system, and *r* and *r′* are mutually logically inconsistent, then the law-applier shall apply the subsumption rule based on the rule which is the most specified of *r* and *r′* (i.e., the one whose set of operative facts is a proper subset of the set of operative facts of the other). (*Lex specialis derogat legi generali.*)

(RP2b) If… inconsistent [=RP2a], then the law-applier shall apply the subsumption rule based on the rule which is the hierarchically higher of *r* and *r′*. (*Lex superior derogat legi inferiori.*)

(RP2c) If… inconsistent [=RP2a], then the law-applier shall apply the subsumption rule based on the one of *r* and *r'* which is most recently issued. (*Lex posterior derogat legi priori.*)

(RP2d) If… inconsistent [=RP2a], then, if *r* is more specified than *r'* and *r'* is more recently issued than *r*, the law-applier shall apply *r*. (*Lex posterior generalis non derogat legi priori speciali.*)

B. Restrictive principles indirectly pertaining to the legal system Restrictive principles can pertain in an indirect way to a legal system, *S*, in two important respects:

(a) by pertaining to the value-basis of *S*, and
(b) by pertaining to the factual basis of *S*.

1. Restrictive principles pertaining to *the value-basis*, or *teleology*, *of S*.

Like the warp in the carpet, the rules of a legal system are tied together by an underlying structure, let us call it "the value-basis" or "teleology" of the legal system. In accordance with our instrumental view of legal orders, we regard legal orders as instruments for achieving, maintaining or abolishing certain social states of affairs.

Let the structure $<S, U_s, V_s>$ be a *legal-teleological model*, where

(i) *S* is a legal system
(ii) U_s is *the utopia of S*, i.e., the total state of affairs (the possible world) where all states of affairs which were intended to be achieved, maintained and abolished by means of *S* are achieved, maintained and abolished respectively, and
(iii) V_s is the *value-basis*, or *teleology of S*, i.e., the set of values which makes U_s the utopia of *S*.

With the aid of this model we can formulate two *teleological restrictive principles* (one negative and one positive):

(RP3) The law-applier must never apply a subsumption rule, *s*, the value-basis of which, v_s, is teleologically irreconcilable with the value-basis of the legal system,

and

(RP4) When constructing a subsumption rule for a case, *c*, the law-applier shall consider the value-basis of the system, and especially the value-basis of rules regulating similar spheres of life as that to which *c* belongs.

RP4 opens to analogical use of existing rules of the system.

There are two, principally distinct, ways of understanding the term "value-basis". The value-basis can be understood (i) in a dynamic way as a set of values, which can change in the course of time, even if the rules of the system are unchanged, and which values are ascertainable in an "objective" manner (i.e., regardless of the intention of the legislator) by law-appliers, or (ii) in a static (conservative) way as the set of values which was in the mind of the legislator when each particular statute, or statutory provision, was issued, and which values are ascertained in a "subjective" (historical, intentional) manner by law-appliers. In the latter case we must accept that national legal systems can have—and, to a large degree, actually have—a non-coherent value basis. RP3 and RP4 can be understood as either objective-teleological or subjective-teleological principles.

2. Restrictive principles pertaining to *the factual basis of S*.

By the term "legal source" lawyers refer to phenomena (texts) such as statutes, court decisions, *travaux préparatoires* of statutes, legal writing, contracts, and also to non-linguistic phenomena like certain habits or customs. The definition of the term is highly disputed in general jurisprudence. With Wedberg I use here the term "the factual basis" of a legal system [5], thus avoiding the metaphorical tinge of the term "legal source".

By the term "the factual basis of *S*" I mean such factors ("basic factors") which appliers of *S* typically refer to in argumentation concerning legal norms, especially subsumption rules.

From the point of view of legality, statutory provisions, as has already been stressed, are the only substantial means of satisfying the four legality conditions. Hence, in this connection we regard statutes as the main basic factor of *S*, and other basic factors, such as precedents or *travaux préparatoires*, as auxiliary basic factors.

Now, if there are any serious defects with regard to the fulfilment of the legality conditions, substitutional legality-warrants can be mobilised in the form of restrictive principles referring to such auxiliary basic factors.

As examples of such conceivable factual basis-related restrictive principles can be mentioned

(RP5) When statutory provisions are so defective from the point of view of some legality condition that a subsumption rule cannot reasonably be based on them, find your subsumption rule in legal decisions (precedents) given by (some specified) law-applying organ(s) of the legal order

(RP6) When…them [=RP5], find your subsumption rule in the *travaux préparatoires* of the statutory provisions in question

(RP7) When… them [=RP5], find your subsumption rule in the legal writing (doctrine) dealing with the legal order in question.

What, now, can be said for and against restrictive principles of the kind RP1–RP7 as substitutional legality-warrants?

As we see, they appear with a Janus-face. On the one hand, they can be regarded as rather the opposite to legality, making room, as they do, for departure from statutory rules. RP3, e.g., prefers a subsumption rule in accordance with the underlying values of the system to a subsumption rule in accordance with the wording of a statutory provision. On the other hand, they put a barrier against sheer arbitrariness.

But are they effective as legality-warrants? I am inclined to be rather sceptical about that.

[5] A. Wedberg, "Some problems in the logical analysis of legal science", *Theoria* (17) 1951, pp. 246–275, at 247–248. Wedberg talks about "the factual basis of legal science", while I use the term "the factual basis of a given legal system", but that difference is of no importance here.

For one thing, they might conflict. It can easily be seen that, e.g., RP1 on the one hand, and RP3 or RP4 on the other, are at a constant risk of collision.

For RP5 to be effective, no small number of precedents must be available. In my country, Sweden, this is seldom the case in most spheres of law, and hence, the production of precedents by the Supreme Court has, for purely quantitative reasons, little general importance from the viewpoint of legality.

As for RP6 and RP7, there is even more reason for scepticism. Apart from the fact that *travaux préparatoires* in their turn also need interpretation (and we might be faced with the problem of interpreting *obscurum per obscurius)* we can, more often than not, adduce equally strong arguments, drawing on them, in favour of each of the opposite parties in a litigation.[6] The same applies to the products jointly referred to as the doctrine.

But the main reason for my scepticism as to the effectiveness of the restrictive principles as legality-warrants is the following. In the preceding Sect. (4.2 above) we emphasised that the core of legalism is conformity. With respect to the restrictive principles this would mean that their value as legality-warrants is ultimately dependent upon their uniform and consistent application by all, or at least most, functionaries entrusted with the application of a given legal system. Such conformity in the adherence to a set of reasonably discernible restrictive principles surely does not exist in my country, and I doubt very much that it does in any other country either.

4.3.3 Technical Devices in the Hands of the Legislator

In this section we shall, in turn, examine the four legality conditions from the point of view of the legislator—both when he aims at perfect legality and when he constructs substitutional legality-warrants. The legislator shall see to it that the law-applier can comply with the law without too many obstacles. His job is to provide a satisfactory legality setting.

I. How to avoid or compensate for lack of statutory provisions

From the legislator's point of view, the simple recipe for curing a lack of law is, of course, to legislate, i.e., to subject certain spheres of social life to statutory regulation. The question of which spheres are most urgently in need of being subject to such a regulation from the viewpoint of the basic law-state values will be discussed in Sect. 4.5 below.

If, however, the legislator, for some reason does not want to, or is not able to, legislate in a substantial manner with respect to a certain sphere of life, are there any substitutional legality-warrants at his disposal, the use of which would lead to a certain degree of second front legality?

[6] See further Å. Frändberg, "Interpretation of Statutes—the Use and Weight of *travaux préparatoires* in Sweden", in *Anglo-Swedish Studies in Law* (eds. M. Andenas and N. Jareborg, Uppsala, 1999), pp. 208–219.

A standard device in this respect is the delegation of legislative power, i.e., to confer competence to issue legal norms on subordinate state organs or private associations.[7] Besides explicit delegation of such competence by statutory provisions, there are also certain forms of delegation in disguise, as it were, or extremely general delegations, e.g., the following.

(1) Delegation by issuing so-called general clauses, i.e., statutory provisions containing very vague, or open, prerequisites, often of an evaluative character and formulated as a standard, i.e., in a way that allows changing interpretations in the run of time while the formulation itself remains unchanged (e.g., "unreasonable", "contrary to faith and honour", "contrary to good commercial custom").

Provisions of this kind can be regarded as delegations, more or less *in blanco,* to the law-appliers to act as legislators by themselves in the field in question. The more such delegation verges on the *in blanco*-side, the more we can regard the issuing of general clauses as pseudo-legislation. Then, until a fairly comprehensive number of legal decisions has emerged, the lack of law is still at hand.

(2) Delegation by conferring, in statutory form, a general competence on courts of law and other authorities to issue binding legal norms, e.g., by giving the Supreme Court of some country competence to produce precedents. Even more diluted forms of delegation exist. Examples are article 1 of the Swiss Civil Code—according to which the judge, when the code is silent, shall apply the rule which he would have issued if he were the legislator—and the aforementioned article 4 of the French Civil Code, subjecting the judge to a general prohibition of the denial of justice, or, in other words, to a duty to create legal rules when statutory rules are obscure or even lacking. Also the modern technique of goal-regulation by directives can be mentioned.

II. How to avoid or compensate for uncertainty of legal provisions

Perhaps the most important uncertainty factors pertaining to statutory provisions are

(i) vagueness
(ii) obscurity
(iii) ambiguity
(iv) complexity
(v) latitudinality.

(1) A statutory provision, p, is *vague* relative to a case c if (i) there is a non-empty set C having as elements every case such that it is totally clear that it is sub-

[7] A strong opponent to delegated legislative power was Locke. In his opinion, "the Legislative's" power of making laws is itself a delegated power from the people and cannot be passed over to others. "The power of the *Legislative* being derived from the People by a positive voluntary Grant and Institution, can be no other, than what the positive Grant conveyed, which being only to make *Laws* and not to make *Legislators,* the *Legislative* can have no power to transfer their Authority of making Laws, and place it in other hands."(*Two Treatises of Government,* The Second Treatise (141).).

sumable under p, (ii) there is a non-empty set C' having as elements every case such that it is totally clear that it is not subsumable under p, and (iii) c does not belong to either C or C'. Example: To decide whether a wooded park is "a forest" according to some legislation on forestry.

(2) p is *obscure* relative to c if sets C and C' in (1) are empty. Obscurity is an important ingredient in a metaphorical use of language—which, indeed, is abhorrent to statutory language, but can be found in "perverted" legal orders. Example: To decide whether a dog has behaved "inhumanly", when applying a rule to the effect that dogs behaving inhumanly shall be taken into custody.

(3) p is *ambiguous* (in a legally relevant, or strong, sense) relative to c if (i) there is some word or phrase, w, in p such that to w can be assigned (at least) two different possible interpretations (meanings), i_1 and i_2, (ii) it is the case that if w is given interpretation i_1, p is applicable to c and (iii) it is the case that if w is given interpretation i_2, p is not applicable to c. Which interpretation shall be chosen? Example: Suppose that "timber" is declared to be contraband goods of war. Shall the provision in question be applied to lumber or to frames used in ships, when application to both is out of the question?

(4) p *is complex* relative to c if p is so comprehensive and so full of details that it is, for that reason, difficult to decide whether p is applicable to c or not. Correspondingly, a statute S is complex relative to c if S is so comprehensive and so overloaded with provisions that it is, for that reason, difficult to find any possibly applicable provision in it.

According to Sir William Dale[8], the legislature of the United Kingdom at times unduly indulges in the art of complexity. As an example we may choose The Sex Discrimination Act 1975, which has 87 sections (!) plus six Schedules. Among the 87 sections we reproduce Sect. 7 below.

7. Exception where sex is a genuine occupational qualification.

(1) In relation to sex discrimination -

  (a) Section 6(1)(*a*) or (*c*) does not apply to any employment where being a man is a genuine occupational qualification for the job, and
  (b) Section 6(2)(*a*) does not apply to opportunities for promotion or transfer to, or training for, such employment.

(2) Being a man is a genuine occupational qualification for a job only where -

  (a) the essential nature of the job calls for a man for reasons of physiology (excluding physical strength or stamina) or, in dramatic performances or other entertainment, for reasons of authenticity, so that the essential nature of the job would be materially different if carried out by a woman; or
  (b) the job needs to be held by a man to preserve decency or privacy because-

[8] W. Dale, *Legislative Drafting: A New Approach,* 1977, pp. 323–324. The example is taken from Dale.

(i) it is likely to involve physical contact with men in circumstances where they might reasonably object to its being carried out by a woman, or
(ii) the holder of the job is likely to do his work in circumstances where men might reasonably object to the presence of a woman because they are in a state of undress or are using sanitary facilities; or

(c) the nature or location of the establishment makes it impracticable for the holder of the job to live elsewhere than in premises provided by the employer, and -
(i) the only such premises which are available for persons holding that kind of job are lived in, or normally lived in, by men and are not equipped with separate sleeping accommodation for women and sanitary facilities which could be used by women in privacy from men, and
(ii) it is not reasonable to expect the employer either to equip those premises with such accommodation and facilities or to provide other premises for women; or

(d) the nature of the establishment, or of the part of it within which the work is done, requires the job to be held by a man because
(i) it is, or is part of, a hospital, prison or other establishment for persons requiring special care, supervision or attention, and
(ii) those persons are all men (disregarding any woman whose presence is exceptional), and
(iii) it is reasonable, having regard to the essential character of the establishment or that part, that the job should not be held by a woman; or

(e) the holder of the job provides individuals with personal services promoting their welfare or education, or similar personal services, and those services can most effectively be provided by a man, or
(f) the job needs to be held by a man because of restrictions imposed by the laws regulating the employment of women, or
(g) the job needs to be held by a man because it is likely to involve the performance of duties outside the United Kingdom in a country whose laws or customs are such that the duties could not, or could not effectively, be performed by a woman, or
(h) the job is one of two to be held by a married couple.

(3) Subsection (2) applies where only some of the duties of the job fall within paragraphs (*a*) to (*g*) as well as where all of them do.

(4) Paragraph (*a*), (*b*), (*c*), (*d*), (*e*), (*f*) or (*g*) of subsection (2) does not apply in relation to the filling of a vacancy at a time when the employer already has male employees-

(a) who are capable of carrying out the duties falling within that paragraph, and
(b) whom it would be reasonable to employ on those duties, and

(c) whose numbers are sufficient to meet the employer's likely requirements in respect of those duties without undue inconvenience.

It is not difficult to agree with Dale that here we find a legislator who "involves himself in extremes of particularity", verging on the ridiculous. Notice also, that this closely knit fishing-net here and there has large rips in the form of highly open provisions, e.g., (2) *(b)* (ii) "reasonably", (2) *(c)* "impracticable" and (2) (*d*) (iii) "it is reasonable".

(5) By *latitudinality* I mean that a provision is equipped with a latitude. Latitudes are mainly used in criminal law, where they occur frequently. The latitude made its breakthrough in the history of law in the Napoleonic *Code Pénal* of 1810. Example: "Any person who... [commits robbery]..., shall be sentenced to at least one and at most 6 years' imprisonment". Closely akin to latitudinality is the use of alternative sanctions.

The opposites to (i)–(v) are respectively

(i') precisation (*p* is made precise)[9]
(ii') clearness (*p* is clear)
(iii') unequivocality (*p* is unequivocal)
(iv') simplicity (*p* is simple)
(v') absoluteness (*p* has an absolute sanction). Absoluteness also excludes alternative sanctions.

It is easily seen that there is a Scylla and Charybdis-dilemma built into the ideal provision-types (i')–(v')—ideal, that is, from the viewpoint of legality. For a legislator trying to avoid (i)-(iii) bears a considerable risk of ending up in complexity, and, hence, in violating (iv') And in trying to avoid (iv), he might land in (i)–(iii).

Usually the task of the legislator is to minimise uncertainty factors. But not always. Often for some reason or another he deliberately makes use of them. From the viewpoint of remedying lack of statutory provisions, a substitutional legality-warrant may be that of issuing provisions afflicted with uncertainty factors. From the viewpoint of remedying the uncertainty of statutory provisions, however, provisions afflicted with uncertainty factors are, of course, the very evil that we set out to cure. An observant legislator must always ask himself with respect to every concrete legislative matter: What is best with regard to the law-state values: to issue a statute afflicted with uncertainty factors or refrain from legislative measures altogether—when, for some reason, clear rules are not attainable?

In order to avoid the dangers (i)–(v) we must require of legislators that they be moderate in their legislative ambitions and of the draftsmen, or legislative technicians, that they develop a keen awareness of linguistic nuances, good literary taste, and an ability to anticipate the reaction of the law-applying organs.

[9] The term "precisation" is used in the more technical sense proposed by A. Naess, *Communication and Argument*, 1966, p. 39: "That an expression U is a *precization* of an expression T means here that all reasonable interpretations of U are reasonable interpretations of T, and that there is at least one reasonable interpretation of T which is *not* a reasonable interpretation of U".

The core of drafting is to make descriptions of generic cases. Two risks are involved here. One is to make such descriptions too wide, the other to make them too narrow (casuistic). In trying to make very wide case-descriptions one tends to expose the statutory language to defects (i)–(iii), and when working with very narrow case-descriptions, the statute in question is exposed to defect (iv). The golden mean between these two extremes is to subject only those situations to legislation that are both socially important and rather frequent (typical cases) and leave other, more or less odd situations, to the law-applying organs—but, in so doing, defining the typical cases with a certain degree of generality.

If this, for some reason or other, is impossible—are there any substitutional legality-warrants available, i.e., non-substantial, auxiliary provisions suited to compensate for uncertainty?

Defects (i)–(iii) can be mitigated by means of a supplementation of statutory definitions, defining terms used in the statute. If well done, such definitions can contribute a lot to a uniform interpretation of the provisions of the statute.

A second type of auxiliary provisions are statutory principles of statutory interpretation, i.e., principles expressed in statutory form, guiding the law-applier's interpretative behaviour.

I am, however, very sceptical about such provisions. After all, there is a decisive difference between ordinary legislation concerning social affairs and legislation concerning argumentation and reasoning, i.e., human thinking. Either such provisions are themselves too uncertain to guide intellectual behaviour or they are too detailed. And a methodological doctrine elaborated in detail—whether in statutory form, court practice or as a programme formulated by academic jurists—would be an intolerable intellectual Procrustean bed. Not surprisingly, known endeavours in that direction in Western legal history have mostly been failures.

A third type of auxiliary provisions are connected with provisions equipped with latitudes. These are probably indispensable in criminal law. On the other hand, there is a risk of a lack of principle when judges mete out individual penalties within the latitudes. There might be a need for a supplementary regulation of "punishmentworthiness"[10]

III. How to avoid or compensate for conflicts between statutory provisions

The most serious kind of conflicts between provisions in a given system of statutory rules is the *normative collision*: according to rule p_1, actions of type A are forbidden in circumstances C and according to rule p_2 actions of type A are permitted, or even obligatory, in C. For a legislator honouring the ideal of consistency within the system, rule conflicts of this kind must necessarily be removed.

Another kind of conflict between provisions is *competition*, (Ger. *Konkurrenz*): according to rule p_1, actions of type A are obligatory in C and according to rule p_2 actions of type A' are obligatory in C $(A' \neq A')$. In a situation of competition it is logically possible to do both an A-action a, and an A'-action a' in C without necessarily violating p_1 or p_2. But doing a & a' in C leads to unwanted states of affairs, and for that reason a choice between p_1 and p_2 might be required from a practical

[10] Cf. N. Jareborg, *Essays in Criminal Law*, 1988, p. 99.

point of view. *a* & *a′* leads to a collective disadvantage, even if *a* or *a′* alone does not lead to any disadvantage. Examples: (i) Suppose that in some country one rule says that children over 12 years old shall attend school 7 h a day and do homework afterwards until the age of 16, and another rule that children over 14 shall work 7 h a day. (ii) According to Swedish law, larceny is defined as a proper subset of theft (every larceny is a (small) theft but there are thefts which are not larcenies). It would be perfectly possible to sentence a person for both larceny and theft and simply cumulate the penalties. But that would, of course, be a foolish thing to do: the *lex specialis*-principle is implied by the legislator as an operative principle in criminal law.

To eliminate collisions is not as easy as it may seem on first glance. National legal orders contain a huge mass of rules, created at different points of time by different kinds of legislatures (parliamentary, governmental, municipal legislation). No one has a comprehensive view of the legal system. However, computer analysis might be an effective instrument for locating normative collisions.

As a matter of drafting technique, in order to prevent collisions it is important to structure the material according to the pattern of principal rule—exception. The priority relation can be further accentuated if the principal rule and the exception are tied together syntactically by conjuntions like "yet", "however", "unless", "except" etc., or if the principal rule and the exception are juxtaposed.

If a principal rule and its exception are located for systematic reasons in different places, or even in different statutes, it would be wise to create separate collision rules (combined with cross-references), serving as substitutional legality-warrants.

In the case of competition, the legislator can choose between the following possible solutions, which can be formulated as a simple strategy:

A. His first choice is (1) whether he shall solve the problem at all or (2) refrain from doing so—thereby leaving the problem to the law-appliers. To refrain from solving a problem is, after all, also a kind of "solving", if the word is taken in the wide sense to include every way of responding when confronted with a problem (problems can be "solved" by being ignored, prevented or solved in a more proper sense of the word).
B. If the legislator chooses to take his stand on competition problems, he has two possibilities: (1) to construct the statute in such a way that no instances of competition occur in it, i.e., to prevent problems of the kind, or (2) to permit instances of competition in it but at the same time to attain solutions of them by auxiliary statutory provisions.

Far from avoiding concurrence, the legislator often intentionally creates it; it might even be regarded as a special technical device. Thus the *lex specialis*-principle is often tacitly understood as an operative principle. When, however, there is the slightest risk of confusion, the legislator should create auxiliary statutory provisions (preference rules)—which can have different degrees of generality—functioning as substitutional legality-warrants.

C. If the legislator chooses alternative B (2)—to solve competition problems in a more proper sense of the word "solve"—he has three possibilities: (1) to let all competing provisions be fully applicable (e.g., by making it possible to sentence a criminal to 150 years imprisonment), (2) to let one provision, or some but not all, be fully applicable, or (3) to subject all competing provisions to some kind of modification with regard to their range of application. In all three cases the solution chosen should be expressed explicitly in the statute.

IV. How to avoid or compensate for the teleological inadequacy of statutory provisions

The very *raison d'être* of a statute is the achievement of its goals. Thus, it is to be expected from a rational legislator that he pay some attention to the question whether or not his product is suitable for its purposes.

We call a statute or statutory provision *expedient* if its observance leads to its goals.

A rational legislator must be able to *justify* a given statute or statutory provision. To justify a statute or a rule is to give reasons also for its expediency.

Usually legislators cannot carry out experiments in this respect before the statute is passed. The testing of the expediency of a given statute must therefore be done in a more indirect way. Probably it is often based on little more than the legislator's everyday experience and common sense.

In order to test the expediency of a given statute, a simple "test schema" of the following kind might be helpful.

Take an obligatory rule of the structure

(R1) If *F*, then *x* shall do *A*

where *F* is some state of affairs (an operative fact), *x* a person and *A* some action-type.

The test schema corresponding to Rl has the following structure (*S* is a social state of affairs regarded as desirable by the legislator and R1 is meant to be a means to achieve *S*):

(J1) If *F* and, simultaneously or later, *x* does *A*: is it satisfactorily probable that *S* will follow?

If a legislator can provide reasons for the answer "yes" to Jl, Rl is justified by him.

For a prohibitory rule of the structure

(R2) If *F*, then *x* may not do *A*

the corresponding test schema has the structure

(J2) If *F* and, simultaneously or later, *x* does *not* do *A*: is it satisfactorily probable that *S* will follow?

An advantage of such test schemas is that different critical arguments against a proposed rule stand out more clearly.

A given rule, *r*, can be criticised by three, principally different kinds of argument, where the last two are questioning the expediency of *r (S* is a social state of affairs regarded as desirable by some legislator and *r* is intended to be a means of achieving *S*).

1. *S* is not a desirable social state of affairs at all.

2. *S* is a desirable state of affairs but following *r* also leads to the undesirable state of affairs *T* and the disadvantage of *T* outweighs the advantage of *S*.
3. *S* is a desirable state of affairs but the fact that the obligation or prohibition of *r* is observed when *F* has occurred (or occurs) does not lead to *S* with a satisfactory degree of probability. In other words, the relation of causality in question does not hold.

Objections of this kind might lead to modifications of the rule proposed with respect to its prerequisites or its theme (i.e., the action-type that is obligatory, prohibited or permitted). An important element of legislative technique is *to calibrate* the rules by modifying their different components in relation to each other until the rules become as expedient as the legislator wants them to be. Such calibrations consist in tentative extensions and restrictions, both upon the set of the operative facts of a provision under consideration and its theme.[11]

A kind of legality-warrant can be mentioned in this connection. It consists in supplementing the proposed piece of legislation with "statutory manifestos", e.g., in the form of preambles, pronouncing the legislative purpose. The idea of this is that such manifestos shall be used as *interpretation rules*. If the legislator introduces such provisions he must be careful not to make them either too empty to serve as a guide or so detailed that they intrude upon the substantial provisions themselves.

4.4 The Limits of Legalism

There is something strange about legalism. Why do we need a special doctrine ordering law-appliers to comply with the law? Is legalism not conceptually redundant? Does it now follow from the normative modalities of each particular legal rule that the law-applier shall apply it in adequate circumstances?

First of all, strictly speaking it does not. Many statutory provisions are not explicitly addressed to the law-applier at all, but to the general public.

But, secondly, even if all statutory provisions actually ordered the law-applier to perform certain actions, there would still be an important problem left. There can be, and indeed are, circumstances where a prudent handling of legal orders requires a looser grip on them. There are important social ideas and principles competing with legalism. With Dworkin we can say that there is a principle ordering law-appliers to comply with the law, but, being a principle, this one, too, has to be weighed against other principles. *Summum ius, summa iniuria.* Legalism has its limits.[12]

Legal orders may exist even if legalism is not all that much adhered to (there is no need to integrate legalism into the definition of "legal order"). On the other hand,

[11] See further Å. Frändberg, "Some Aspects on Rationality in Legislation", in *Juristische Logik,Rationalität und Irrationalität im Recht. Rechtstheorie,* Beiheft 8, 1985, pp. 123–137, at pp. 131–132.

[12] The modern *locus classicus* for discussions on this topic is Judith Shklar, *Legalism,* (1964, rev. ed. 1986).

as we defined the concept "valid legal order" in Sect. 2.3, validity in fact amounts to conformable adherence to legal rules, i.e., if legality is upheld, the legal order is valid. But even if legal orders may exist without legality, there would be little point in having the former without the latter. After all, legality is that fixed centre around which the whole of legal life revolves. A radical criticism, therefore, of legalism must in fact amount to a criticism of the particular *legal* way of organising society on the whole.

Shklar eloquently draws our attention to how deeply impregnated Western culture is by legalistic ideas:[13]

> To see the deep roots that legalism and trials have in Western culture one need think only of the part which legal imagery plays in literature, in metaphor, and in religious discourse of every kind. The court of love, the court of conscience, the trial of wits, the court of honour, Judgment Day—how much these phrases tell us about ourselves! How many trial scenes appear in dramas and novels! How central to our everyday speech and to our imagination is the picture of a contest between diametrically opposed wills, judged according to some general rule! Even fate as we think of it behaves legalistically. The trial, the supreme legalistic act, has served us with an image around which we have structured a vast variety of experiences—ethical, religious, and aesthetic.

However dominant legalism is in Western societies, though, it is not uncontested. Equity, fairness and teleological considerations have played no small role in Western legal life either.

Earlier in this monograph we have claimed that legality is a necessary condition for the maintenance of the four basic law-state values. In that respect legalism is the corner-stone of the law-state thinking. But legality is certainly not a sufficient condition. There are other necessary conditions too, and the fulfilment of these might be obstructed by legality. In other words, *legalism can sometimes conflict with law-state thinking*. Then the latter sets certain absolute limits to the former.

This kind of conflict occurs when some law-state value is violated *by statutory means*. Then legalism may reinforce that violation.

Strict legality may obstruct legal equality. Suppose that some statute contains highly undue discriminatory provisions with respect to a certain group of people. To comply with these provisions is to assist in discrimination, i.e., to violate the value of legal equality.

Strict legality may obstruct legal certainty. At first, it might seem strange that this would be the case. To comply strictly with statutory provisions—does that not inevitably lead to certainty? Yes, mostly, of course. But there are situations, admittedly not particularly common, where a clash of that kind is possible. Such situations pertain to conflicts, unsolved by the law, between particular legal rules or between legal systems. In the last, declining years of the Soviet Union a state of legal instability reigned, referred to by Gorbachev as "the war of the laws". It was a battle over legal supremacy between federal legislation and the legislation of each union republic, each of which declared statutory products of the other invalid, and there was great confusion as to which kind of law one should rely upon. Let us assume

[13] Shklar, *op. cit.*, p. 180–181.

a society of this kind, where (i) the authorities in some sphere of law sometimes strictly comply with federal legislation and sometimes strictly comply with that of the republic, and (ii) the authorities have law-applying competence according to both legal systems. From the viewpoint of the ordinary citizen it might then be difficult to predict what would happen to him legally; and, consequently, it would be easier for him if the authorities complied with only one of the competing systems in that legal sphere.

Strict legality may obstruct legal accessibility. Suppose that the purpose of some statute in some society is effectively to block access to legal means (e.g., access to remedies or to presenting proof before a court of law). To comply with that statute is to assist in creating a state of lawlessness, i.e., to violate the value of legal accessibility.

Strict legality may obstruct legal security. Suppose that some statutes give state organs the authority to torture people, arrest and detain them for an indefinite period of time, confiscate their property on arbitrary grounds, etc. To comply with these statutes is to assist in torture and the like, i.e., to violate the value of legal security.

Faced with situations of this kind, the law-applier encounters a dilemma. Either he is not complying with the law (and not violating any law-state value) or he violates some law-state value (and complies with the law). It is in accordance with law-state thinking that, in this predicament, he ought to choose the first alternative.

This, however, is easier said than done. An obstructing judge in a country like Hitler's Germany or Stalin's Soviet Union risks a prison camp, or even his life and the safety of his family. And most of us are not made of the stuff that heroes are made of. For all practical purposes, law-state thinking is, paradoxically enough, made for, in the main, civilised societies. The real brutes, once in power, are more or less beyond its reach. Of course all this does not affect the law-state values as such.

Thus we have found that law-state thinking itself sets absolute limits to legalism. Another important question concerning limits to legalism, now to be approached, is whether and how legalism must lower its pretensions in extraordinary situations, such as distress.

First of all it must be said that, in this connection, we must always be on our guard against references to such situations for the purpose of excuse. The first thing a dictator or oppressor does when accused of excesses he cannot bluntly deny is to invoke distress, state necessity, and the like. This being said, let us turn our attention to societies where the law-state ideology is taken seriously. In such societies the question asked becomes relevant in a state of war (or danger of war), including the aftermath of war (*Silent enim leges inter arma*), when under threat of outrageous terrorism, and also in more serious economic crises.

Many countries, e.g. Germany, have constitutional or ordinary statutory regulations addressed to states of emergency, ready to become effective when such a state of affairs is present. In that way legality, at least, is preserved even if some law-state values have to yield a bit under this legislation. This device is probably the only one available for the task of counteracting pure arbitrariness in a state of war.

For Shklar, there are degrees of legalism.[14] (This, I guess, amounts very much to my contention that "legality" is an ideal-type concept.) And, as is always the case with ideal-type concepts, it might well happen that the best becomes the enemy of the good. This insight is inevitably brought to the fore when we study Shklar's well-founded arguments in favour of the Trial of the Major War Criminals by the Military Tribunal at Nuremberg, 1945–1946.

This Trial has been criticised on legalistic grounds. Neither the Tribunal itself nor the rules of criminal law under application existed beforehand; nor were there any rules according to which these things could legally come about. Everything was a purely *ad hoc* construction.

Now Shklar argues that, although "a political trial", the Nuremberg Trial in fact promoted "legalistic values".[15] In the light of a strict principle of legality, according to which "the existence of prior law" is the only thing that can justify a criminal trial, "then the Trial was simply unjust".[16] But, maintaining this, we disregard that there can be degrees of legalism; we cling to an inflexible idea that either "a decision is valid in terms of a prior legal norm or it is not, and nothing in between will do".[17] But this idea is not workable in an extraordinary situation of the kind at hand: "What would domestically, in Britain or the United States, have been a dilution of legalistic values, however, was in a totally different social situation a positive ideological contribution to legalism. It was a legalistic way of coping with violence, vengeance, disorder, and even the future of German politics."[18]

Why legalistic? If I have it right, Shklar's main reason is that this was the best possible approximation to ideal-type legality under the circumstances, all other alternatives considered. After all, which alternatives were open to the victors? To do nothing? Impossible. To shoot the leading Nazis on the spot? That could have made them martyrs and is, in addition, an alternative even far removed from perfect legality than is the Trial. As Shklar puts it: "There are no civilized responses that are fitting, and certainly no legal norms can cope with what the Nazis did to Europe".[19]

Another argument of hers is that we must differentiate among political trials. What is wrong with a political trial is not that it is "political", but that it is used in the service of persecution; not that horrors are performed by the courts but that they are performed at all. So when, in extraordinary circumstances, a political trial serves not inhumane but humane values, the fact that it is "political" does not amount to very much.[20]

---

[14] *op. cit.*, p. 166.
[15] *op. cit.*, p. 145.
[16] *op. cit.*, p. 157.
[17] *op. cit.*, p. 166.
[18] *op. cit.*, p. 147.
[19] *op. cit.*, p. 167.
[20] *op. cit.*, p. 145.

A third argument is that the Trial was a fair trial. The defendants had German counsel, chosen by themselves. It certainly was not a mock trial (some defendants were acquitted of one or more or even all charges).[21]

Fourthly, the perhaps most valuable effect of the Trial was the securing for the future of an enormous evidential material. As Justice Jackson, one of the American judges of the Tribunal, put it, the object of the Trial was to "establish incredible events by credible evidence".[22]

Fifthly, the Trial "replaced private, uncontrollable vengeance... taking the power to punish out of the hands of those directly injured".[23] I find this an extremely important argument.

Finally, we have the argument—especially stressed by the Americans—that merely eliminating the Nazi leaders without establishing the evidence of their deeds would have had disastrous effects on the stability of post-war Europe, and most of all in Germany.[24]

In other words, the Nuremberg Trial was from the point of view of legalism like a medicine able to cure a sick person, while it would have made a healthy person sick. We must always bear in mind that, from the viewpoint of law-state thinking, legality has no intrinsic value, its only value is as a means.

4.5 Legal Subordination. Constitutionalism

I. Legality, in normal circumstances, is a necessary condition for the maintenance of the law-state values. A necessary condition for legality proper, in turn, is that there actually be statutory material in relation to which law-appliers can behave legally. Thus, in every sphere of law where legality is important, subordination to statutes is equally important. Therefore legalism also claims legal subordination.

From the point of view of law-state thinking it is natural that the protection of its basic values through statutory regulation is in focus. Law-state thinking has, as it were, a legislative programme. This section is devoted to some reflections upon this programme.

One important thing must be pointed out right from the beginning. Legal inequality, uncertainty, inaccessibility, and insecurity can be brought about, or at least reinforced, by legislation alone. Then, of course, we are rather better off without any such legal subordination at all. Just as is the case with legality, legal subordination can sometimes conflict with law-state thinking. Also in this respect law-state thinking sets certain absolute limits to nomocracy.

This being said, how, if at all, can legal subordination serve the value of legal equality to begin with?

[21] *op. cit.*, p. 168.

[22] *op. cit.*, p. 168.

[23] *op. cit.*, p. 158.

[24] *op. cit.*, p. 159.

This value—in contrast to the other law-state values—might well seem to be immune to demands for subordination. The only thing, it could be said, that the legislator has to observe, *if he chooses to legislate at all*, is to forbear from discriminating unduly in the law (i.e., violate equality in the law).

However, apart from the obvious fact that legislation may counteract certain undue discriminatory tendencies in society, codification of legal positions serves the purpose of providing us with explicit standards for ascertaining whether the value of legal equality has been violated. By means of legislation, legal positions are laid bare, exposed to scrutiny from the point of view of legal equality.

With regard to equality before the law, an important condition of the realisation of that value is the existence of rules regulating procedural matters such as fair trial and the evaluation of evidence. This calls for legal subordination of important parts of procedural law.

Can legal subordination serve the value of legal certainty? Obviously, yes. The lack of law in spheres of life as such affected by law leaves room for arbitrariness. In the first place, legal certainty—from the point of view of law-state thinking—has its greatest importance when it comes to certainty with respect to statutes that safeguard the three other law-state values. But as an independent law-state value, it also has importance far beyond that. How much legal certainty, then, can reasonably be claimed in legally organised societies, and in which areas of law?

An attempt to answer this question in a general way would, only produce trivialities. It is often argued that the deprivation of personal liberty or of property by means of criminal sanctions, social or medical care, or taxation requires an especially high degree of legal certainty, and that is certainly true. But no less important for the ordinary citizen is to be able to acquire clear information when it comes to questions, the answers to which might influence the direction of the rest of a person's life, such as: "How big a pension can I expect as a widow?" or "Under what conditions can I be admitted to study medicine at Uppsala University"?

Can legal subordination serve the value of legal accessibility? The creation and composition of "law-ways" lie mainly within the field of procedural law. Due to the technical character of this area, its inevitable wealth of detail and, hence, its need for precise rules, subordination to statutory regulation is essential.

Deficiencies concerning legal accessibility strike at the very idea of legal orders. All rights and duties rationed out by private and adminstrative law would be an empty gesture if they could not *be realised* by "second-order law", i.e., procedural and executory law, providing "law-ways" for whoever is seeking vindication of his right. If such second-order rules did not exist, or were highly uncertain, the rules of private and, to no small degree, also administrative law would be no more than *leges imperfectae,* and the legal order itself little more than mockery. Fundamental moral reasons demand that if the legal order gives you a right, it should also give you a remedy. *Ubi ius, ibi remedium.*

Can legal subordination serve the value of legal security? Yes, most certainly. From the point of view of law-state thinking, regulation of state coercion and violence is, for obvious reasons, the most important of all kinds of legal subordination. This will be developed further in Chap. 8.

II. Throughout the history of Western law-state thinking—in antiquity, in the Middle Ages, in the era of classical natural law and from the Enlightenment and onwards—the idea of subordination of *supreme power* in society (be it that of a monarch, an oligarchy or a democratically elected parliament) under laws, in modern times mainly under written constitutions, has been central.

This idea is commonly referred to by the term *constitutionalism*. Within the conceptual framework of this monograph, constitutionalism is a part of the general claim of legal subordination contained in nomocracy. Constitutionalism is included in nomocracy. Hence, law-state thinking, also with respect to constitutionalism, sets an absolute limit at a line, the transgression of which would violate some law-state value. (This presupposes that there might well exist both good and bad constitutions.)

Why is constitutionalism a law-state value? The answer to that question lies in the relation between supreme power and the basic law-state values.

In Sect. 3.5 above, I argued that power restriction is the most important purpose of a constitution. An important law-state-informed reason for that lies in the law-state paradox formulated in the same Chapter (Sect. 3.3 above): the state is both a threat against the law-state values and a protector against such a threat. This paradox reaches its peak with supreme power. In supreme power lies the competence to legislate, and legislation can be the most dreadful weapon brought to bear on individual human beings. From the point of view of law-state thinking, the task of constitutions is to minimise that threat and maximise the protection. In Sect. 3.5 I have specified to some extent the desirable content of a constitution aiming at power restriction.

Constitutionalism does not presuppose democracy, nor does democracy presuppose constitutionalism. Constitutionalism, however, always imposes certain limits on democracy. Constitutionalist democracy is, as Neil MacCormick puts it, "democracy qualified, not democracy pure and simple".[25]

To regard the legal order as a strategic alternative (see p. 62 above) is, speaking in general terms, an idea more likely to present itself to persons sharing in supreme power rather than to persons engaged in public administration and administration of law. The exercise of supreme power is (with relatively few exceptions) politics, and politics is, for good reasons, regarded both by politicians themselves and by the public as a game between conflicting interests in society or as the implementation of some ideological programme. No wonder then, that the rules of the game may sometimes be conceived by some as somewhat cumbersome. Power is not only an external phenomenon—a relationship between power-holder and subject—but also an internal, emotional quality in the mind of the power-holder. A constituent of such a state of mind is a tendency to experience discomfort when faced with physical or cultural limits to some element of power in one's possession—an insight fully obvious to classical writers such as Hobbes, Locke and Montesquieu .

[25] N. MacCormick, "Constitutionalism and Democracy", in *Internationales Jahrbuch für Rechtsphilosophie und Gesetzgebung.* Aktuelle Problem der Demokratie, 1989, pp. 17–28, at p. 28.

For this reason it is of the utmost importance that the constitutional (legal) element receives its due on the institutional level of supreme power—in the form of competence to carry out judicial review for some specified, or for all, courts of law, or—not least—constitutional organs integrated into the political institutions themselves, and manned by politicans (with judicial assistance), e.g., parliamentary standing committees on the constitution—something that can contribute to the maintenance of respect for the rules of the game among politicians themselves. And this is fully applicable also to politicians in a democracy, since their psychology is no different from the psychology of other human beings.

From the point of view of the individual, we can distinguish between strong and weak constitutionalism. Strong constitutionalism means that individuals can, by themselves, mobilise constitutional provisions, e.g., by claiming judicial review, claiming damages or even instituting a prosecution. Weak constitutionalism means that the individual does not have such a possibility: the constitution, even if it includes a bill of rights, is merely a kind of standard addressed solely to holders of supreme power.

The opposite of constitutionalism is the emancipation of some human being or beings from the law. A king, for instance, is "placed above the law"—*princeps legibus solutus*—and is at the same time the source of the law. This state of affairs prevailed in the classical European autocracies of the seventeenth and eighteenth centuries. Constitutionalism is, historically, a reaction to this. Constitutionalism is the emancipation of law from the holders of supreme power. Already in ancient Greece the idea that the law is an impersonal ruler was accurately articulated: *nómos basileús*—the law is the king.

Chapter 5
Legal Equality

5.1 Clarifying the Concept "Legal Equality"

5.1.1 *Introduction*

Already very early in history the close connection between law and certain ideas of equality had been perceived and discussed. Of all general values attachable to law, the value of equality seems to be the one closest to law. If there is one single value about which one might be tempted to say that there is a necessary connection between it and the law that would be the value of equality. Alas, history offers a great abundance of violations of that value by legal institutions in the name of law. However close the connection is between law and equality, it is certainly not a necessary one (whatever that would amount to). Indeed, for that very reason, legal equality is a law-state value.

The basis for this close connection between law and equality is something we find in what are perhaps the two most rudimentary qualities of law: the generality of its rules and the crucial role of the legal process (adjudication). If we have general rules, singling out *sets* of situations, the very functioning of these rules presupposes that they are complied with by everyone who is normatively addressed by a rule in such a situation. The idea of the legal process, for its part, is based upon the generality of legal rules. The administration of law within the framework of the legal process is not a matter of free decision-making, it is decision-making in accordance with general rules. The administration of law is a matter of regularity. This state of affairs is suited to promoting legalism. If there are general rules, the law-applier shall keep himself within their scope. Legalism, further, is suited for promoting the idea of impartiality. If a case falls within the scope of the general rule, it should not matter which persons "belong to" that case. The idea of impartiality, finally, is suited for promoting ideas of equality. Impartiality is a matter of disregarding legally-non-relevant circumstances that favour or disfavour a party in a litigation. The value of equality is one important argument for having a regime of general rules and an institutionalised legal process.

Å. Frändberg, *From Rechtsstaat to Universal Law-State,* Law and Philosophy Library 109,
DOI 10.1007/978-3-319-06784-1_5,

Why, more exactly, is legal equality a law-state value? It is a law-state value since (i) undue discrimination is a violation of a life of human dignity, (ii) undue discrimination, as a matter of tragic fact, has often been perpetrated in the name of law by legal institutions, and (iii) only legal institutions can remedy and prevent undue legal discrimination. Those responsible for the maintenance of legal equality are legal functionaries, notably legislators and law-appliers.

5.1.2 The Basic Components of Equality

Equality (EQ) is a relation having the following structure:

(EQ) *x* as regards *F* ranks as equal with *y* as regards *G*,

where *x* and *y* are individual human beings or collectives of such—*x* and *y* are *the subjects* of EQ—and *F* and *G* are entities or properties attributed to the subjects, be it rights, duties, rewards, punishments or whatever. *F* and *G* are *the objects* of EQ. (The relation can easily be extended to cover more than two subjects or objects.) The subjects and objects of EQ are the basic components of EQ. Equality meeting the demands of law-state thinking requires equality with respect to both the subjects and the objects involved.

5.1.3 Legal Equality With Respect to Subjects

It must be possible to ascertain whether an individual's legal equality has been violated, i.e., whether he or she has been *unduly discriminated against legally* (a concept that will be clarified in Sect. 5.2 below). Undue discrimination is a relation having the following structure:

(UD) *x* as regards *F* is unduly discriminated against as compared to *y* as regards *G*.

Suppose that, in some society, members of a certain caste, C, share some facilities equally among themselves, perhaps even with an extreme egalitarianism regulated by the law of that society, while no member of that society outside C has access to these facilities. Suppose further, that somebody argues that this is not *legal* discrimination, due or undue, at all, since the status of individuals outside C is not regulated by law at all with respect to these facilities.

From the point of view of law-state thinking, this answer will not do. The answer would amount to the viewpoint that some human beings are situated outside the scope of the law and are regarded as legal objects rather than subjects (e.g., slaves, the Helots in Sparta or Jews in Nazi Germany). A basic principle of law-state thinking, fundamental to the value of legal equality, is what we may call *the principle of universal legal subjectivity*, meaning that every human being shall be treated as a legal subject with respect to his or her capability of having legal rights and duties. The question whether or not a person is in a certain legal position should always be answered under the condition that the person in question *can be* in that legal position. From the point of view of legal discrimination this means that everyone is capable of being legally discriminated against duly or unduly. Nobody is outside the law—and, hence, every human being is entitled to law-state protection.

The idea that all human beings have equal value (formulated in the Universal Declaration of Human Rights, Art.1, enacted by the U.N. General Assembly in 1948) is fundamental here. But then it is important to be clear about what that idea can reasonably mean and what it reasonably cannot mean. It cannot reasonably be taken to mean that all human beings are equally valuable.[1] That would amount to the absurdity that Hitler was as valuable as Albert Schweitzer and Stalin as valuable as Shakespeare. From an abundance of different points of view, and in innumerable different respects, some persons are more valuable to some people than are others. So the idea must mean something else. It can perhaps best be understood as another (less clear) formulation of the principle of universal legal subjectivity and its law-state consequences. It can be formulated more generally in this way: *Every human being shall be treated with respect where a life of human dignity is concerned.* In fact, the very point of the equal value idea is to assure equal treatment *irrespective of* how valuable a person is from some point of view.

A special relationship between subjects involved in a UD-comparison is an *agonistic* (as opposed to a *non-agonistic*) situation (from Greek *agôn,* contest, trial). (I do not use the word "antagonistic", since that word has a wider meaning than is intended here.) By an agonistic situation I mean a formalised opposition (hostile or friendly) between two (or more) *parties* such as, e.g., the participants in a game, the competitors in a race or the parties in a litigation, where the game, the race and the litigation constitute a formalised opposition. Not least in this last example does the kind of legal equality called equality before the law come to the fore.

Finally, another important law-state principle pertaining to legal equality with respect to subjects must be mentioned, viz. the idea that the state shall act as a private law subject when the state is dealing with private law matters, e.g., when the state is renting or buying a house, or functioning as a shareholder in a private limited liability company. The state should be equal to (should have no special privileges as compared with) a private adverse party in a legal process. Let us refer to this idea as *the principle of the state's subordination to private law* (including civil procedure). Its importance with respect to the value of legal equality is obvious.

This principle is well formulated by Hobbes. "If a Subject have a controversie with his Soveraigne, of Debt, or of right of possession of lands or goods, or concerning any service required at his hands, or concerning any penalty corporall, or pecuniary, grounded on a Precedent Law; He hath the same Liberty to sue for his right, as if it were against a Subject; and before such Judges, as are appointed by the Soveraign".[2]

[1] Cf. I. Hedenius, *Om människovärde* [On Human Dignity], 1982, pp. 12 ff.

[2] Th. Hobbes, *Leviathan* [1651] Chap. 21. Quoted from C.B.Macpherson, ed., 1968, p. 271.

5.1.4 Legal Equality With Respect to Objects

Let us now take up the objects of equality (F and G). We shall make a simple but important distinction between two different situations:

1. Monoobject-based equality: $F=G$. This is the case when x and y are sharing *the same thing* equally, e.g., cutting a cake into equal pieces, or sharing an inheritance or a debt in equal parts.
2. Polyobject-based equality: $F \neq G$. What matters here is not sharing a thing in equal parts. This kind of equality has to do with *two (or more) different things* being equivalent.

The equivalence principle—expressed by the ancient Egyptian symbol of scales in balance—is deeply rooted in Western legal thinking and is brought to the fore in all fields of law. In the law of contracts it takes the form of equivalence as fair exchange (e.g., goods should be paid for by a sum equal to their value). In the law of torts it takes the form of equivalence as fair compensation (redressing the balance). In criminal law it takes the form of equivalence as (fair) proportionality, i.e., proportionality between the suffering of the victim and the suffering of the offender by his being punished. An extreme form of equivalence as proportionality in criminal law is the most radical variant of the principle of retaliation, viz. the "mirroring" punishment ("an eye for an eye").

Perhaps the distinctions made here could shed some light upon the Aristotelian distinction between distributive and corrective (or commutative) justice. Distributive justice seems to be related to monoobject-based equality, while corrective justice is about polyobject-based equality. Corrective justice seems to be relevant mainly in agonistic situations, while distributive justice is relevant mostly in non-agonistic situations.

5.1.5 Discrimination

Fundamental to the idea of legal equality is the concept *discrimination*. It is here conceived as a value-free concept: to discriminate is taken to mean that some distinction is made within the category of human beings or within some subcategory of human beings. Discrimination is an indispensable component of law. The very function of law is fulfilled by discriminating for social purposes between categories of human beings: between children and all others, bakers and all others, criminals and all others, mentally handicapped and all others, etc.

An advantage of regarding the concept "discrimination" in a value-free (neutral) way is that it provides us with a framework within which we can make meaningful distinctions based on evaluative considerations. Crucial for our purpose here is the distinction between *due* and *undue legal discrimination. Undue legal discrimination is the kind of discrimination that violates the ideal of legal equality.* By ascertaining what undue discrimination is, we have ascertained what the ideal of legal equality amounts to.

Hence, the opposite of due legal equality (i.e., undue legal equality) amounts to undue legal discrimination and the opposite of undue legal equality (i.e., due legal equality) amounts to due legal discrimination. This might seem strange. But, as will be argued in Sect. 5.1.8, also undue legal equality is a kind of undue legal discrimination. For that reason, in the following we shall not use the expression "undue legal equality". "Legal equality" as the name of a law-state value means, of course, "due legal equality".

The clarificationof the idea of undue legal discrimination is inseparable from the justification of the ideal of legal equality (to be dealt with in Sect. 5.2). Suffice it, for the moment, to say that undue legal discrimination is legal discrimination that violates a life of human dignity.

5.1.6 The Symbiotic Nature of Legal Equality

Undue discrimination, apart from being a violation of the value of legal equality, is always also a violation of some other value. Legal equality has a symbiotic character of being necessarily tied to another value ("the host value"). Undue discrimination is making some evil even worse. Suppose that, just because you belong to a special class of people, you are unduly deprived of a certain right that other people have. Having this right would be something good for you and, hence, to be deprived of it is something evil for you. To this evil is connected the additional evil of being unduly discriminated against in relation to certain other people. Or suppose that you are subjected to a penalty for a certain offence while some other person, who has committed the same kind of offence, is unduly exempt from penalty or receives a less severe one. To the evil of penalty is added the evil of undue discrimination. In this way the host value and the value of legal equality are connected.

The host value is the value attached to objects of EQ:*F* and *G*. The host value can be a positive value (attached to a right or a reward) or a negative value (attached to a duty or a punishment).

Of course, undue discrimination can be more or less severe. The combination of (i) the degree of mischief attached to the deprivation (or inflicting) of the host value and (ii) the degree of mischief attached to the discrimination as such determine the degree of mischief attached to a certain undue discrimination as a whole. For that reason it is important to keep the host value and the value of legal equality apart. It might well be the case, for instance, that the deprivation of the host value is of little importance to a person while the humiliation of her being unduly discriminated against owing to that deprivation is profound. It might also be the case that undue legal solutions (in legislation as well as in the administration of law) are regarded as undue discrimination, although this is not always the case. In this chapter we shall concentrate on undue discrimination as such.

Examples: (1) Suppose that women of a certain country do not have the right to vote. Not having the right to vote is a violation of the (host) value of having the right to vote. The insult to women that stems from not having the right to vote while men have this right is a violation of the value of legal equality (or, in other words, an undue discrimination). (2) Suppose that the respected managing director A gets a one-year sentence for smuggling currency to the value of ten million kronor, while young B gets a three-year sentence for stealing a TV set, in both cases by means of a correct application of valid statutes. There are good reasons to regard this piece of legislation as a violation of the value of equality in the law. The host value is the negative value of being imprisoned. And in addition to that, B is unduly discriminated against in comparison to A.

5.1.7 The Proper Direction of Legal Equality

Closely connected to the distinction between host value and undue discrimination is the question of what might be called the proper direction of legal equality.

Fundamental to the idea of equality is uniformity, or equal treatment. If you are duly equally treated, you are equal. (You are not unequal only because some persons *think* you are inferior to others in some respect.) But uniformity can move in two different directions and they stand in opposition to one another, to wit:Either some object of equality should be assigned to all, or to none.

In the Slovakian town Spisske Podhari, a decree was issued the 1st of July 1993 prohibiting "citizens of gypsy extraction and other suspect persons" from staying outdoors between 11 p.m. and 4.30 a.m.[3] This is an example of undue discrimination. It could be countered in either of two ways. Either it should be the case that no one is allowed to stay outdoors during that period of time or that everyone is allowed to do so. In both cases undue discrimination would be eliminated.

This seems to indicate that the choice between these two directions is irrelevant from the point of view of legal equality. What we are faced with would rather be a matter of an ordinary choice between two opposing (host) values. But things, however, are not always that easy. The question concerning equality could be considered in different ways, depending upon whether or not the *proper* direction is chosen.

It seems obvious that the proper direction in our example is that all should be allowed to stay outdoors during the period of time mentioned—there was no indication that a declaration of a state of emergency was called for. Then undue discrimination is at hand as soon as any person or group of persons is deprived of this right without due reasons. But if the proper direction is chosen, due reasons to make exceptions are in fact—exceptional. Suppose, on the other hand, that the improper direction (prohibition for all) is chosen. Then we are faced with the strange situation that *due* reasons to make exceptions are not exceptional at all but for the most part outweigh the reasons for upholding the rule—since there are no due reasons for that rule at all.

From this it follows that, when an improper direction is chosen, it might be appropriate in some—admittedly extreme—situations to make as many exceptions as possible, even at the cost of what would normally be regarded as undue discrimina-

[3] Reported by the Czech news agency CTK the 10th of July 1993.

tion. No one, I guess, would think that rescuing certain groups of Jews from Nazi Germany constituted undue discrimination against those Jews not thus saved, even if the criteria for the choice of those to be rescued were not particularly honourable. Laws having such a cruel content should apply to no Jew. *Owing to the improper direction of the host value, the value of legal equality is perverted.*

5.1.8 Direct and Indirect Legal Discrimination

Since Aristotle the ideas of equality and justice are often summarised in the formula "Treat like cases alike and different cases differently". This formula indicates four possibilities:

1. Like cases are treated alike.
2. Like cases are treated differently.
3. Different cases are treated alike.
4. Different cases are treated differently.

Legal equality prevails in case (1) and (4). What usually enters one's mind when thinking of unequal treatment is no doubt unequal treatment of type (2), whether or not it appears in the law or arises before the law. Discrimination of this type we might call *direct discrimination* (the distinction made here between direct and indirect discrimination seems to me to correspond to how these terms are used, at least sometimes, in the discussion in the field of legal science on discrimination, e.g., discrimination based on gender). For instance, statutory law contains provisions to the effect that Jews shall be deprived of rights that other people have, or that a judge bullies one of the parties in a legal process.

Unequal treatment of type (3), *indirect discrimination, m*ight sometimes be more difficult to distinguish. As regards direct discrimination, the law *contains* (the legislator constructs, or the judge invents on his own responsibility) some discriminating criterion (prerequisite) which, if undue, should not be there. The scope of application is too narrow. As regards indirect discrimination, on the other hand, the law *does not contain* any discriminating criterion that should be there in order to prevent the law from being unduly discriminating. The scope of application is too wide. Take, for instance, an employer who, without good reason, demands from employees that they must be able to cope with every step in a chain of production. One single step happens to be of such a kind that women, for physical reasons, are unable to cope with it. Let us assume that, from the point of view of the employer, the condition in question facilitates the planning of the production a bit but is of no particular importance to him. But it definitively excludes women and is therefore a case of undue discrimination. This undue discrimination is most easily cured by, in addition to the order in question, discriminating between men and women to the effect that women are exempt from fulfilling the step in question.

This example also shows that what could be characterised as direct or indirect discrimination respectively is sometimes not easy to decide. If the employer had had no reason whatsoever to impose this condition upon his employees, the situation would better be qualified as a case of direct discrimination and it would be better if the order were abolished altogether.

In situation (1) direct legal equality and in situation (4) indirect legal equality prevails.

Of course, the set of different cases, unlike the set of like cases, is a very strange, extremely broad and open kind of set. For example, a murder and the payment of a debt are different cases. But when we talk about different cases in the discussion about legal equality we are in fact talking about different sets of cases which are (proper) subsets of sets of—in some wider respect, however strained it may be—like cases (the universe of discourse).

A standard trick used by political villains for persecuting and harassing a certain category of human beings is to invent discriminatory criteria—used as prerequisites in legal rules—thereby being able to lean on the principle of different treatment of different cases. A horrifying example is the Nazi idea of *Volksgenosse* (roughly "compatriot").[4] Item 4 of the programme of NSDAP reads: "Staatsbürger kann nur sein, wer Volksgenosse ist. Volksgenosse kann nur sein, wer deutschen Blutes ist… Kein Jude kann daher Volksgenosse sein", and item 5 adds: "Wer nicht Staatsbürger ist soll nur als Gast in Deutschland leben können und muß unter Fremdengesetzgebung stehen", ["Only a compatriot can be a citizen. Only a person of German blood can be a compatriot… Hence, no Jew can be a compatriot. A person who is not a citizen can live in Germany only as a guest and is subject to laws concerning aliens", my trans.].

5.1.9 Discrimination in Disguise

It might happen that some discrimination is effected explicitly in the law and that this discrimination causes another case of discrimination, intended or not intended by the legislator. If intended, the legislator more often than not tries to hide an undue discrimination behind a more or less due one. In both cases—but more seriously, of course, in the case of intentionally disguised discrimination—this amounts to nothing less than legal functionaries' abusing the legal order, the handling of which they are entrusted with. For that reason devices of this kind are violations of the law-state thinking.

Discrimination in disguise is also sometimes referred to as "indirect discrimination" in the literature. But then it is important to realise that indirect discrimination as defined in Sect. 5.1.8 above is not identical with indirect discrimination as discrimination in disguise. Discrimination in disguise can also be of the direct kind, and I think it usually is. Suppose that an employer without good reasons demands a minimum height of 175 cm from his employees. This causes the undue discrimination in disguise that most women are deprived of the possibility of gaining em-

[4] A. Azolla, "Die rechtliche Ausschaltung der Juden aus dem öffentlichen Leben im Jahre 1933. Ein Beitrag zur Vorgeschichte eines Genozids", in *Recht und Justiz im „dritten Reich"*, ed. R. Dreier and W. Sellert, 1989, pp. 104–117.

ployment.[5] But the discrimination in disguise in this example is of the direct kind of discrimination (like cases treated differently).

From real life there are, unfortunately, outrageous examples of discrimination in disguise. In the first period of Hitler's reign the Nazis tried to cloak to some degree their discrimination of Jews—before abandoning all restraint and pressing ahead with a naked dictatorship. Arguing that Jews were overrepresented in certain professions, higher education, and in schools (which, in fact, they were not), the Nazis pretended that equality (!) demanded a *numerus clausus* with respect to Jews.

5.1.10 Equality Before the Law. Equality in the Law. Equality Through the Law

1. *Equality before the law.* It counts as an outrage when an individual is unduly discriminated against in legal affairs by legal authorities (the state) themselves. Such discrimination occurs when certain people are placed "above the law" by allotting to them advantages not allowed by the law, or exempting them from burdens or penalties imposed by the law—or when some people are placed "outside the law" by depriving them of rights granted to them by the law, or inflicting upon them burdens or penalties not allowed by the law.

The decidedly metaphorical expression "equality before the law" means that *all* human beings to whom a certain legal rule is applicable (i.e., all human beings in situations described by the prerequisites of the rule) shall be treated in the way indicated by the legal consequence of the rule. No one belonging to that category of people shall be placed "above" or "outside" the law. Equality before the law is a matter of the uniform application of the law.

2. *Equality in the law.* As has already been pointed out, in order to organise social life, legal orders must inevitably discriminate between different categories of people. Of course, "equality in the law" can not be taken to mean that no discrimination whatsoever is allowed in the law. As a law-state principle it can only mean that the law must have content such that if the law is faithfully and strictly applied to all cases falling under it, no individual is a victim of undue discrimination (to be dealt with in Sect. 5.2 below).

3. *Equality through the law.* Now and then legislation is used for the very purpose of attaining a state of equality between certain categories of people in society. Equality shall be attained through the law. Different legal-technical arrangements have been invented for that purpose.

Equality through the law is not the same as equality in the law. The latter prevails when there is no undue discrimination in the law, i.e., where there is no undue

[5] The example is borrowed from L. Lerwall, *Könsdiskriminering. En analys av nationell och internationell rätt* [Discrimination on Grounds of Sex – An Analysis of [Swedish] National Law and International Law], 2001, p. 142.

discrimination created and maintained by the legislator. The former is a means of counteracting undue discrimination outside the law and its handling by legal functionaries. This is the case, e.g., when women or members of a certain race, although not unduly discriminated against in the law itself or through its application by legal functionaries, are nevertheless discriminated against by fellow-human beings. Unlike equality in the law, and before the law, equality through the law is not a value by itself, but a means of attaining a certain level of equality in the society generally.

Equality through the law is neither a law-state value nor a means of attaining a law-state value. A violation of the value of equality in the law is an abuse by legal functionaries (the legislators) of the legal order: undue discrimination is introduced into or maintained in the legal order. If, on the other hand, the legislator for one reason or another does not take measures in order to attain extra-legal equality, he is not abusing the legal order—undue discrimination is not introduced into or maintained in the legal order.

But could not the legislator's refusal to take measures in order to achieve equality through the law be a greater evil than allowing some, perhaps only slightly undue, discrimination in the law? Yes, of course. But that does not make it a violation of the fundamental law-state value—protection of individuals through the law from being violated by legal functionaries (the state) by means of the law.

And one is wise to recall that attaining equality in the law would be no small achievement indeed. An elimination of all unduly discriminatory elements in the law would surely be an immense improvement of any legal order.

It might happen that some devices for achieving equality through the law come into conflict with the value of equality in the law, e.g., affirmative action, preferential treatment and quota systems. I shall deal with that kind of conflict in Sect. 5.2 below.

5.1.11 Procedural Legal Equality

The judicial process is a cornerstone of the legal order, and the way it is handled by its functionaries, notably the judges, is a crucial test of the extent to which a given society lives up to being a law-state. Let us differentiate between five standard kinds of undue procedural discrimination (before or in the law).

1. A party is discriminated against with respect to his accessibility to process. A spectacular example is the so-called *mort civile* (civil death), introduced into French law by *Code pénal* of 1810, meaning that criminals who committed certain serious crimes lost their status as legal entities. They had no party capacity and were not allowed to give evidence. *Mort civile* was abolished in 1854. In the Swedish process concerning tax assessment, to take a less severe but still not a particularly flattering example, the taxpayer had, until 1994, the duty to pay his litigation costs even if he won the litigation, a piece of legislation well suited to discourage taxpayers from seeking to vindicate their rights.
2. A party is discriminated against with respect to a fair trial. Many of us have seen the secretly photographed, horrifying films from a crumbling Nazi Germany,

where the notorious judge of "the people's court", Roland Freisler, in the last days of the *Reich*, is roaring wildly at the defendants, who are forced, among other humiliations, to take off their trousers. Threats and sarcasm are thrown into their faces and the boundary between the prosecutor's role and the judge's is completely ignored. Similar reports are given by eyewitnesses of the mock trial against Sinjavski and Daniel in the Soviet Union in 1965. Equality before the law is satisfactorily attained only within a scheme of adversary litigation. Inquisitive litigation, not drawing a clear dividing line between prosecutor and judge, is, for obvious reasons, dubious from the point of view of equality before the law.Fundamen*tal f*or attaining equality before the law is the observance of the principle *Audiatur et altera pars*.

3. A party is discriminated against with respect to the evaluation of evidence. This is the case, e.g., when, in comparison with other people, greater importance is attached regularly to testimony given by policemen, or less importance is attached to testimony given by Romani, without any individual examination in each case.
4. A party is discriminated against with respect to the interpretation of law. Suppose, for instance, that courts of law in tort cases would have demands above the standard with respect to what shall be considered negligence when the state is the defendant, with the result that it would be more difficult to get damages from the state than from private legal subjects.
5. A party is discriminated against with respect to the choice of legal sanction—whether criminal, civil or administrative. It is widely held, for good reasons it seems, that blacks in the American South are discriminated against by being more severely punished than caucasians for the same type of crime.

As regards procedural legal equality we can differentiate between two kinds, *intraprocedural* and *interprocedural* equality. Intraprocedural equality pertains to the relation between the parties in each individual process, i.e., between plaintiff or prosecutor on the one hand and defendant on the other. Interprocedural equality prevails when there is conformity in treatment of parties of the same kind wherever the legal order in question is applicable, e.g., that drunken drivers or fathers in trials concerning the custody of their children are treated equally under Swedish law irrespective of whether they have been tried, say, in the district court of Stockholm, Gothenburg or Malmö.

5.2 Undue Discrimination and a Life of Human Dignity

Why and when is legal equality a value? How can we justify the value of legal equality, i.e., by clarifying our intuitive response to this question?

The question cannot be answered by any analysis, however thoroughgoing, of the concept of equality itself. Neither can it be answered by mechanically enumerating traditional grounds for serious undue discrimination, such as race, gender, religion, origin, nationality, language, etc. And it cannot be answered by merely stating that if some constant qualities of men, above all hereditary characteristics, are used as discriminating criteria, the value of legal equality is violated.[6] The answer is to be found deep in the human soul.

Of course, it would be a preposterous presumption to think of myself as capable of fathoming even slightly the immense depth and elusiveness of the human soul. But the fact that we find undue discrimination revolting even when it happens to completely unknown or even imagined persons clearly shows that we are dealing here with something very fundamental in our mental life. For that reason it is important to try to investigate it, and the following is a most humble effort in that direction.

The basis of the law-state idea, and hence of the value of legal equality, is individualism, not tribalism or some other kind of collectivism. Of course, undue discrimination is often, not to say usually, directed against some *kind* of individuals, e.g., those who belong to a certain race, gender or religion. But the sufferers of undue discrimination are always individuals.

Legal equality is a value, since undue discrimination is violating a life of human dignity. To discriminate against an individual unduly is to undermine that individual's dignity; it is to degrade him, to belittle him, to inflict an indignity upon him. Georges Simenon, a man who more than most has penetrated the human soul, writes, drastically but to the point: "On peut tout faire à un homme, même le tuer, mais pas l'humilier" ["One can do anything to a man, even kill him, but not humiliate him", my trans.].[7]

Let us outline the picture of a man's life of human dignity. Such a picture provides a humanistic basis for—or justification of—the value of legal equality (as well as the other fundamental law-state values). Let us proceed by means of a contrast. From a display of the ugliness of undue discrimination a picture of a man's life of human dignity will, hopefully, emerge. We find that picture outlined in many old cultures. In ancient Greece it took the form of a high reverence for the virtues of moderation (*sôphrosúnê*)and justness (*dikaiosúnê*) and a deep contempt of overweening pride and arrogance, *hubris*.

Undue discrimination is a form of the abuse of power. The abuse of power is something ugly in three respects; let us call them (i) *the insult of abuse of power*, (ii) *the arrogance of abuse of power*, and (iii) *the decadence of abuse of power* respectively. In this chapter we shall concentrate on the insult, arrogance and decadence of undue discrimination.

The insult of undue discrimination affects, of course, in the first place the individual who is the immediate object of its negative consequences, but also the compassionate witnesses thereof. In the Soviet Union there was a time when it was forbidden to import or possess gramophone records from Western countries. People who violated that prohibition were punished. But within the reigning *Nomenklatura* itself there was no shortage of Western records—and what public prosecutor dared to prosecute people in those circles? The immediate objects of the insult of undue discrimination were ordinary Russians longing for Western records of the kind the

[6] See, e.g., J.C. Smith, *Legal Obligation, 1*976, p. 122.

[7] G. Simenon, A *la recherche de l'homme nu, 1*976, p. 14.

Nomenklatura was enjoying. Another such immediate object of insult would be the Jewish advocate in Germany in 1933, who was not allowed to practice his profession due to the *numerus clausus* imposed for the sole purpose of persecuting Jews. Further examples would be the aforementioned Romani of Spisske Podhari, the Swedish taxpayer who is the winning party in a tax process but nevertheless has to pay his own litigation costs, Julij Daniel in the mock trial of 1965, an "ordinary" witness whose testimony is regarded *per se* as less reliable than that of a policeman and a black who is prosecuted for a crime in the American South seeing white criminal defendants receiving lighter sentences for equivalent or even worse crimes.

What, then, is "the insult" in these cases? It consists, as far as I can see, of three components: the deceitfulness of undue discrimination, the erroneousness of it, and the powerlessness of it.

Undue legal discrimination surely has its causes. It can have its roots in hostility, contempt, feelings of superiority, fear or dislike, or in belief in prejudiced doctrines about reality. By the deceitfulness of undue discrimination I mean the insult of being betrayed by the power-holders' use of the law as a means for private or otherwise irrelevant ends. An adequate response to this is anger.

There is erroneousness of undue discrimination when the grounds of discrimination are erroneous. *x* is hostile to *y* although *y* is no real enemy of *x*. *x* despises *y* although *y* is not despicable. *x* feels superior to *y* although *y* is not inferior to *x*. *x* fears *y* although *y* is no threat to *x*. *x* dislikes *y* although *y* does not deserve *x's* dislike. *x* believes that *y* threatens the stability of the nation since *y* is a Jew, although the belief that Jews threaten the stability of nations is false.

Feelings and beliefs of these kinds are, as we all know, not exceptional, and of course they cannot be made unlawful. But when they influence legal activity in a discriminatory direction the insult becomes at once more concrete and more serious. And if erroneous, the insult is even greater. You are treated worse than others owing to the power-holders' mistaken perception. An appropriate response to this is wounded feelings and anger—for being misunderstood, for not being given due respect for your merits, for being the subject of simplification and prejudice, in certain extreme cases for not even being counted as a human being. This is the erroneousness of undue discrimination.

The powerlessness against undue discrimination lies in being deserted, at the power-holders' mercy, exposed to their spite or prejudice. Also to this aspect of insult anger is an appropriate response.

The arrogance of undue discrimination lies with those who indulge in discriminatory legal deeds and their sympathisers. But also the non-discriminated (the privileged) run the risk of being afflicted with it. To violate another individual's life of human dignity is, in addition, to violate one's own life of human dignity. Respecting others is a part of one's own self-respect. It is a characteristic of a life of human dignity to forbear from violating others by unduly discriminatory means.

Components of this kind of arrogance are conceit, pomposity, *hubris*—in extreme cases self-apotheosis ("*L'état c'est moi*"). There is also an element of ruthlessness in it: to treat another individual as if that individual were at one's own free disposal is indeed the very height of arrogance. Just because most of us—besides being of intrinsic value, at least to ourselves and to those close to us—are means to other people's ends, restrictions must be laid upon human rampage.

Why is the arrogance of undue discrimination (violation of somebody else's life of human dignity) a violation of the arrogant person's own life of human dignity?

The answer is the following: Because of the ugliness of it. Conceited, pompous, pretentious, corrupt, deceitful, dictatorial power-holders are not only dangerous, they are ugly to behold. Power to discriminate between human beings tends to bring out a propensity for arrogant behaviour in those who have such a power. The essence of arrogance is an overestimation of oneself, and to overestimate oneself is to violate one's own life of human dignity. Overestimating oneself is to transgress the border of moderation and self-control (*sôphrosúnê*), and, from a humanistic point of view, that is something ugly to behold.

The decadence of undue discrimination, especially when more advanced and comprehensive kinds of it prevail, consists in the decadence of the victims or potential victims of undue discrimination. It lies in the coming-into-existence of a great number of dejected, cringing, obsequious, self-pitying, self-denying beings, regarding each other with suspiciousness and envy.

These three aspects of undue discrimination are hideous contrasting pictures, bringing out the beautiful picture of a human being's life of human dignity in full relief.

It is, no doubt, easier to ascertain whether discrimination before the law is undue or due than discrimination in the law. The mere placing of someone outside the law, thereby giving the adverse party an undue favour, is violating his life of human dignity. In the case of equality in the law, the task can be much more difficult.

As was touched upon in Sect. 5.1.10 above, it might happen that devices for achieving equality through the law conflict with the value of equality in the law, notably affirmative action, preferential treatment and quota systems. Finally, I will say something about that problem.

As we all know, the conflict is this. The technical device as such of attaining equality between certain categories of people through the law by means of, e.g., a quota system, consists in creating of a new discrimination in the law, and that discrimination might be undue.

From the viewpoint of law-state thinking and its underlying value-basis in the idea of a life of human dignity, there are very good reasons to be sceptical about these devices. They might be ideologically counterproductive. (I will not dwell upon the factual effectiveness of devices of this kind. Whether they have a mere cosmetic effect or are highly efficient—which, or so it seems, they are not—would not affect all that much a judgment made from a point of view of principle.) As a reason for this scepticism the following could be argued. Let us, as a paradigmatic example, take the case where, by means of preferential treatment with respect to women's access to higher education, a more qualified man is passed over by a less qualified woman.

1. The discrimination is a violation of the man's life of human dignity. His qualifications are given less weight.
2. The discrimination is a violation of the woman's life of human dignity. It is a gross insult to her that she is not judged on her merits but is treated in a patronising manner like a child.
3. The discrimination is a violation of the life of human dignity of other women who are judged on their merits. Their qualifications, too, are thereby depreciated.

Law-state thinking has strong claims on the methods used to attain equality. Equality through inequality is to be looked upon with suspicion. The cardinal rule must be that, when eliminating inequality, no new kind of undue inequality may be created. Other methods must be tested.

Chapter 6
Legal Certainty

6.1 Clarifying the Concept "Legal Certainty"

For many reasons it can be difficult for an individual to ascertain which legal position he happens to occupy, or will occupy, if some event occurs. He is then more or less in a state of legal uncertainty. An important law-state value is that the opposite of this, legal certainty, prevail. It is the task of legislators as well as law-appliers in a law-state to achieve and maintain legal certainty.

Legal certainty prevails in a society (i) when individuals without undue difficulty can get correct information, based on the law, of legal positions and the legal conditions for legal positions, according to some legal system (*availability*) and (ii) when they safely can rely upon such correct information (*reliability*). In the present chapter I shall try to clarify this concept.

The term "legal position" is used according to the common use of it as clusters of rights and duties (see Sect. 2.2 above.) Legal positions are best articulated in Hohfeldian categories.

Statements based on the law about legal positions I call *P-statements*. Often P-statements are statements (predictions) about future legal positions—positions not existing now but allegedly in the future if some legal action is performed, some natural occurrence takes place or the law is changed. But sometimes we also want to know in which legal position, in one respect or another, we happen to be just now, as matters now stand. Hence, we can make a distinction between categorical P-statements of the type

(P_c) person x is in legal position p

and hypothetical P-statements of the type

(P_h) x is in p and, if event e occurs, x will be in position p'.

We say that a rule r is formally valid at time t if and only if it is issued and not repealed at t according to the criteria of issuing and repealing given in the sources of law doctrine of the society in question, e.g., if it is expressed in a statutory provision which is in force or in a precedent regarded as binding according to some doctrine

Å. Frändberg, *From Rechtsstaat to Universal Law-State,* Law and Philosophy Library 109, DOI 10.1007/978-3-319-06784-1_6,

of precedent. We say further that a legal position is formally valid if it follows deductively from a formally valid legal rule in conjunction with a sentence stating an adequate operative fact (cf. Sect. 2.2. above). A P-statement about the existence of a position *p* is true if and only if *p* is formally valid.

That P-statements are true can be more or less probable, especially if they are predictions of some future legal state of affairs or are about matters of a legal character that are unregulated. Legal certainty is a matter of degree.

As we see, the relation between a P-statement and the law is two-fold. On the one hand P-statements are based on the law, on the other they are about legal positions. Statements about legal positions not based on the law are not P-statements. That is to say, however probable a statement is with respect to the existence of some legal position, it is not a token of legal certainty if it is not based on the law. It might for example be probable because of knowledge of the ways in which certain legal functionaries can be corrupted. Neither are statements about non-legal-phenomena P-statements.

To what kinds of questions do we wish to have answers, where the answer is an (individual or generic) legal position (or the legal conditions for it) and the answer provides us with a certain degree of legal certainty?

Legal availability—with respect to some person, *x*, some action or actions (intended or under consideration), *a*, *a'* etc., some situation (actual, anticipated or imagined for the sake of theoretical interest), *s*, some geographical place, *loc*, some point of time, *t*, and some legal system(s), *L*, *L'* etc.—means to have fairly certain information at hand regarding answers to questions like the following:

(i) *x* is in *s*. What is *x's* legal position in *s* according to *L*? (What is *x* allowed, forbidden or under an obligation to do according to *L*?)
(ii) *x* wants to do *a*. In what circumstances is *x* allowed to do *a* according to *L*?
(iii) *x* is in *s* and wants to do *a*. Is *a* permitted, forbidden or perhaps obligatory for *x* in *s* according to *L*?
(iv) *x* is in *s* and has a choice between *a* and *a'*. Which one has the legally (not necessarily the same as personally) more advantageous legal consequences for *x* according to *L*? (For instance, which alternative, *a* or *a'*, leads to lower taxes?)
(v) *x* knows that it is forbidden (obligatory) to do *a* in *s* according to *L*. But what happens to *x*, according to *L*, if *x* does (forbears to do) *a* in *s*?
(vi) *x* is in *loc* at *t*. Is *L* for that reason the applicable legal system when it comes to questions of the type (i)–(iv) (with the phrase "according to *L*" omitted)? To be subject to the jurisdiction of a certain legal order is regarded as a legal position.
(vii) *x* is in *loc* at *t*. Which of *L*, *L'*, *L''* etc. is (are) for that reason the applicable legal system(s) when it comes to questions of the type (i)–(v) (with the phrase "according to *L*" omitted)?

Answers to questions of these types are bits of legal information derived from legal rules, e.g.

to (i) x is allowed to do a, forbidden to do a' and obligated to do a''

to (ii) in s

to (iii) forbidden

to (iv) a

to (v) 2–5 years imprisonment

to (vi) yes

to (vii) L, or L and L' ($L \neq L'$).

In light of this, we can talk about "legal certainty relations" ("LC-relations", for short). LC-relations are states of affairs (individual or generic) like the following (p, p' are legal positions, e some event):

1. x has by means of L legal certainty, when being in p, that x is in p
2. x has by means of L legal certainty, when being in p, that, if e occurs, x is in p' according to L
3. x has by means of L, L' etc. legal certainty, when being in p according to L, that x is in p' according to L'
4. x has by means of L, L' etc. legal certainty, when being in p according to L, that, if e occurs, x is in p' according to L'.

Legal availability prevails when individuals without undue difficulty can ascertain whether some alleged legal position is formally valid or not. However, legal availability is only a necessary condition for legal certainty. Another necessary condition is legal reliability. And a necessary condition for a P-statement to be reliable is that the rule or the position to which it refers is materially valid. Let us define material validity as follows.

A rule, r, is materially valid in society S at t if and only if r is applied by the adequate authorities in S at t in the great majority of cases, if a case falling under r is submitted to any such authority. A legal position, p, stated by r, is materially valid if and only if r is materially valid and p follows deductively from r in conjunction with a sentence stating adequate operative facts. The clause "in the great majority of cases" is justified by the argument that a rule does not become invalid if not applied in some rare cases, due to, e.g., ignorance on the part of the law-applier or that the application of the rule would lead to disastrous consequences when applied to some very special case to which the rule is applicable. An ideal-type material validity is unattainable—and, for that matter, not even desirable.

Legal reliability prevails when individuals can rely upon the fact that legal rules and positions are materially valid when they are formally valid—or, in other words, that legalism is strictly adhered to. Ideally, legal certainty demands that, if formal validity is ascertained, no further investigations about material validity are needed.

To sum up. We can say that a society guarantees a person legal certainty to some legal question of any of the types just listed when

A. the legal system of the society is capable of providing an answer (i.e., it has an answer) to the question (*capability*),
B. the answer is clear (*comprehensibility*),
C. the answer is easily obtainable to her (*obtainability*), and
D. she can rely upon the answer (*reliability*).

"*Availability*" is used as an umbrella term for capability, comprehensibility, and obtainability (A–C). The greater availability and reliability there is with respect to any question of a legal character, the more legal certainty pertains in that society.

Legal availability is not the same thing as legal accessibility (to be investigated in Chap. 7). The former pertains to the possibility of acquiring correct information about the content of the law by means of the legal sources. The latter pertains to the possibility of having a certain legal problem decided and having the result of such a decision executed by legal authorities.

Before we proceed, some words must be said about the relationship between legality and legal certainty. Legality, I argued in Sect. 4.1, prevails in a society to the same degree as the legal system of that society is complied with by the officials to whom the rules of the system are addressed. Legalism I characterised as a normative idea according to which legality should prevail. But *why* should legality prevail? I have found it proper to answer this question in the following way. Legality should prevail because a state of affairs where legality is realised is a necessary condition for the realisation of the four basic law-state values, one of which is *legal certainty*. This way of conceiving the concepts involved implies that legality and legalism on the one hand, and legal certainty on the other, are not the same thing. However, among the basic law-state values, legal certainty is the one that comes closest to legality. This is so due to our insistence that legal certainty means certainty *based on the law*. As a consequence, factors obstructing legality are also factors obstructing legal certainty (in the following called LC-defects).

The next Sect. (6.2) deals with LC-defects. In Sect. 6.3 some thoughts about the justification of the value of legal certainty are presented. Finally we discuss relations between legal certainty and some other values (Sect. 6.4).

6.2 Factors Obstructing Legal Certainty (LC-Defects)

Let us, as a preliminary to our justificatory argumentation concerning the value of legal certainty (Sect. 6.3 below), make use of the contrast-method. We shall contrast certain common defects in the law and in the handling of law with the ideal of legal certainty. By displaying these defects, the value of legal certainty will, I hope, stand out clearly.

The LC-defects are the following:

I. *Incapability*. (Defects violating A.)
LCD1. Legal certainty is defective due to the fact that the legal system does not contain any rules which answer the question.

II. *Incomprehensibility.* (Defects violating B.)
LCD2. Legal certainty is defective due to the fact that the legal rules are vague, obscure, ambiguous, have built-in latitudes or conflict with one another.
LCD3. Legal certainty is defective due to the fact that the legal rules (the legal system) are complex.
III. *Unobtainability.* (Defects violating C.)
LCD4. Legal certainty is defective due to the fact that it is difficult to acquire legal information.
IV. *Unreliability.* (Defects violating D.)
LCD5. Legal certainty is defective due to the fact that the official authorities cannot maintain the efficacy of the legal order.
LCD6. Legal certainty is defective due to the fact that the legal order is perverted by the authorities.
LCD7. Legal certainty is defective due to the fact that legal rules have retroactive force.
LCD8. Legal certainty is defective due to the fact that the law is under constant change at short notice or no notice at all.
LCD9. Legal certainty is defective due to the fact that the *res judicata* principle is not upheld.
Let us say a few words about each of these.[1]

LCD1. *Legal certainty is defective due to the fact that the legal system does not contain any rules which answer the question.* It might well happen that the legal system does not contain any rule which answers the legal question raised. Now, in most Western societies legal life is governed by a fundamental principle, viz. the prohibition of *déni de justice* (denial of justice). This principle—which made its first appearance in the history of law in the French *Code Civil* of 1804 (article 4)—says that it is forbidden for the judge to refuse to decide a case by appealing to the fact that the legal system in question does not contain any rule for the case at hand, or to the fact that the rules are obscure in this respect. In this predicament the judge is obligated to create a rule with the aid of which the case can be decided (although the French doctrine of legal sources feigns that it is not a matter of creating a rule but of applying a somehow already existing rule). A main reason for this principle is, of course, that people shall not be left without legal protection. (Also noteworthy is that a great many legal claims, e.g., in criminal law, are to be dismissed if not based on legal rules in force. Dismissal, however, is a decision of the case after trial.)

Let us refer to the class of cases (situations, problems) which are explicitly regulated by the rules of a legal system, *L*, as *the direct scope of L*, to the class of cases which the courts established by *L* have to decide according to the prohibition of *déni*

[1] My list of LC-defects has a certain resemblance to Lon Fuller's "eight principles", expressing "indispensable conditions for the existence of law at all", in that on the basis of LCD1-9 just as many corresponding principles can be formulated to the effect that these defects shall be avoided, and this set of principles and Fuller's partly overlap. However, the two sets function in different contexts. I do not claim that my principles are conditions for the existence of a legal system. They pertain exclusively to the value of legal certainty. Neither do I regard them as belonging to an "inner morality of law". Lon Fuller, *The Morality of Law*, 2nd ed., 1969, pp. 38–44.

de justice as *the total scope of L* and to the class of cases which belong to the total but not to the direct scope of *L* as *the indirect scope of L*. It could then be said that a legal system guarantees legal certainty in proportion to how great a part of its total scope is occupied by its direct scope. This kind of legal certainty can be characterised as a quantitative type of legal certainty.

It goes without saying that to achieve a maximum quantitative legal certainty is not a desideratum. The price would be too high: Legislative machinery working up to the boiling point in order to regulate even the most unimportant and far-fetched situations which may arise. The result would no doubt be horrifying. On the other hand, it might be a disaster if vital social relations within a large group of people are left unregulated.

The problems involved here have sometimes brought about a kind of legal magic. In the nineteenth century, French lawyers belonging to the so-called Exegetic School regarded—overwhelmed by the systematic and comprehensive character of the Napoleonic codes—the written law as complete: it could answer any legal question. This fiction inevitably led to the use of highly strained methods of interpretation, behind which the law-creating role of the courts of law was concealed.

If your question belongs to the indirect scope of the applicable legal system, you have a more modest kind of legal certainty, which also can be characterised as indirect. Then there is no answer to your question, that is true, but you can *get* an answer from the courts of law or other authorities entrusted with the administration of law. You are not placed in a lawless state of affairs. You might find that too modest a form of legal certainty, but consider then for a minute or two what a society would be like, if access to legal institutions were denied to people with claims of a legal nature outside the direct scope of the legal system—thus without even having *a chance* to vindicate their claimed rights. That would indeed be a violation of both legal certainty (for it is impossible to ascertain your legal position) and legal accessibility (for it is impossible to gain access to courts of law). But, of course, this is an utterly weak kind of legal certainty.

LCD2. *Legal certainty is defective due to the fact that the legal rules are vague, obscure, ambiguous, are equipped with latidudes* (in the sense of that term when used in criminal law, e.g., "at least one year and at most four years of imprisonment") *or conflict with each other*. In Chap. 4 (pp. 82 ff. above) I have tried to be precise about what I mean by vagueness, obscurity, ambiguity and latitudinality, and also in what way legal rules can conflict with each other. The prohibition of *déni de justice* applies to such situations as well.

Extremely vague rules are the ones expressed by so-called general clauses, i.e., statutory provisions containing prerequisites referring to standards like "unreasonable", "contrary to faith and order", "contrary to good commercial custom", etc. In addition to being vague, such provisions often, not to say generally, confront the law-applier with a choice based on evaluation. If the provisions are more or less empty of substantial content, they can be regarded as delegations, more or less *in blanco*, of the legislative competence from the legislators to the law-applying authorities. In the case of such pseudo-legislation, no extensive quantitative legal certainty is obtained until a fairly comprehensive number of precedential decisions are at hand.

When it comes to rules equipped with latitudes, we are also faced with a problem concerning the degree of legal certainty. The defendant's legal certainty may consist in knowing for sure that he will be convicted of crime *c* and that he will be sentenced to at least two and at the most six years of imprisonment. But he cannot reasonably predict that he will be sentenced to three years and six months imprisonment. Perhaps knowledge of internal practices within the courts of law might be of some help (although such practices may differ between different courts of law within the same legal order)—which knowledge, then, is in fact based more on sociological facts than on the law.

There are several kinds of conflicts between legal rules and between legal systems ("conflict" is used here in the usual weak sense). Let me mention four. (a) A case might "have a connection to" two or more different national legal systems. Such conflicts are solved by second-order preference rules of the kind we study in private international law. (b) Another type of conflict can occur in an intertemporal perspective. A case can have a connection both to an older and a younger momentary legal system within the same intertemporal legal system (e.g., Swedish law at any time), which is the case when one statute succeeds another on the same topic. Also here second-order preference rules (transitional rules) decide the choice. (c) Further, the choice of law might concern the choice between statutory provisions and law constructed by private parties themselves, usually in the form of contracts. This is the case when statutory provisions are optional. Which rules are optional is indicated by other statutory provisions, functioning as second-order preference rules. (d) Finally, legal rules might collide or compete with each other (concerning these phenomena see pp. 86 ff. above). Here the very systematics of a statute can indicate how the choice is to be made. Otherwise, the law-applier must resort to general derogatory principles, e.g., *Lex specialis derogat legi generali* (see pp. 78 f. above). In all these situations, the guarantee of legal certainty is that *the second-order preference rules* ("choice of law-rules"), or their substitutes, themselves are clear, unambiguous, etc.

In Chap. 4, I have given reasons for the view that what I there called auxiliary legal sources—precedents, preparatory material and legal doctrine—are of little help as legality warrants (pp. 80 f. above). The same arguments are valid with respect to legal certainty. The principle of statutory interpretation known as the principle of literal (linguistic, logical-grammatical) interpretation is, as it is usually formulated, worthless as an aid in hard cases (the reason for that harsh statement is given on page 77 above). It is better conceived of as identical with legality principles L1 and L2 (p. 59 above), i.e., a principle forbidding reductions, extensions and analogies. As such, it can of course be of some value as a warrant for legal certainty. As for the other traditional principles of statutory interpretation—intentional, systematic and purposive (teleological)—I think that, on the whole, it would be an illusion to conceive of them as legal certainty warrants. Law-appliers are usually not even obligated to use them.

After all, however, it would certainly be absurd to claim legal certainty in detail in every situation. In practice, we must often rest content with a "be-on your-guard" kind of legal certainty. This means knowledge of certain danger zones, such that if you enter one of them, you are wise to provide yourself with the necessary legal information (especially since ignorance or mistake of law is usually an irrelevant excuse in the eyes of the law).

LCD3. *Legal certainty is defective due to the fact that the legal rules (the legal system) are complex*. An overzealous legislator, aiming at perfect clarity, ends up in complexity. In this way he increases legal certainty in one respect, viz., that of the precision of the legal information, but decreases it in another, viz., that of the comprehensibility of this information (see the horrifying example on pp. 83 ff. above).

The totality of the legal system is so complex that no one can have precise knowledge of it. But any individual might well be exposed to an innumerable quantity of rules belonging to it. This brings to the fore the relationship between complexity and expertise knowledge.

To be sure, we are not able to cope by ourselves even with our most basic needs. We cannot produce our own food, make our own clothes or build our own houses, not to speak of curing our own diseases. So it is not particularly surprisinging that we, faced with problems of a legal character, often have to resort to legal expertise. Already at an early stage in the history of law professional legal advisers make their appearence. This being so creates, however, new obstacles to legal certainty, e.g., costs, difficulties in finding adequate expertise and possible conflicts between the clients' interests and the experts' own interests. (Of course, I am not claiming that complexity is the only reason for seeking legal advice.)

For this reason I find it realistic to argue that a satisfactory degree of legal certainty prevails, in the case of people using legal advice, when the legal certainty *ex ante* is smaller than the legal certainty *ex post* (i.e., after having acquired legal information)—when the legal uncertainty caused by information obstacles of the kinds mentioned have been subtracted from the latter. If legal certainty *ex post* is small, that fact can be an incentive for people to seek extra-legal solutions to their problems in the form of, e.g., mediation or negotiation.

Still, however comprehensible the rules are, legal certainty is not guaranteed if these rules are not also obtainable.

LCD4. *Legal certainty is defective due to the fact that it is difficult to acquire legal information*. In the centuries of absolutism in Europe, it was not uncommon that statutes and legal decisions were not published, and also that the reasons for legal decisions were secret. Unpublished statutes and official directives were frequently used in the Soviet Union. It is one of the great achievements in the struggle for legal culture that this state of affairs has radically changed. The credit for this achievement belongs to no small degree to the Enlightenment and the liberal tradition emanating from it.

But the idea is older than that. Isidore of Seville (560–636) argues in his *Etymologiae* that the word *lex* (law) is derived from *legere* (to read), since the law is written, and this statement is taken by Thomas Aquinas as a justification of a claim of promulgation of laws. As soon as there is written law, it is, he says, continually promulgated.[2] In Thomas Hobbes's legal philosophy, publication plays a crucial role. The sovereign's command "is Law onely to those that have means to take notice of it"—"... so also every man, from whom any accident, not proceeding

[2] Thomas Aquinas, *Summa Theologica. Treatise of Law*. Q. 90, Art. 4.

from his own default, hath taken away the means to take notice of any particular Law, is excused, if he observe it not; And to speak properly, that Law is no Law to him".—"The Law of nature excepted, it belongeth to the essence of all other Lawes, to be made known, to every man that shall be obliged to obey them, either by word, or writing, or some other act, known to proceed from the Soveraign Authority... Nor is it enough the Law be written, and published; but also that there be manifest signs, that it proceedeth from the will of the Soveraign".[3] For Hobbes, publication with respect to positive law is a necessary condition for securing that *the will of the sovereign is made known to the public*, and that, in turn, is a necessary condition for the individual to be under an obligation to obey the law. This is a radical intertwining of positivism and the idea of legal certainty. Beccaria praises the art of printing "which makes the community, and not only a few, administrator of the holy laws".[4] For Beccaria, the laws must be published in order to remind us of the original social contract. "If there were no permanent testimony of the social contract, how could the laws hold out against the inevitable forces of time and passions?" "The notoriety of every law ought to be as extensive as its binding force", exclaims Bentham, and adds: "No axiom can be more self-evident: none more important: none more universally disregarded. Considering how obvious it is a man may be ashamed even to mention it: and to think how little chance there is that the mention that is made of it will be attended to. Yet till it is attended to and the grievance remedied, the business of legislation is from the beginning to the end of it a cruel mockery, and every legislator without thinking of it a Caligula, or rather in this respect even worse than a Caligula. Caligula published his laws in small characters, but still he published them: he hung them up high but still he hung them up. How many laws in this enlightened age that are neither hung up nor published!"[5]

Obtainability means not only publicity but also a satisfactory distribution. Authorities shall be supplied with relevant texts without delay and such texts shall be easily obtainable by lawyers and private citizens. The Swedes can rejoice at three annual (private) editions of the central statutes in all relevant fields of the law. In the last decades legal obtainability has acquired a new, most efficient servant: Internet.

However available rules are, though, legal certainty is not secured if these rules are not also reliable.

LCD5. *Legal certainty is defective due to the fact that the official authorities cannot maintain the efficacy of the legal order*. When I say that the authorities cannot maintain the efficacy of the legal order, I mean, roughly, that the authorities are incapable of seeing to it that the rules of the legal system are followed, on the whole, by the citizens. The causes of such an inability are in this connection irrelevant. It might be the case that the authorities would gain greater observance of the laws if more resources were at their disposal. It might also be the case that the authorities most eagerly strive for such an observance or that they do not care.

---

[3] Thomas Hobbes, *Leviathan* [1651], Penguin English Library, 1982, pp. 317 ff.

[4] Cesare Beccaria, *Dei delitti e delle pene* [On Crime and Punishment], 1764, § 5. (My trans.)

[5] Jeremy Bentham, *Of Laws in General*, 1970, ed. H.L.A. Hart, p. 71.

Suppose that you are going to visit a certain country and you acquire the (correct) information that pickpocketing is severely punished according to the laws of that country. You also read in a newspaper that a pickpocket was hanged the other day. Then you arrive there and notice that pickpocketing is going on everywhere all the time.

The information you received before you left for that country was, of course, reliable in the sense that it was a true statement about the content of the law of the country. But it was not reliable in the practically important sense that you were safe in adjusting to it. In that respect your legal certainty was precarious.

Naturally, we are everywhere confronted with a certain amount of legal uncertainty of this kind. For instance, the risk of detection of certain crimes, e.g., blackmail, is regularly low. Impotence of the authorities to maintain efficacy on a large scale is to be found in old states in decay and in new nations without any established state authority.

If such a decay proceeds far enough, what is likely to happen is that people begin to take the law into their own hands, citizen guards are formed, military tribunals take over a part of the administration of law, and perhaps sooner or later "a saviour" is ready for entry behind the scenes. In the history of the last years of the German Weimar Republic we see the pattern: an antidemocratic and disloyal judiciary and public administration, rivalling private armies, *Fehmgerichte* in a new version pronouncing death-penalties and, finally, the complete destruction of democratic institutions perpetrated by the Nazis. It has often been argued that a "positivistic" view of law (in the nowadays common, but improper, sense of strict, orthodox legalism) contributed to this. But probably it was the absence of such a positivism that contributed to the fall of the democratic *Rechtsstaat* in Germany. The servants of the law did not uphold the legal order. But now we have already come to the next defect.

LCD6. *Legal certainty is defective due to the fact that the legal order is perverted by the authorities*. What I have in mind when I say that a legal order is perverted by the authorities is that they do not take the legal order seriously: they sometimes follow its rules and sometimes they do not, their decisions being more or less *ad hoc*, and you cannot, by means of the established legal sources alone, know for sure when they will do one thing and when another.

When this is the case on a large scale and with the tacit consent of the legislator, the legal order is nothing more than a facade. In societies where this is going on, the activities of the courts are often controlled by some extra-judicial body, e.g., a political party in a monopoly position.

This kind of perversion can be arbitrary or even capricious—or "ideological", i.e., based on some idea or prejudice, or all of that at the same time. The examples are unfortunately abundant. According to the law of the land you are allowed to leave your country, but you are forcibly prevented from doing so (Pasternak). According to the law of the land you are allowed to stay in your country, but you prove to be inconvenient and therefore ousted (Solzhenitsyn). According to the law of the land you are entitled to university studies, but you are a Jew, so there will be no studies. According to the law of the land, you have a right to attend religious services, but you are a Baptist and if you visit your chapel you will be beaten. But not always, mind you. If you are entitled to university studies and are both a Jew and a devoted member of the Party, then you might be welcome to lessons—and, after all, there is no need to be too pedantic about the rules of admission either.

In a totalitarian society where law is perverted in this way, life for many of its best members takes the shape of a Kafka-like dream. Legal certainty, there, is little more than a distorted reflexion of the law-state idea of legal certainty—just an insight, registered with resignation, that almost everything involves a risk.

LCD5 and LCD6 are consequences of a disrespect for the idea of legalism on the part of the servants of the law. Legality—conformity between the law and its application—based on respect for and loyalty to the law, is the very heart of the legal order. For what is the point of the legal project if the law is not loyally applied by those who have precisely as their task that? A widespread discrepancy between the law and its application is a rot that does harm in a profound way to the legal way of organising society.

LCD7. *Legal certainty is defective due to the fact that legal rules have retroactive effect* (in criminal law thereby violating the subordinate legality principle *Nullum crimen, nulla poena sine lege praevia*). What is questionable about retroactive legislation from the point of view of legal certainty is, roughly speaking, (1) that things happen to you which you did not have reason to expect would happen to you—since those things were not the legal consequences of your actions at the time when you performed them, and (2) that what you had reason to expect would happen as a result of your actions when you performed them did not happen—although what you had reason to expect were the legal consequences of your actions at the time of their performance. And what is more, (3) you can do nothing about it afterwards, since the consequences that you did not have reason to expect are exclusively determined by actions *already performed*. With respect to the past we are all fatalists, are we not?[6]

There are situations where the claim of legal certainty has less importance and may yield to other, opposite values. For instance, the important prohibition of retroactive legislation within criminal law has in many legal systems a significant exception—the so-called retroactivity *in mitius*. If the law has changed between the time of the crime and the time of the pronouncement of the sentence, the new law shall be applied retroactively if that is more favourable to the defendant than the application of the law in force at the time of the crime, due to mitigation of the range of punishment or decriminalisation.

Retroactivity can also be an efficacious remedy in extraordinary situations, where the task of the legislator is radically and resolutely to disarm an older legal system. This is the case when it is a matter of tidying up after, e.g., a dictatorship that has violated the most basic values of humanity and the law-state ideas, such

[6] "Retroactivity" and other transitional (intertemporal) concepts are investigated in Å. Frändberg, "Retroactivity, Simulactivity, Infraactivity", in *Time, Law and Society* (J. Bjarup, M. Blegvad, eds.). ARSP-Beiheft 64, 1995, pp. 55–72. Reprinted in Å. Frändberg, *Rättsordningens idé*, 2005, pp. 131–150.

as Nazi Germany. In order quickly and efficiently to remove the "pathological" parts of the system, retroactive legislation might be a powerful instrument. Even restitutive retroactive legislation might then be appropriate, e.g., in order to restore property that has been outrageously confiscated to the deprived (see LCD9 below). Such steps can be compared to that of a doctor curing a sick person with a medicine that would make a healthy person sick.

LCD8. *Legal certainty is defective due to the fact that the law is under constant change on short notice or on no notice at all.* The reason for this is obvious. Legal certainty presupposes a certain degree of "legal permanence". To be sure, there are extraordinary situations where an element of surprise is crucial, e.g., when, in an economic crisis, measures like price-freezing and exchange restrictions are deemed necessary. But in a law-state such measures must always be looked upon as extraordinary.

LCD9. *Legal certainty is defective due to the fact that the* res judicata *principle is not upheld.* Here, too, the reason is obvious. If legal decisions that have gained legal force could constantly be taken to court again and again and be reviewed repeatedly, we could never rely upon the legal positions in which we find ourselves, even if constituted by legal decisions given by courts of law. Without *res judicata*, a state of legal chaos would ensue and legal certainty would surely stand little chance.

Violating the *res judicata* principle (*ne bis in idem*) can take the extreme form of restitutive retroactivity (see LCD7 *supra*), i.e., repealing old decisions that have gained legal force and deciding the cases according to new law. This is, of course, a most extraordinary measure. However, it is not unknown in Western legal history. The inheritance act passed by the French revolutionary legislators in the month of *Nivôse* year II (1793–1794) had retroactive force from the 14th of July 1789 (a date surely not chosen by chance) and all decisions made according to older law after this date were repealed.[7]

6.3 Justifying Legal Certainty

The justification of the value of legal certainty lies in the fact that measures tending to undermine it can involve violations of a person's life of human dignity. But not every infringement of legal certainty (LC-defect) is a violation of an individual´s life of human dignity. Some of them are trifles; others are well justified by the efficient accomplishment of some important legislative goal. And even if the legislator is mistaken in some case about such a motive, it may be the case that his measure is not regarded as a violation of somebody's life of human dignity. But where shall we draw the line? It is easy to draw in principle, but much harder to draw in practice. The limit is where a life of human dignity is violated. That this limit is extremely

[7] P. Roubier, Le droit transitoire, 2nd ed., 1960, p. 286.

difficult to draw in practice, however, does not mean that it is beyond the scope of rational discussion. Let me examine several points of view on the topic.

LCD5 constitutes a special case. Suppose, in some country, that legislators, the judiciary, the police, and all other legal bodies are most eager to uphold the efficacy of the legal order and do so in strict accordance with the law-state values. Suppose further that their efforts are by and large in vain. The causes for that might be that the country is ethnically divided and tribes are fighting each other with violent means, that a powerful maffia controls the society, that widespread anarchy prevails or still something else. Then it cannot be said that, since the legal reliability, and hence the legal certainty, is almost non-existent, the officials and other servants of the law are therefore violating this value, i.e., are harming the law-state. This society would be more accurately described as a lawless one, where the most basic conditions for the existence of a law-state are lacking. Legal certainty is not damaged by the authorities but by society itself. The task there is not to preserve a law-state, but to make such a state possible.

Also LCD1 differs from the other defects. Is it possible that the legislator can violate a person's life of human dignity simply by forbearing to legislate? Must a claim of legal subordination be added to the claim of legality as a warrant of legal certainty? Let me mention two situations where this can be the case. The first has to do with the issuing of imperfect laws or symbolic legislation. Suppose that valuable rights are granted to people in statutory provisions with corresponding duties imposed on others. Suppose, further, that the legislator out of, e.g., malevolence or cowardness fails to stipulate sanctions for neglecting these duties. Here, with good reason, it can be said that the legal order has been used fraudulently. If such things take place on a large scale as a deliberate policy, the whole legal order is something of a fake. Potemkin village was, for example, not an unknown phenomenon of this kind in the legal life of the Soviet Union. The second situation is the following. Suppose that, within a certain sphere of societal life, some people are treated by others in an outrageous way. Suppose further that this sphere is not covered by statutory regulations and that decisions handed down by the courts of law within it are outrageous too. Also in this case it can be said, with good reason, that the legislator, by forbearing to legislate, is violating peoples′ lives of human dignity (and then, of course, not only because legal certainty is lacking). The perpetual function of the law (see p. 18 above) requires legal subordination for its realisation, i.e., rules guaranteeing legal security, which rules must fulfil the demands of legal certainty, too.

If we compare ordinary crimes that can be committed by ordinary people to the power-holders' manipulations of the law, what comes closest are different kinds of fraud. (With respect to the value of legal security (Chap. 8), on the other hand, what comes closest are crimes against life, health, liberty, and peace.)

Among the remaining defects, special attention should be given to LCD7 (retroactivity). Here the character of fraud is particularly conspicuous. The unrighteous blow comes abruptly for the exposed, heretofore settled in peace under the existing law, and then all of a sudden is inexorably forced by stronger powers into another, less advantageous legal position, the whole thing not unlike the fate of a tragic hero in a Greek drama.

Manipulating legal certainty can have many and various manifestations. A grave instance is harassment of the population or some part of it. Further, it can be a matter of those in power having a nonchalant attitude towards the citizens. Or it can be a result of good, though misdirected, intention. The violation of a life of human dignity is of course, generally speaking, greater in the two first cases. In these cases the result can also be a widespread self-depreciation (cringing to the powers that be) among those exposed to manipulation of the law. But the possibility of violation of a life of human dignity is definitely not absent in the third case either.

6.4 Value Relations

The relation between legality and legal certainty has already been touched upon (pp. 116 f. above). Let me first add something about the relations between legal certainty and the other law-state values, and then something about the relations between legal certainty and the demands of values outside that group.

The law-state values, in their mutual relations, tend either to reinforce or deprecate each other (in the sense stated in Sect. 3.2.2 above; see also Sect. 8.3 below). Here I shall dwell a little upon the kind of deprecation that I called *betrayal* of a value.

Peczenik has argued that the use of the term "legal certainty" (the Swedish term is "*rättssäkerhet*") in the sense of "predictability" is absurd. He says: "German Jews under Hitler´s rule could by the help of statutes in force at the time easily predict that they would be persecuted, but it would be absurd to call such a predictability legal certainty".[8] The reason for that is of course that Hitler´s laws were morally unacceptable.

Is this argument persuasive? First of all, in order to accept a linguistic usage that renders it possible to say that legal certainty prevailed in Nazi Germany with respect to the legislation directed against the Jews, it is important to be more precise. In fact, the Nazi action against the Jews can be divided into three "parts": (1) Actions based on legislation which was applied, by observance of the legality principle, according to the wording, (2) actions based on an absurd interpretation of existing law, thereby usually reinforcing barbarism, and (3) actions performed by special courts, police, and other authorities without any legal authority whatsoever. Even if it were possible to a great extent to predict what would happen in all three cases, it is only with respect to (1) that we can talk about legal certainty at all, i.e., predictability based on law.

What might have prompted Peczenik to take this position, although he does not explicitly say so, is that he might have feared that the positively charged word "legal certainty" one way or another would contribute to exculpate outrages performed by the state legalistically. To say that the Jews to a certain extent had legal certainty in

[8] A. Peczenik, *Vad är rätt? Om demokrati, rättssäkerhet, etik och juridisk argumentation.* [What is law? On Democracy, Legal Certainty, Ethics and Juridical Argumentation] 1995, p. 97. My trans.

Nazi Germany could be understood as an embellishing picture of the Hitler regime. However, if one is careful in explaining what is meant, I do not see any particular danger here.

More important is another aspect, which speaks in favour of a linguistic usage which allows one to say that the German Jews to a certain extent had legal certainty and which pertains to relations between values. The fate of the Jews makes topical the relationship between the value of legal security and the value of legal certainty. The same problem can also be raised with respect to other values. Suppose that a democratically elected legislative body allows the torture of individuals belonging to some minority and issues laws to that effect. How shall the relationship between the value of democracy and the value of legal security be described? Or suppose that the legislator institutes laws which are unduly discriminating and that the courts of law apply these laws by strictly observing the principle of equality *before* the law. How shall we clarify the relationship between the value of equality in the law and equality before the law in this situation?

In the first of these examples (the German Jews), legal security is sacrificed while legal certainty is upheld. In the second one legal security and legal equality are sacrificed while democracy is upheld. In the third one equality in the law is sacrificed while equality before the law is upheld. Generally speaking, we can formulate our question thus: With respect to two values, v_1 and v_2, what happens to v_1 if v_2 is sacrificed while v_1 is upheld?

As far as I can see, what might happen—and happens in the examples—is that the sacrifice of one value can violate—*betray*—another value, even if the other value is upheld (by which I mean that actions are performed which cause the existence of the valuable state of affairs). What was legal certainty worth for a Jew in Nazi Germany? Only the victims' certainty of imminent suffering and the oppressors' certainty that they could pursue this business with impunity. What has happened is that by violating legal security legal certainty has been betrayed. Although upheld, the latter loses its value because the former is violated. Legal certainty is not designed for such situations. And what is there in a democracy that would make torture less unpleasant than torture used in a dictatorship? Nothing. The violation of legal security and legal equality has betrayed democracy in so far as it is used for such purposes, however loyally democracy is adhered to. Finally, what does equality before the law mean if the law itself contains deeply undue discrimination except that this discrimination is consolidated and even reinforced by strict adherence to equality before the law? The undue discrimination in the law has betrayed the equality before the law, the value of which has turned into its opposite.

To describe the realities in these situations by saying in the first case that no legal certainty existed, in the second that no democracy existed, and in the third that no equality before the law existed in the spheres concerned seems to me to be highly misleading. It is as if one with words could conjure away unpleasant value conflicts. If we find it important to achieve and maintain a high degree of realised law-state values and democracy, it is also important to have a realistic conception of the conditions under which these values thrive. A vital part of such realism is to be conscious of the very important difference between, on the one hand, that a value is violated by not being upheld, but on the contrary obstructed and, on the other, that a value is violated by being betrayed, although upheld. For this reason it is better to say that the German Jews in a certain respect had legal certainty than to say that they did not.

So I recommend a linguistic usage that allows such conflicts to stand out more clearly. It makes us realise in a more distinct way that, in order to live in a good society, it is not enough that values like legal certainty and democracy are maintained. We must also be watchful and on guard against such a value's being betrayed by the violation of some *other* value.

Let me finally say a few words about the relationship between legal certainty and values outside the scope of other law-state values and democracy. I shall do so by pointing to some situations where the legislator has reason to use some LC-defects as a legislative technique for good purposes. What I have in mind is a "defect" of type LCD2, viz. vagueness. Sometimes legal rules that are too precise might be an obstacle to obtaining some important end. There are situations where the legislator must give the law-applier a certain amount of discretion so that all relevant aspects of the individual case are considered. This is especially the case when the task is not to put a legal label on some occurrence in the past, but to form an opinion of how to obtain some desirable state of affairs in the future. Typical examples are the custody of a child and the meting out of criminal sanctions in individual cases. In such kinds of cases the law-applier is faced with (i) relevant circumstances pertaining particularly to the individual case, (ii) which circumstances are manifold, and (iii) he has to consider different possible outcomes in the future, and (iv) evaluate them.

One could ask: If this is so, why issue statutory rules on such matters at all? Why not delegate the whole thing to the courts of law or other authorities? But that, of course, would be too rash a solution. Legislation is necessary in order to have written formulations of some general, basic guiding principles, thrashed out, with the assistance of experts, in the legislative process and given democratic authority. The vagueness can range over a wide span, from general clauses with formulations like "unreasonable" and "contrary to faith and honour" to more specific formulations in statutory principles. As an example of the latter can be mentioned Chap. 3 Art. 6 in the Swedish Penal Code, where guidelines are given for deciding whether an assult is "gross" or not: "When estimating whether the crime [an assault] is gross it shall particularly be taken into consideration whether the act was fatal or whether the offender had inflicted grave bodily injury or severe illness or otherwise shown particular ruthlessness or brutality" (my trans.). Suppose that the offender has inflicted severe illness on his victim but the court does not sentence the offender for gross assault but only for assault. The court has hereby not necessarily breached the provision. Other circumstances, giving reasons for not regarding the act as gross, might have been conclusive. Statutory principles of this kind have been breached only if the court has *not taken into consideration* circumstances of the type mentioned in them. From the point of view of legal certainty, such discretion is situated on a scale between decisions where there is no law at all and application of very precise rules.

Chapter 7
Legal Accessibility

Ubi ius, ibi remedium.

7.1 Introduction

In this chapter I shall try to clarify (at least some aspects of) the sphere of thought connected with the term "legal accessibility."

The venerable dictum *Ubi ius, ibi remedium*—wherever there is law, there is (or should be) a remedy—indicates that a legal order, including even the most advanced set of legal rules, is still incomplete and defective if no "law-ways"are accessible to persons with legal claims based upon the rules, making it possible for them to "realise" these claims. Legal accessibility is an important component of the legal protection of the individual, and it is necessitated by the very existence of a legal order—where no legal order exists, there is no need, or even room left, for legal accessibility.

But what does "legal accessibility" signify? Of course, every legal order in fact has some legal organisation (set of legal bodies), however rudimentary, itself constituted by legal rules, accessible to a larger or smaller sphere of individuals, and fulfilling the task of realising the law. Therefore, there are reasons to regard legal accessibility as an inevitable companion of legal orders.

In Sect. 7.2 I shall try to clarify what can reasonably be meant by saying that a person has access to some such body. This will be done in terms of what I call *the accessibility relation.*

However, even if some kind of "law-ways", or remedies, are provided by any legal order to persons subject to it, that obviously does not mean that this legal order satisfies some given standard of what can be demanded from legal orders with respect to legal accessibility. Law-state thinking has, indeed, strong claims upon legal orders in this respect. It is directed against abuse of the legal order by state organs. And a powerful resource of those in power for violating individuals if they so wish (or out of sheer ignorance) is to abstain from offering acceptable remedies, or even denying to certain people the use of such remedies.

Å. Frändberg, *From Rechtsstaat to Universal Law-State,* Law and Philosophy Library 109,
DOI 10.1007/978-3-319-06784-1_7,

In order more precisely to formulate these claims, we must say something about how legal accessibility can be *justified* as a value from a law-state point of view. In Sect. 7.3 I shall put forward some ideas in that respect. In the light of these justificatory reasons for legal accessibility, I shall then formulate some claims that law-state thinking can have upon legal accessibility (Sect. 7.4). I conclude the chapter by saying something about relations between legal accessibility and some other values (Sect. 7.5).

7.2 Clarifying the Concept "Legal Accessibility"

My task in this section is to clarify the very idea of legal accessibility. What I propose is a conceptual (or pure) theory, capable of being applicable to any legal order whatsoever.

A natural point of departure is that *access* here means access to (actions performed by functionaries of) legal bodies, and that *remedies* are "the keys" opening access to legal bodies.

An important distinction, as I see it, can be drawn between *offensive* and *defensive accessibility*. A person has offensive accessibility if and only if (i) if she has some legal claim upon another person (natural or legal, including the state itself), (ii) she has access to legal bodies for, ultimately, having her claims vindicated, if valid. And a person has defensive accessibility if and only if (i) if she is a person against whom a legal claim has been made, (ii) she has access to legal bodies for defending herself against such claims, making it possible for her ultimately to free herself from some legal burden if her objections hold. While a person endowed with offensive accessiblity has *remedies* at her disposal, we say that a person endowed with defensive accessibility has *counter-remedies* at her disposal.

Let us spell out an *accessibility relation* (A_l) in the following way. A_l reads "accessibility according to legal order *l*." (To begin with, we disregard the distinction between offensive and defensive accessibility.)

(A_l) Person *p*, with respect to issue *i*, has access to functionaries of body *b* by means of remedy *r*, to the effect that *b* is to perform some to *i* relevantly corresponding remedial measure *m*.

Example: According to Swedish law, buyer B, with respect to receiving compensation for delayed delivery from seller S, has access to some judge of court C by means of instituting a claim for compensation, to the effect that C passes a sentence whereby it either approves or dismisses the claim on its merits.

The example describes *a potential legal position*. B is in the potential legal position that if he institutes a claim for compensation, then some judge of C shall hand down a judgment whereby he either approves or dismisses the claim on its merits. If B actually has instituted a claim for compensation, he is in the *actual legal position* that some judge shall hand down a judgment whereby he either approves or dismisses the claim on its merits.

From the viewpoint of principle we are, of course, more interested in *kinds* (or *types*) of issues, remedies etc. than in individual ones. As variables for kinds we use *P* for kinds of persons, *I* for kinds of issues, *B* for kinds of legal bodies, *R* for kinds of remedies, and *M* for kinds of remedial measures. Changing A_l to a relation between kinds, A_L*, we have

$$A_L*(P, I, B, R, M).$$

Relations of type A_L* are *generic potential positions*. Example: According to some legal order, buyers in general, with respect to receiving compensation for breach of contract on the part of the seller, by means of civil action, have access to some judge of a civil court of first instance to the effect that the court in question will hand down a judgment whereby the judge either approves or dismisses the claim on its merits.

Generic potential accessibility positions are legal consequences of general legal rules, whose antecendents (requisites) describe the conditions for accessibility. They belong, of course, mainly to procedural law.

Our task in the following is to clarify A_L*. Let us begin by commenting a little on each one of the different kinds separately.

i. *P* covers kinds of human beings and collectives of human beings. To be sure, it is not completely unreasonable also to include (certain kinds of) animals here. If so, the accessibility of animals to law must of course be handled by human beings. In the Middle Ages animals were subject to punishment, and in the future it might well be the case that animals get certain rights of their own. But here we shall leave aside the case of animals. As we all know, the extent of persons enjoying legal accessibility varies greatly between legal orders, especially in a historical perspective. And likewise the degree of accessibility can differ a great deal between different kinds of persons with respect to some individual legal order.
ii. *I* covers kinds of legal issues. Here we use the term "issue" in a very wide sense. We shall let it denote any legal claim in any legal form whatsoever directed to some person from another person, any answer in legal form to such a claim from the adversary, declaratory claims, criminal prosecutions, defences, and so on. The variations between and within legal orders are remarkable.
iii. *B* covers all kinds of legal bodies, both legal authorities in a strict sense (courts of law, prosecution authorities, the police force) and private bodies such as bar associations, as well as legal authorities in a wider sense, viz. parliaments, governments and administrative agencies which are all constituted by legal rules. The variations between and within legal orders are remarkable.
iv. *R* covers remedies in the widest possible sense. It includes the right to plead before a court (standing to litigate), the right to furnish proofs, and to bring forward arguments, the duty to communicate claims, proofs, and arguments delivered by a party to the adverse party (of special importance with respect to defensive accessibility), the right to have a judgment executed, the right to appeal to a higher instance, the right to constitutional review or other forms of control (e.g., through *ombudsmen*), the right to be granted a new trial, the right to appeal to an international court of law, etc. The variations between and within legal orders are remarkable.

Remedies are means to the end of coming into one's right.

Remedies are normative phenomena. They can be articulated in terms of Hohfeld elements (claims, duties; liberties, no-rights; competences, liabilities; immunities, disabilities).

v. The actions by which remedies are performed (e.g., the action of making a claim, fulfilling a duty or exercising a competence of a remedial character) we call *remedial measures*. To institute a claim for compensation is a remedial measure. If a person has a remedy right to have the proofs presented to a court of law evaluated, then the evaluation of this piece of evidence is a remedial measure "realising" that right. To execute a judgment is a remedial measure.

We can talk about *chains of remedies and remedial measures*. Using our example above buyer B has a right (a remedy) to institute a claim for compensation. He exercises this right by doing that, and thus performs a remedial measure. The judge then has a duty (as well as a competence) either to approve or dismiss the claim on its merits. If he, e.g., approves the claim, he is performing a remedial measure. Now B can claim execution, which is a remedy. If he does so (thereby performing a remedial measure), the executory authority has a duty to execute (which is a remedy). And, finally, if the authority executes the judgment, it has performed a remedial measure. When this last remedial measure has been performed, it could be said that B has come into his right. Now he has been compensated as well as possible. Execution of a judgment is, we say, *the ultimate remedial measure*.

We see that some remedial measures are in the hands of private individuals, while others are in the hands of the authorities. Usually the first remedial measure is performed by private individuals, looking after their interests. But sometimes the first step can be taken *ex officio* by the authority. Then the authority becomes a kind of representative of the private individual. Other measures can only be performed by authorities (evaluating evidence, handing down a judgment, performing an execution). In civil law issues, the triggering of the ultimate remedial measure is usually in the hands of the private individual (e.g., to demand the execution of the judgment). In criminal law issues, on the other hand, it is usually not the injured party who decides whether the defendant shall be punished or not.

Finally, what do I mean by the expression "a measure relevantly corresponding to some issue?" Let me give some examples. To approve or dismiss a claim on its merits is a measure relevantly corresponding to the issue of receiving compensation for delayed delivery. To have an execution performed, thereby giving the buyer money from the seller equivalent to his loss, is a measure relevantly corresponding to the issue in question. But if a wife, suing for a divorce from her violent husband, is instead awarded damages from him, or the husband is instead punished for assault, these measures do not relevantly correspond to the issue of being divorced. In order for a remedial measure, *m*, to be relevantly corresponding to issue *i*, *m* must either be the ultimate remedial measure for realising *i* or *m* must be a member of a chain of remedial measures giving the interested party a possibility of acquiring the ultimate remedial measure performed.

Let us now turn to defensive accessibility. We shall use the word "claimant" ("C" for short) as an umbrella term for both plaintiffs in civil cases and prosecutors in criminal cases. The adverse party we shall call “the defendant” (“D” for short). Defensive accessibility consists in giving D counter-remedies to C’s remedies. Counter-remedies provide D with counter-moves to C’s moves. That C has a remedy *r* and D no counter-remedy to *r* is not only a violation of the value of legal equality. It is also a violation of the value of legal accessibility.

The counter-position of D involves all components of A^*, including the reference to a legal system. Let us take them in order.

1. It might seem strange to talk about a counter-legal order, *cl*, to another legal order, *l*. But in spite of this terminology it might well be, and in fact sometimes is, the case that a remedy used by C according to *l* can be met by a counter-remedy used by D according to l' ($l' \neq l$).
2. The counter-class of persons of kind C is the class of persons of kind D.
3. To every issue can be formulated a counter-issue, usually only rejecting the former.
4. To talk about counter-bodies to some legal bodies likewise sounds a bit strange. Usually the body to which a remedy is directed is also the body to which counter-remedies are directed. But that is not a necessary (conceptual or logical) state of affairs. It is possible to think of a counter-remedy directed to another authority to the effect that the case shall be transferred to that authority. If the line of demarcation between the competences of two different bodies is obscure, that might even encourage lawyers to transgress the borderline for strategic reasons.
5. To talk about counter-remedies comes more naturally. To the right to plead before a court corresponds the right to reply to a charge. To the right to furnish proofs and bring forward arguments corresponds the right to reject these proofs and arguments and provide one’s own proofs and arguments. A necessary condition for this is the right to be informed of the proofs and arguments presented by the adverse party (communication). To the right to have a judgment approving a claim corresponds a right to have a judgment rejecting that claim, or even to have it dismissed on formal grounds (not on the merits). To the right to have a judgment executed might correspond a right to a stay of execution. To the rights of appeal to a higher instance, to constitutional review or other forms of control, to be granted a new trial, to appeal to an international court of law etc. correspond the same rights for the adverse party.
6. Nor does it seem particularly strange to talk about counter-measures. Counter-measures are the actions by which counter-remedies are performed.

7.3 Justifying Legal Accessibility

In Sect. 7.2 I tried to clarify what legal accessibility is. We now turn our attention to legal accessibility as a law-state value. For that purpose we need a standard or standards by means of which we can evaluate the quality of legal accessibility guaranteed by different legal orders and the handling of them from the point of view of law-state thinking. But in order to be able to formulate any such standards we must first shed light on the question of how legal accessibility can be justified, i.e., what it is that makes accessibility a (positive) value. Some ideas addressed to this issue will be presented in this section.

As a point of departure I shall, by way of contrast, describe some situations where the value of accessibility appears to be violated, and why we conceive of them as repugnant.

Complaints about alleged violations of legal accessibility are not rare phenomena. It is significant that Article 6 of the European Convention on Human Rights, protecting legal accessibility, is the most frequently invoked article of the convention.

Violation of a person's legal accessibility means the absence of a remedy corresponding to his issue (claim), or the existence of certain facts preventing him from making use of such a remedy.

Let me give some examples of violations of a person's legal accessibility, chosen for their illustrative force from the case law of the European Court of Human Rights.[1] In all cases mentioned the state has not satisfied the requirements laid down in Article 6.

I. *Violation of standing to litigate and the right to have one's say in the trial proceedings.*

   1. I. and C. were prosecuted for assault and sentenced to imprisonment. Although present at the proceedings, they were not heard by the court (Ilisescu and Chiforec v. Romania, 1 December 2005).
   2. Z. was sentenced by a district court for participating in an illegal demonstration. He appealed to a regional court, which rejected the appeal on 4 May 2000. Notice to attend this session was sent by mail on 3 May 2000. Z. had probably not received the notice until the proceedings were already over (Ziliberberg v. Moldavia, 1 February 2005).

II. *Violation of the right to obtain the attendance and examination of witnesses.*

   3. Z. was denied confrontation in the first instance as well as in the court of appeal with two persons, who had incriminated him. In no stage of the proceedings did Z. have a chance to hear these persons. Although their testimonies were of great importance for the conviction, the French authorities made no attempt whatsoever to find them (Zentar v. France, 13 April 2005).

III. *Violation of the right to appeal.*

   4. A medical board declared that M. suffered from a physical disability of "the second degree". After that M's health deteriorated and another medical board classified his disability as being of "the first degree". A month after that decision the central medical board of the department of public health changed the classification back to "second degree". M. appealed to the Supreme Administrative Court, which dismissed the appeal on purely formal grounds (Mihailov v. Bulgaria, 21 July 2005).

[1] I have for this purpose profited from Hans Danelius's excellent case law surveys regularly published in *Svensk Juristtidning*.

IV. *Violation of the right to have a judgment executed.*

5. P.-B. had four children, of whom their father had custody. P.-B. had been granted a right of access to her children. The father refused to bring a daughter to the place where she and her mother were supposed to meet. French authorities did not help in executing the judgment (Plasse-Bauer v. France, 28 February 2006).

V. *Violation of the right to have access to evidence.*

6. E. and L., having been prosecuted for a crime, did not have access to certain evidence, and this made it more difficult for them to defend themselves, although the judges adjudicating the case had access to this evidence (Edwards and Lewis v. United Kingdom, 27 October 2004).

VI. *Violation of the right to appear before a court of law.*

7. V., being prosecuted for a crime, delivered a medical certificate, stating that he was unable to attend the main hearing. In spite of this, the court carried out the hearing. His counsel, who was present, was not allowed to defend his client, the client himself being absent. The same thing happened in the court of appeal (Vigroux v. France, 19 May 2005).

VII. *Violation of the right to have objections taken into consideration by courts of law.*

8. V. applied to the authorities to have back land owned by his family and occupied by the Soviet army returned to him. The authorities replied that, according to two decrees from 1960 and 1968, ownership had been transferred to the municipality. V. argued before a court of law that these decrees were unconstitutional. The court dismissed his claims without taking up his objections (Vasilescu v. Romania, 8 February 2006).

VIII. *Violation of the right to public court proceedings.*

9. M. had, as a treasurer of an association, made incorrect payments. M was ordered by the *Cour des comptes* to compensate for these payments. No public proceedings were held in the *Cour des comptes*. The European Court emphasised that public proceedings protect individuals against the secret administration of justice (Martinie v. France, 12 April 2006).

IX. *Violation of the right to have access to legal authorities within a reasonable time.*

10. C. was suspected of embezzlement. In May 1996, property belonging to him was seized. Ten years later C. had still not been prosecuted or even summoned to interrogation. The examining magistrate had also refused to give C. more detailed information about the development of the preliminary investigation. (Casse v. Luxembourg, 27 April 2006).
11. S. owned land that was expropriated by the authorities in 1974. S. complained about the compensation at a court of law in 1976. The case was finally decided in February 2002 (Stornaiuolo v. Italy, 8 August 2006).

X. *Violation of the right to have access to legal authorities at reasonable costs.*

12. K. instituted a claim for compensation against the municipality P. A regional court imposed on K. as a court fee the amount of an ordinary annual salary without taking into consideration the financial position of K. (Kreuz v. Poland, 19 June 2001).

XI. *Violation of the right to receive a fair trial through obstruction, negligence, incompetence or harassment*

13. M. was prosecuted before a French *cour d'assises* for rape and theft. The proceedings began on 3 December 1998 at 9.15 a.m. and were completed 5 December at 8.30 a.m. On the second day (4 December) the proceedings ended at 12.30 p.m. at the request of M's counsel. They were taken up again at 1.00 a.m. the following night and continued till 4.25 in the morning. The proceeding had then lasted for altogether15 h and 45 min. The judge and the jury deliberated between 6.15 and 8.15 a.m. 5 December (Makhfi v. France, 19 October 2004).
14. S. was prosecuted for an offence against the Bankruptcy Act. In the proceedings he was defended successively by several public counsels appointed by the authorities. There was nothing to suggest that these counsels were familiar with the case; despite this fact, they did not ask for a suspension of the proceedings in order to study the facts of the case. The first two of them had claimed and been granted examination of witnesses but the subsequent ones did not ask that these these examinations be carried out (Sannino v. Italy, 27 April 2006).
15. F. was plaintiff in a civil procedure and lost the case. She complained at the European Court of Human Rights that the local court had not been correctly composed according to Russian national law. While the proceedings were under way at the European court, Russian police ordered F's representative at the European court and her translator to prove that they had paid a tax on their fees from F., although they were not suspected of any crime (Fedotova v. Russia, 13 April 2006).

All these cases are examples of the violation of the value of legal accessibility. By way of a contrast we might be able to formulate in words what it is that makes legal accessibility a value. On the basis of such a formulation we can then try to lay down some standards by means of which we can measure the quality of the handling of legal orders by legislators, judges, prosecutors, lawyers, police officers and other legal functionaries. Both tasks are problematic. Let us begin with the first one. The second one will be discussed in Sect. 7.4.

As is the case with other law-state values such as legal equality, the justification of legal accessibility cannot be articulated in a "mechanical" manner by reference to some fixed criteria related to, e.g., different types of access. It is to be found in the human mind and is strongly connected to our capacity for empathy. It must be expressed in a picture rather than in the form of principles.

As I see it, violations of the value of accessibility are violations of a life of human dignity for individuals. This is the justificatory ground for that value. The justificatory ground is itself of an evaluative and a normative character. The picture is a picture of an ideal state of affairs. Violation of accessibility is something ugly to behold. The person who is unable to appreciate that ugliness for what it is cannot embrace legal accessibility as a value. I think most people are capable of seeing it when they encounter it.

However, I shall not undertake to paint such a picture. Instead, I shall use the examples given as pictures of the ugliness of violating legal accessibility. From these pictures, by way of contrast, the ideal picture may emerge in all its beauty and purity.

Violating legal accessibility is a kind of abuse of power. It is ugly in three respects. Let us call them (i) the insult of violating accessibility, (ii) the arrogance of violating accessibility, and (iii) the decadence of violating accessibility. (See the corresponding idea concerning the value of legal equality in Chap. 5.)

The insult of violating legal accessibility consists in the combination of two evil things: deceitfulness on the part of the functionaries and powerlessness on the part of those subject to them.

Individuals are deceived by being deprived of something, the deprivation of which can be characterised as a violation of a life of human dignity, and which the state could provide if it chose to. Let us illuminate the aspect of deceit on the part of the functionaries by using our examples. A party is thus deceived, in example 1 of being listened to, in example 2 of being able to participate in the proceedings, in example 3 of having witnesses questioned, in example 4 of being able to plead his case before a court of law, in example 5 of having judgements executed, in example 8 of having objections in matters of law taken into consideration, in example 9 of having a public hearing, in example 10 of having access to proceedings within reasonable time, in example 12 of being able to vindicate his right although lacking financial means, in example 13 of having a trial which is fair (not sabotaged), in example 14 of having a decent (not negligent or incompetent) defence, and in example 15 of being able to use legal remedies without being harassed when so doing.

A life of human dignity is violated when the individual exposed is powerless with respect to all these deprivations—when she can do nothing about it by legal means. In all our examples this was the case with respect to national law.

The arrogance of violating legal accessibility consists in using one's power to tamper with remedies. It shows itself in all the examples. In example 1 by failing to listen to a party as though he were not there, in example 2 by assuming a nonchalant attitude to a party, in examples 3 and 6 by regarding oneself as free to pick and choose persons to be questioned, in example 5 by first granting a person a right only to refuse later to help this person in having this right realised, in example 7 by not showing due consideration for a person's bad health, in example 8 by not listening to the party's objections, in example 9 by keeping the proceedings secret, in examples 10 and 11 by not bothering to carry out one's obligations to a party with respect to his right, in example 12 by imposing unreasonable costs on a party, in example 13 by sabotaging one's right to a fair trial, in example 14 by being careless vis-à-vis one's duties and in example 15 by trying to influence a party by means of harassment, i.e., by extortion.

In many of our examples the person violated is a criminal, in some of them even a rather nasty one. This might lead some of us to believe that the value of legal accessibility is a rather dispensable one. It could be said that these people get what they deserve, and that's all there is to it. But—quite apart from the possibility that they are in fact innocent—it is a mark of civilised society to treat even those unfortunate human beings decently. To be sure, their level of civilisation cannot be used as a standard for the behaviour of the servants of law.

The decadence of violating accessibility pertains in the first place to the victims of such violations. If legal authorities neglect, in various respects, individuals who are claiming their rights, this can have serious effects on the morale of the people. Citizens may be inclined to yield to the authorities, to become reduced to flatterers or self-pitying human beings, humiliating themselves in order to have the authorities' ear. A sense of frustration (emerging not least from situations of the types exemplified in examples 10–12), leading to people obstructing the legal order, might spread. In the case of state terror (example 15), people can be even more inclined to yield to the powers that be. But there are dangers in the opposite direction, too. Private persons might be tempted to bribe legal functionaries to tamper with remedies. Then decadence in the form of corruption and humiliation on the part of the authorities spills over into society.

The absence of these three defects justifies the value of legal accessibility in a society equipped with a legal order. The greater the number of defects in a society, the greater the degree of lawlessness. The fewer number of defects found in the society, the more the society will be informed by the value of legal accessibility.

7.4 Law-State Standards of Legal Accessibility

Thus, we have found the justificatory criterion of the value of legal accessibility as a law-state value in the superior value of a life of human dignity. Now the question arises: which law-state standards that meet this criterion can be formulated?

First of all, it must be emphasised that the connection between the superior value and these standards is necessarily rather vague. To present this connection in a strict and precise manner would be an unwarranted simplification and also an over-intellectualised approach to the matter.

Let us formulate the standards with respect to each component of *the accessibility relation* A_L*.

1. *With respect to persons.* Everyone shall be granted a remedy to the issue he might want to pursue.

2. *With respect to legal issues.* To each possible legal issue shall correspond an adequate legal remedy.

3. *With respect to legal bodies.* Authorities and other bodies shall be adapted to the issues they are meant to handle. As regards individual rights, the ultimate arbiter shall be a court of law. Borderline cases here are special courts of law, tribunals, and the like. Military tribunals are repugnant from the viewpoint of the value of legal accessibility as are, of course, secret organs. A far-reaching separation of powers between state organs, each with well-defined competences, facilitates access to law (see further Chap. 9).

In order to achieve legal accessibility certain conditions related to legal bodies must be fulfilled. There are certain obstacles to access, the absence of which is a necessary condition for having legal access. Let us, in this respect, make a distinction between external and internal obstacles.

External obstacles are obstacles "outside" the legal bodies themselves, obstructing access to these bodies. Geographic distance is one such obstacle. Suppose, e.g., that you want to appeal a judgment and the court of appeal is situated far away from your place of residence, in another part of your country. Another external obstacle is lack of economic means. Or it might be the case that you fail to understand the language spoken in the proceedings. Or you might be deaf.

Legal accessibility as a law-state value requires absence of external obstacles. This means reasonable geographic proximity to such legal bodies before which you must appear in person. Otherwise it must be possible to reach authorities by mail, phone, e-mail or fax. The legal order shall also provide adequate legal aid as well as competent legal interpreters.

Internal obstacles are obstacles in a more direct way pertaining to the legal body itself. Legal accessibility includes some requirements of utmost importance concerning legal proceedings. Thus, the proceedings must not be obstructed by exaggerated formalities and unnecessary delays. Legal functionaries should behave politely and, if the situation so requires, should be in possession of a certain degree of courage where standing up for the law-state values is concerned. Intimidation and disrespect might well deter people from seeking their rights. These requirements, and many others to the same effect, are included in the general requirement of a fair trial.

4. *With respect to remedies.* The remedies—and counter-remedies—offered by the legal order shall be clearly stated in the form of statutory law. There shall be no uncertainty inherent in them concerning which issues they are remedies (counter-remedies) for, which bodies they are addressed to, and the character of the remedial measure they provide. Individuals shall be given a free choice to decide for themselves whether they want to use the remedial measure or not. Hence, the legal rules stating the conditions for access to some remedy, and the remedy itself as a legal consequence (*remedy rules*), are best framed as competence rules and liberty rules. The corresponding rules addressed to the authorities, on the other hand, should be competence rules and duties. The remedy rules shall not be encumbered by hindrances in the form of unnecessary formal requirements.

Indispensable remedies are standing to litigate, the right to produce legal arguments and evidence, the right to appeal (also to international courts of law), and the right to enforcement. In addition to this, there are extraordinary remedies in certain cases (relief for a substantive defect) and judicial control in the form of constitutional review or examination performed by *ombudsmen* and other bodies with a controlling function.

5. *With respect to remedial measures*. The very description of the accessibility relation A_L* in Sect. 7.2 stated that the remedial measure shall relevantly correspond to the issue. The reason for this is that I find it misleading to talk about "accessibility"at all if this is not the case. I also gave some examples indicating what I mean by "relevantly corresponding." The perfectly corresponding measure is a measure which creates (restores) the state of affairs that the party desired. But this is in most cases impossible. Then the corresponding measure is a matter of compensation (usually measured in money) or, with respect to criminal law, punishment.

The remedial measures shall also be efficient. By this I mean that they shall be (i) expedient, i.e., suitable for their purposes, and (ii) observed by their addressees.

Of utmost importance is that the remedial measures are backed up by all the superior force state power can mobilise. As John Locke would have said (and in fact implied), why else would people abstain from taking law in their own hands?

6. *With respect to counter-measures*. What has just been said about remedial measures bears upon counter-measures as well. But in addition to that, the counter-measure shall also relevantly correspond to the remedial measure that it is a counter-measure to. For instance, if an execution has begun, an adequate counter-measure to it is to try to block the execution. But it is not an adequate counter-measure to sue the adverse party for trespassing.

Without any doubt the most important requirement concerning counter-measures is *communication*. What is it then that shall be communicated? It is information. For every remedial step a party takes, information about that step shall be given to the adverse party. Claims, objections, evidence, expert opinions, legal argumentation—everything shall be delivered to the adverse party.

Communication is of course facilitated if issues and their corresponding counter-issues are handled by the same organ (let us call it "the principle of joint handling").

7.5 Value Relations

1. *The relation between legal accessibility and the other basic law-state values*. There are two disastrous gaps which must never be tolerated in a valid legal order informed by law-state values. One is the rift between what the law says and how the servants of the law in fact handle the law (the discrepancy between formal and material validity, due to disrespect of legalism, described in Chap. 6). The other is

the gap between what the legal order promises and what it keeps—the gap between *ius* and *remedium*. Promising *ius* and not giving *remedium* is a large-scale betrayal of those subject to the law. And it betrays the other law-state values as well. Without legal accessibilty, legal equality (in the law as well as before the law), legal certainty and legal security come to very little. The reverse holds, too. Violations of legal equality, legal certainty and legal security make legal accessibility worth less.

As for legal equality, equality before the law (procedural legal equality) is, for purely logical reasons, impossible without legal accessibility to bodies that make it possible to violate or uphold equality before the law.

As was pointed out in Chap. 6 (p. 124 above) extreme legal accessibility might violate legal certainty. If the *res iudicata* barrier is not upheld, the scope of legal accessibility expands at the cost of infringements of legal certainty. A variety of alternative legal remedies to choose between can also create legal uncertainty. The best becomes the enemy of the good.

2. *The relation between legal accessibility and values other than the basic law-state values.* Some legal orders embrace the principle *De minimis non curat lex, i.e.*, the legal order does not take account of trifles. This principle is directed against legal accessibility. What, then, are the opposing values that challenge legal accessibility by means of this principle? One is the value of the economy of work. Dealing with important matters must not be obstructed by trifles. Another, related to the value of economy of work, is to deter opinionated, dogmatic persons from using the legal order, at least in small matters. Litigation must not become a mockery. The lust for litigation—well known since the days of ancient Athens—is an inescapable companion to the legal way of solving problems and the psychology of it would be worth a close study. The legislature would, in fact, be wise to create safety-valves outside the courts of law by means of which those lusting for litigation can let off steam. In Sweden, the *justitieombudsman* has that function to no small degree.

Legal accessibility may be a hindrance when the safety of the state is at stake. Two risks are prominent in this connection. One is the risk of leakage in the legal process of vital information, which must be kept secret. The other is the risk of delay in the case of vital decisions if they are in the hands of courts. (On the other hand, delay can in certain situations be strategically valuable.)

Chapter 8
Legal Security

8.1 Clarifying the Concept "Legal Security"

There are forms of abuse of the legal order on the part of the state which without any doubt can be said to violate the idea of the law-state but which cannot be described as violating either legal equality, legal certainty or legal accessibility (although often combined with violations of them). These forms of abuse are in fact a main concern for law-state thinking.

What I have in mind is the state's use of the legal order to attack individuals' in life or limb, damaging their health or property, obstructing their freedom of movement, or subjecting them to harsh or degrading treatment, and similar outrageous measures. Let us sum up all such measures under the term "legal insecurity".

It seems to me that legal insecurity in a certain important respect differs from legal inequality, legal uncertainty and lawlessness (legal inaccessibility). To be sure, all of them subject individuals to suffering of various kinds, and are apt to violate the individual's life of human dignity. But with respect to the latter, there is an element of *deceit* on the part of the state, which is lacking in the former. You seek to vindicate your right, but you are unduly discriminated against in so doing, or the legal order does not give you clear answers to legal questions of importance to you, or you are not granted access to legal bodies. You are let down by the legal order in matters closely related to the handling and functioning of the legal order itself. Legal insecurity, on the other hand, is brought about by means of the state's *attacking* the individual's body, belongings or personal environment, thereby making him insecure (exposed to state interference, deprived of things or possibilities) with respect to these. Legal insecurity has devices—and remedies—of its own.

Legal inequality, legal uncertainty, and lawlessness are, of course, no legitimate means in the hands of legal functionaries in a law-state. But certain infringements of the body, freedom, and belongings of individuals, notably sanctions and procedural coercive measures, e.g., detention, are such means.

While legal equality, certainty, and accessibility may have a hint of formalism or abstraction attached to them, physical and mental security is a value more intimately connected with our very life-sustaining instincts. Infringements on it often mean pure pain. We usually take testimony about violations of this value far more

Å. Frändberg, *From Rechtsstaat to Universal Law-State,* Law and Philosophy Library 109,
DOI 10.1007/978-3-319-06784-1_8,

to the heart than violations of other values. It is, indeed, the value closest to the perpetual function of legal orders—that of preserving the peace (see p. 18 above).

In spite of these differences, however, legal security is a law-state value in the same sense as legal equality, legal certainty, and legal accessibility are law-state values. The idea of legal safety is directed against abuses of the legal order with respect to the very handling, or use, of it. It is in the first place a matter of abuse of the traditional arsenal of means of achieving compliance with the legal rules, notably sanctions.

In this section we are concerned with the very concept of legal security. We shall try to mould a notion of legal security which is fruitful while also preserving our basic intuitions of what legal security means. In Sect. 8.2 we shall formulate a justification of the value of legal security. In Sect. 8.3 we focus on possible conflicts between legal security and other values and discuss the balancing of them. In Sect. 8.4 we formulate certain principles guiding that balancing. Here we also present some ideas about how the realisation of legal security can be warranted by means of legislation.

Let us introduce a concept: *the individual's personal sphere* (*IPS* for short). This concept is taken to be a purely descriptive, non-normative one. *IPS* embraces the individual's body, his efforts to satisfy his necessary living conditions, his personal premises (not least his own home), his range of movement, his property, and his personal communication with other individuals and the documentation thereof.

Now, infringements (attacks) of *IPS*—legitimate or illegitimate—can be undertaken by other individuals as well as by state organs. To protect *IPS* from illegitimate infringements undertaken by other private persons is the task of the legal order at large and falls outside the scope of law-state thinking. Protection of the *IPS* from illegitimate infringements undertaken by the state, on the other hand, is a claim on the legal order made by law-state thinking. The ideal of legal security, as a component of law-state thinking, concerns the borderline between legitimate and illegitimate infringements of *IPS* on the part of the state and makes claims about how to draw these borderlines. *IPS* delimits the scope of application of the idea of legal security.

Legal orders claim state monopoly of violence. With certain specified exceptions, a private person has no right to engage in violence on her own. The exceptions usually concern necessity situations, in the first place self-defence, and situations of immediate urgency, where self-help can be allowed (e.g., when encountering into a thief in the very act of stealing).

However, the state monopoly of violence can be extended to embrace the whole area of *IPS*, not only attacks on a person's body (her life, limbs and health). For good reasons it can be argued that modern states, through the legal order, with certain specified exceptions, claim a monopoly of infringements of, e.g., persons trying, illegally, to provide themselves with food, drink or clothing (violating the monopoly may be committing the crime of illegal self-help, or whatever it is called in different criminal codes); the main exception in such cases being self-help in the very act of, e.g., somebody's stealing. (Another matter is that the person protected by the state monopoly possibly is committing a crime herself, e.g., a theft). The state might also be said to claim a monopoly with respect to entering another person's home without permission (violating it being trespassing; the main exception of the state monopoly being evicting a trespasser provided that only reasonable force is used), with respect to infringements of a person's range of movement (detention; violating the monopoly being unlawful deprivation of liberty, kidnapping etc.; the main exception also in this case being legally allowed self-help), with respect to infringements of a person's property (violating it being, e.g., theft; the main exceptions to the state monopoly being different kinds of necessity, e.g. putting out a fire, and cases of *negotiorum gestio* in legal orders where that legal institute is accepted) and, finally, with respect to infringements of a person's private correspondence by letters, on the Internet etc., or infringements by tapping her telephone calls, bugging her home etc. (violating the monopoly being, e.g., offences against secrecy of correspondence and illicit bugging or wire-tapping; a possible exception to the state monopoly being, e.g., parents' interference with small children's use of the Internet in order to protect them from sexual offenders). The state has a monopoly in these situations in the same sense that it has a monopoly of physical violence (in all situations with legally specified exceptions). Hence it is reasonable to argue that modern states usually claim *monopoly of infringements of individuals' personal sphere* (*IPS*)—whether they are "law-states" or not.

Intrinsically, there is no difference between infringements of *IPS* performed by servants of the state acting as such and infringements of *IPS* performed by criminals. The difference between them lies in the relationship of these actions to the legal order. The former but not the latter are allowed, or even prescribed, by the legal order and are, at best, justified with respect to upholding peace and order in society without violating the law-state values. And the servants of the state have in their hands a far more effective tool than the criminal does: the legal order.

It must be emphasised that the principle of state monopoly of violence—and its extended variant *the principle of state monopoly of infringements of IPS*—are not law-state principles. They are claimed also by states that cannot be said to be law-states in any reasonable sense of the word. They are in fact inseparably connected with what I refer to as the perpetual function of legal orders.

The relationship between the principle of state monopoly of infringements of *IPS* and the law-state ideas is, rather, an antagonistic one. No one has expressed it better than John Locke (cf. p. 28 above). If ordinary citizens are deprived of the legal possibility to violate the *IPS* of others in order to claim their right (self-help), and all power in that respect is in the possession of the state, that is all the more reason then to subject the state to severe restrictions and control in order to prevent abuses of this monopoly, or the individual will be even worse off than without the monopoly. This is a vital aspect of the basic law-state idea.

As our bodies—and, indeed, our minds—are not made of stone, and our bodily capacity of both fleeing and fighting is highly limited, specimens of our species are dangerously vulnerable. Since time immemorial, this fact has given human beings a—too often irresistible—temptation to achieve their goals and move their positions forward by use of violence on, or intimidation of, others. That this temptation can be reinforced and yielding to it justified owing to the fact that the person who is tempted is in possession of power, counts as a tragic fact that tells us something about the darker side of human nature.

Since the efficacy of legal orders depends in the last resort upon the use of violence and coercion, it is not difficult to explain the temptation for the ill-disposed powers that be to tamper with the legal order. A perverted use of state power may even stand out as a legitimate use of it. Especially tempting in this respect is criminal law and procedural coercive measures (e.g., arrest, detention and travel prohibition) and that for two reasons: (1) an established, working order for repression is already there, ready to be used, and (2) the powers that be can take advantage of attitudes of repugnance extant directed at ordinary criminals when using criminal and procedural law against, e.g., political enemies.

Let us introduce a notion: *naked (or natural) infringements (attacks) of IPS*. Naked infringements are common to pre-legal, legal and illegal infringements of *IPS* alike and are essential to them all. Naked infringements are "natural actions", i.e., actions stripped of any legal qualification. Naked infringements are, e.g., killing, hitting, stabbing, cutting, and hacking (all different kinds of naked violence), sending off by force, expelling, locking up, and stopping a person from moving where she wishes (all different kinds of naked restriction of movement), entering homes or places of work without consent, and grabbing things from others (all different kinds of naked encroachment), and bullying, frightening, and threatening (all different kinds of naked harassment). Common to all kinds of naked infringements of *IPS* is suffering on the part of the persons attacked.

The historical development from a pre-legal society into a legally organised one is not a process of the elimination of naked violence, or the naked infringements of *IPS* on the whole. Naked infringements of *IPS* enter into the legally organised society and become an instrument in the service of the legal order. What has changed in the process is not the nature of naked infringements of *IPS* but the conditions and forms of its use, notably monopolisation in the hands of the state. Decapitation is decapitation whether it takes place in a pre-legal, primitive society, or is a murder or an execution of a criminal according to law.

The driving forces that result in infringements of *IPS* in pre-legal and illegal situations are, e.g., emotional excitement and impulses, desire for revenge, cruelty, hatred, and greed, and its means, e.g., taking advantage of superior physical strength, taking by surprise, and evil scheming.

How, then, shall "legalisation" (incorporation in the legal order) of infringements of *IPS* be characterised? Important features of the state's handling of it are the following.

1. Infringements of IPS are gradually—and not unexceptionally—monopolised by the state.
2. Instrumentalisation of infringements of *IPS*. They become a tool for attaining certain social goals, in the first place social peace and order.
3. Infringements of *IPS*, and the conditions for their use, are specified and formulated in general terms in statutes. Natural means are arrayed in legal dress. Law uses human nature.

4. Infringements of IPS are institutionalised, i.e., handled by state agencies.
5. Infringements of IPS are meted out in individual cases (by courts of law).
6. Institutionalisation of infringements of *IPS*, notably violence, leads to what we can call a "de-psychologisation", or "de-emotionalisation", of infringing *IPS*. Institutionalised infringements are drained of emotions, violence becomes non-aggressive. The hangman is not aggressive or spiteful. He does his job and having satisfactorily performed his duties he goes, like the clerk, home for supper. De-emotionalisation can be seen as a step towards civilisation, and in certain respects it is. But it also involves obvious dangers. Institutionalisation and legalisation provide an excuse för outrageous deeds and de-emotionalisation can corrupt. Suffice it to refer to the functionaries of the Nazi death camps or to Adolf Eichmann for an example.

I wish I could have added humanisation of infringements of *IPS* as a point (vii). However, although this often is the case, it is not universally so. Functionaries of the state can be as bestial and inventive with respect to such infringements as any outlaw. That is why legal security is a crucial law-state value. *The ideal, or principle, of legal security makes certain claims and imposes certain important restrictions upon legalisation of infringements of IPS.*

It seems to me that legal infringements of *IPS—irrespective of whether they are justified or not according to the principle of legal security*—can be assorted into four groups.

1. *Violence*. I restrict the use of the word "violence" to physical violence. We sometimes talk about, e.g., mental torment as "violence", but for the sake of clarity I will keep these things conceptually separate and, hence, I use different terms for them. Examples of legal violence are capital punishment, torture or a policeman bringing a thief by force into a cell.
2. *Restraints on freedom of movement (including choice of residence) and activities*. Examples: Arrest, detention, imprisonment, travel prohibition, compulsory commitment for medical care, "area restriction" forcing, e.g., an alien to remain in a certain area or duty to report his whereabouts—and, with respect to activities, restraints on reading, watching TV, using computers or making telephone calls. Also shadowing falls under this heading.
3. *Intrusion*. Examples: Search of premises, physical examination, personal search (of clothes etc.), sequestration, attachment, seizure, wire tapping or violation of the privacy of correspondence.
4. *Harassment*. Examples: Frightening persons in order to make them abstain from using their legal access to courts of law or to give evidence; policemen bullying and humiliating people, perhaps with the tacit consent of their superiors; having arrested persons spend their time in darkness or creating severe security regimes like the one the USA practiced on detainees in Guantánamo. Especially frightening are deeds performed in secrecy. The unfortunately rather common use of degrading sexual actions and allusions are harassments that tell us something less than flattering about mankind.

Threatening is an efficacious form of harassment. We can draw a distinction between immediate and mediate threats. An immediate threat is "pure" harassment, e.g., when a person says to another: "I' ll cut your throat!" without adding or implying "unless you do (forbear from doing)…". A mediate threat is finalistic and conditional. It has the logical structure "If you do (forbear from doing) action *a*, I shall bring about that something unpleasant, *u*, happens to you". It is logically connected to an imperative: "Do (forbear from doing) *a*!" issued by the person who threatens. There are strong similarities between mediate threats and warnings, and it might sometimes be difficult to distinguish between them. The typical warning has a conditional structure very much like the one of the mediate threat: "If you do (forbear from doing) *a*, then *u* will happen to you". Another similarity is that both mediate threats and warnings (e.g., "If you don't bring your umbrella, you will be soaking wet") provide the addressee with an option, e.g., "leaving town or getting one's throat cut" and "bringing one's umbrella or becoming soaking wet". The difference is that the one who warns usually is not declaring that he shall bring it about himself that *u* ("If you do not bring your umbrella, you will be soaking wet"). Another difference is that a warning is "weaker" than a threat in the respect that it is not logically connected to an imperative addressed to the one who receives the warning. It is rather logically connected to advice ("If I were you, I would bring the umbrella", or something like that). It seems obvious to me that both kinds of threats belong to the wider category of frightening. Frightening in its turn belongs to a wider category of harassment. Every act of frightening is an act of harassment, but the reverse does not hold. Harassment can be, e.g., humiliating, making fun of, irritating, and provoking.

To this list *compulsion* might been added. My reason for not including compulsion is that I do not regard it as an independent infringement on *IPS*. It is symbiotic to the above-mentioned ones. The logical structure of an act of compulsion is the following: "Person *x* forces person *y* by means of *c* to do (abstain from doing) action *a*". *c* is a variable for some means of compulsion. By compulsion *x* is prompting *y* to do (not to do) *a*. This he accomplishes by using some means of compulsion. But there are no such means peculiar to compulsion. Our notion of compulsion is a finalistic or teleological one, indicating that some means are used for some ends (but not indicating which means). In this respect there is a similarity between mediate threat and compulsion. (On the other hand, violence, restraints of freedom of movement, intrusion, and harassment (apart from mediate threats) do not conceptually imply anything finalistic—although they are used instrumentally in the hands of the law). The means themselves (e.g., compulsion by means of violence) fall outside the scope of the notion. What is implied by "compulsion" is only that the means shall be sufficiently strong that in practice they more or less render it necessary for the person exposed to them to do *a*. Compulsion may be performed by means of violence, restraints of freedom and activities, intrusion, and harassment. Compulsion by means of mediate threat gives "formally" the addressee an option, but the alternative sought by the person making the threat is rendered necessary in the way just mentioned (an example of illegal compulsion by means of mediate threat is blackmail).

The borderlines between and among the four kinds of state infringements on *IPS* are sometimes subtle. Two or more of them are often combined in one and the same continuous activity. For instance, (i) violence and restraints on freedom of movement are combined when a culprit is pushed into a cell by force or beaten up by policemen in the arrest, (ii) violence and intrusion are combined when officials procure a means of entering a house for the purpose of searching the premises by beating up the house-owner, (iii) violence and harassment are combined when executions are performed publicly or torture is combined with sexual degradation (Abu Ghraib), (iv) restraints on freedom of movement and intrusion are combined when a prisoner's mail is opened, (v) restraints on freedom of movement and harassment are combined when a detainee's religious beliefs are scorned by the warders and (vi) intrusion and harassment are combined when a policeman performing a physical examination of a person in order to find drugs abuses that person sexually.

It seems reasonable to differentiate between different *forms* of state infringements of *IPS*. Let us distinguish between (a) infringements performed by state agencies in compliance with statutory law, (b) infringements performed by state agencies without statutory support, and (c) infringements within the realm of the state monopoly performed by private persons or bodies without statutory support *but with the tacit consent of the state*. (a) to (c) indicates a kind of scale, where (a) is the strongest ("safest") form of state infringement of *IPS* and (c) the weakest ("most unsafe").

By far the most important way of allowing infringements of *IPS* by state agencies in compliance with statutory law in times of peace is *criminalisation*. Each time a new crime is introduced in the penal code, the field of state violence and other infringements on *IPS* is inevitably expanded. It seems to me that legislating politicians, with all their good intentions and concern for our moral standards, are not always fully aware of this. What criminalisation can do is at best to uphold rudimentary peace and order in society. As a tool for promoting a more subtle, delicate private morality, it is remarkably ill-suited. Criminalisation ought to be a last recourse (*ultima ratio*), used only if the worse comes to the worst. The Swedish Penal Code (Chap. 6, art. 11) criminalises "purchase of sexual service." This crime is committed by the person who purchases for himself a casual sexual encounter for a consideration. The sanction is a fine or imprisonment for a maximum period of 1 year. (It must be borne in mind that prostitution is not prohibited in Sweden, and that rape, "purchase of sexual acts from a child", procuring and trafficking are criminal offences according to Swedish law). Since this crime was added to the Swedish criminal law in 1999 little, if anything, has changed with respect to the extent of prostitution and, if anything has changed at all, it may even be for the worse. Not even the commission preparing the law believed that criminalisation would lead to a decrease of prostitution. The purpose was merely to create a moral attitude. For the sake of this vain hope, state infringements of *IPS* were meddlesomely ordained.[1]

[1] For an illuminating discussion of this topic see D. Husak, *Overcriminalization. The Limits of the Criminal Law*, 2007.

It is not the many weak persons whom we should crack down on by means of the criminal law, it is the (much fewer) evil ones. Punishment, as I have just stressed, is a heavy artillery and a last resort. Other methods must be tested first, e.g., with respect to prostitutes, providing jobs in other professional fields, combatting against drugs and the treatment of drug addiction. Not least of all, legislators must become more aware of the fact that a certain amount of immorality in society is inevitable and that there is very little they can do—or should do—about it. For instance, it is not easy to understand why a person, of her own free will, taking every sanitary precaution, could not prostitute herself without being, herself and her customers, punished for it. In his classic work *Dei delitti e delle pene* [On Crime and Punishment] Cesare Beccaria argues with reference to Montesquieu: "*Ogni pena che non derivi dall' assoluta necessità, dice il grande Montesquieu, è tirannica; proposizione che si può rendere piú generale cosí: ogni atto di autorità di uomo a uomo che non derivi dall'assoluta necessità è tirannico*" ("Every punishment that is not derived from absolute necessity is, says the great Montesquieu, tyrannical—an assertion that can be rendered more generally like this: every authoritative action by man against man that is not derived from absolute necessity is tyrannical)."[2] It must be taken into consideration that even a short term of imprisonment can have disastrous consequences for the convicted and his relatives.

Although warranted by statutory law, or even by the constitution, the private use of violence can be streched very far. The Second Amendment to the United States Constitution states that "…the right of the people to keep and bear Arms, shall not be infringed." If that—which seems to be taken as self-evident—implies that the people also have a right to use arms in certain situations, the state's yielding its monopoly of violence is, indeed, far-reaching.

With respect to *the form* of a state infringement of *IPS*, law-state thinking only accepts (a). (More about that later in this chapter.)

An intermediate step between state infringements of *IPS* according to statutory law and private persons or bodies taking law in their own hands with the tacit consent of the state is willfulness on the part of official agencies other than the sovereign legislator, such as the police and the armed forces. This is to a large extent a matter of blurring the division of power between different state organs and will be discussed further in Chap. 9.

States sometimes make concessions with respect to their monopoly of *IPS*-infringements and allow private persons or bodies to perform actions of this kind. Such concessions are, in civilised societies, given in legislative forms. The widespread—and, indeed, not unproblematic—use of private security companies exercising police functions and the establishment of prisons under private management are usually warranted by legislation. In less scrupulous societies a statutory warrant is regarded as an unnecessary obstacle. In its most abhorrent forms the state gives, by means of its tacit consent, free rein to people willing to do any dirty job whatsoever when freed from responsibility for their deeds. Outstanding examples are

[2] C. Beccaria, *Dei delitti e delle pene*, 5th ed. (the Haarlem-edition), 1766 [1970], § II. Diritto di punire. My trans.

the harassment of Jews performed by hordes of Nazis in Hitler's Germany and the red guards' outrages in China during the so-called Cultural Revolution. From the *Machtergreifung* in 1933 and onwards German thugs were free to burn synagogues, plunder Jewish shops and harass or even kill Jews. As Ian Kershaw puts it: "Hitler had to do no more than provide the general licence for barbarism. There was no shortage of ready hands to put it into practice."[3] The outrages performed by the red guards in China ranged from material damage such as destroying archaeological sites, burning libraries and smashing Ming-porcelain to stopping people on the street to cut their hair, breaking ladies' "decadent" high heels or forcing people to balance with their arms folded on their back and placing signs with accusations around their necks—and, worst of all, to the uninhibited killing of alleged dissidents. The police force was ordered not to keep the youth back.

8.2 Justifying Legal Security

A main tenet of the present book is that the four basic law-state values are ultimately justified by securing a life of human dignity for individuals in their dealing with the state—or, in other words, by securing that the state does not expose them to degradation or compel them to forms of self-abasement. What I have said in the three previous chapters about justification applies *mutatis mutandis* to legal security, too.

As a justification of legal security—as well as of legal equality, legal certainty and legal accessibility—a reference to the value of a life of human dignity might, however, seem unpardonably vague. And vague it is, indeed. But claiming exactness with respect to the justification of general values amounts, as far as I can see, to a misguided over-intellectualisation of the problem. The value of a life of human dignity seems to me to be the most reliable beacon we have recourse to in these troubled waters.

But is the value of a life of human dignity really the most plausible justification as regards legal security? Another candidate, which might be considered as even more plausible, presents itself immediately. It could be said that information of *the pain* that the victim of a violation of his legal security is affected by arouses *sympathy*, or even *compassion,* for the victim in those who have a normal emotional life and are without biases that would lead them astray. And because of that sympathy or compassion, we incorporate the value of legal security into our total set of values. This is not a justification in the sense that one idea is justified by another idea. Sympathy and compassion are not ideas. The justificatory phenomenon here is pure emotion. Fair enough; sympathy and compassion need no justification. This special kind of justification is, one could say, an ostensive justification in that it only points out instances of pain, saying "Just look at it!".

A utilitarian might even say that the justificatory ground for the value of legal security is related to the (inflicting of) pain itself rather than to the sympathy aroused

[3] I. Kershaw, *Hitler. 1936–1945. Nemesis* (Penguin Books, 2001), p. 250.

by it. But that objection reflects, I think, a shortcoming of utilitarianism. Referring to the principle of maximisation of utility and minimisation of pain will not do as ultimate justifications, for the question still remains: Why shall we maximise the utility and minimise the pain of others? In order to answer this question we must transcend utilitarianism itself. Natural sympathy and compassion as well as capacity for insight into the value of a life of human dignity is a good answer to this question.

Is the mental experience of what it is to live a life of human dignity (whether it is the life of others or your own) an emotion or an idea? It seems to me that it has connections to both. It is an idea in so far as the assimilation of it, as opposed to sympathy, requires a certain amount of thinking. But a necessary and indeed its most important, component is an emotion. You cannot understand what a life of human dignity is without embracing the thought of it with positive emotions. In that respect the experience of it is like an aesthetic experience.

The difference between a justification in terms of "the sympathy with sufferers of pain" and a justification in terms of "the life of human dignity" must not be exaggerated. For the appreciation of a life of human dignity is also founded on sympathetic insight. But with regard to infringements of *IPS* performed by the state, I find the justification consisting exclusively of sympathy with the victim's pain too narrow. Some important aspects are excluded. The justification based on sympathy with a life of human dignity includes sympathy with the victim's pain but it takes these other aspects into consideration, too.

What I have in mind are two things, one concerning the victim (the sufferer) and one concerning the perpetrator (the one who inflicts suffering upon the victim). The victim, on the one hand,—when the perpetrator is the state—is exposed to pain and humiliation in an inextricable amalgamation. In addition to sheer pain, he is subjected to the degradation of being powerless against the state and, at worst, he counts for nothing. The perpetrator, on the other hand—i.e., the representative of the state—violates his own life of human dignity by using his power over the victim with arrogance, *hubris*.

Sheer pain is more prominent in connection with use of state violence than in connection with restraints on freedom of movement and activities, intrusion, and harassment. But the violation of the victim's life of human dignity can be equally strong in all four cases.

Legal security is a value, since legal insecurity involves a violation of a life of human dignity. As in the foregoing chapters we proceed by means of contrast. From a display of the ugliness of legal insecurity, a picture of what a man's life of human dignity signifies will, I hope, emerge—just as we proceeded with respect to undue legal discrimination, legal uncertainty, and lawlessness.

Let me first give some examples of obvious violations of legal security. I will then try to show why they are violations of legal security by explaining how they violate an individual's life of human dignity.

A. Examples concerning the use of violence I. "An Islamist rebel administration in Somalia had a 13-year-old girl stoned to death for adultery after the child's father reported that three man had raped her.[4] Amnesty International said the al-Shabab

[4] Quoted from http://www.guardian.co.uk/world/2008/nov/02/somalia-gender.

militia, which controls the southern port city of , arranged for a group of 50 men to stone Aisha Ibrahim Duhulow in front of a crowd of about 1,000 spectators. A lorryload of stones was brought to the stadium for the killing. Amnesty said that Duhulow struggled with her captors and had to be forcibly carried into the stadium. 'At one point during the stoning, Amnesty International has been told by numerous eyewitnesses that nurses were instructed to check whether Aisha Ibrahim Duholow was still alive when buried in the ground. They removed her from the ground, declared that she was, and she was replaced in the hole where she had been buried for the stoning to continue,' the human rights group said. 'Inside the stadium, militia members opened fire when some of the witnesses to the killing attempted to save her life, and shot dead a boy who was a bystander.' Duhulow's father told Amnesty that when they tried to report her rape to the militia, the child was accused of adultery and detained. None of the men Duhulow accused was arrested."

II. In recent times an abundance of examples are provided by the use of violence committed by officials of the U.S.A. within the framework of "the Global War on Terror", proclaimed by President George W. Bush after the terrorist attacks on the World Trade Center in New York on 11th September 2001.[5]

The pictures from Abu Ghraib prison in Baghdad have been disseminated throughout the world: Seven naked bodies, twisted as to form a coil, buttocks and genitals photographed. Bodies bound together on the cellblock floor. "The naked body wearing only the black hood, hands clasped above its head: Pfc Lynndie England, she of the famous leash, frames the body … grinning back at the camera, pointing to its genitals with her right hand, flashing a thumbs-up with her right hand."[6] Seven hooded men getting their head beaten on the walls and doors—hooding used for preventing prisoners from seeing, to disorient them and to prevent them from breathing freely. Tight handcuffing causing skin lesions. "Beatings with hard objects …, slapping, punching, kicking with knees or feet on various parts of the body … Exposure while hooded to loud noise or music, prolonged exposure while hooded in the sun over several hours, including during the hottest time of the day when temperatures could reach … 122 °F … or higher; Being forced to remain for

[5] For detailed information, see *Report of the International Committee of the Red Cross (ICRC) on the Treatment by the Coalition Forces of Prisoners of War and other Protected Persons by the Geneva Conventions in Iraq During Arrest, Internment and Interrogation* by Delegates of the International Committee of the Red Cross, Feb. 2004, *Article 15-6 Investigation of the 800th Military Police Brigade* (The Taguba report) by Major General Antonio M. Taguba, 2004. For presentations and commentaries of these and other investigations, see Mark Danner, "Torture and Truth", *The New York Review of Books*, Vol. LI, Number 10, 2004, pp. 46–50, *ibid.*, "The Logic of Torture", *The New York Review of Books*, Vol. LI, Number 11, 2004, pp. 70–74, *ibid.* "Abu Ghraib: The Hidden Story", *The New York Review of Books*, Vol. LI, Number 15, 2004, pp. 44–50, and Anthony Lewis, "Official American Sadism", *The New York Review of Books*, Vol. LV, Number 14, 2008, pp. 45–49. About use of torture by US officials see also Jane Mayer, *The Dark Side: The Inside Story of How the War on Terror Turned into a War on American Ideals* (2008). My examples are taken from Danner'sand Lewis's articles.

The most terrifying among chambers of horrors exposing outrageous use of violence by state functionaries—as well as restraints on freedom of movement and activities, intrusion and harassment—are, of course, the regimes of Hitler and Stalin. For the latter, see Anne Applebaum, *Gulag—a History*, 2003.

[6] Danner, "Torture and Truth", p. 46.

prolonged periods in stress positions such as squatting or standing with or without the arms lifted." According to the Red Cross report its authors themselves witnessed "the practice of keeping [prisoners] completely naked in totally empty concrete cells and in total darkness". An image shows a prisoner "who was placed on a box with electric wires attached to his fingers, toes and penis."[7] A policy emanating from Major General Geoffrey Miller to be practiced in the Guantánamo prison includes "the use of dogs, stress positions, yelling, loud music, light control and isolation."[8] Another device is known as waterboarding. The prisoner is pushed by force under water, inflicting partial suffocation, and making him believe that he might be drowning. Asphyxiation is "a—perhaps the most—terrifying threat faced by human beings." It was also used in the Spanish Inquisition and by Japanese prison officials in World War II.[9]

B. Examples concerning restraints on freedom of movement and activities "For more than 2 years Mr. Padilla [an American held in solitary confinement as an alleged enemy combatant] was detained in a navy brig on the order of President Bush, without being charged with any offense and without access to counsel. He was kept in a cell with nothing to read except, for a short time, a copy of the Koran, and no sense of time or daylight and no interaction with anyone except his interrogators. When he was once taken to a dentist, his eyes and ears were covered to maintain the sensory deprivation."[10] "An al-Jazeera cameraman, Sami al-Haj, was on his way to Afghanistan in 2001 when he was stopped by a Pakistani official and turned over to the United States. He was held for 6 years at Guantánamo—and questioned not about Al-Qaeda but about al-Jazeera. (He was released in 2008.)"[11]

C. Examples concerning intrusion Representatives of the Red Cross reported after frequently visiting Abu Ghraib: "Arresting authorities entered houses usually after dark, breaking down doors, waking up residents roughly, yelling orders, forcing family members into one room under military guard while searching the rest of the house and further breaking doors, cabinets and other property. Sometimes they arrested all adult males present in a house, including elderly, handicapped or sick people. Individuals were often led away in whatever they happened to be wearing at the time of arrest—sometimes in pyjamas or underwear…"[12]

D. Examples concerning harassment Mr. Hayder Sabbar Abd is one of the prisoners who was photographed when treated in a humiliating way in Abu Ghraib prison in 2003. "He … saw himself, as degraded as possible, naked, his hands on his genitals, a female soldier, identified in another report as Pvt. Lynndie England, pointing and smiling with a cigarette in her mouth. Mr. Abd said one of the soldiers

---

[7] Ibid. p. 47.

[8] Mark Danner, "Abu Ghraib: The Hidden Story", p. 48.

[9] Anthony Lewis, "Official American Sadism", p. 45, n. 1.

[10] Ibid. p. 45, n. 3.

[11] Ibid. p. 47.

[12] Quoted from Mark Danner, "Abu Ghraib: The Hidden Story", p. 45.

had removed his hood, and the translator ordered him to masturbate while looking at Private England. 'She was laughing, and she put her hands on her breasts,' Mr. Abd said. All the while, he said, the flash of the camera kept illuminating the dim room that once held prisoners of Mr. Hussein…."[13] The Red Cross report mentions as one of the "methods of physical and psychological coercion": "Being paraded naked outside cells in front of other persons deprived of their liberty, and guards, sometimes hooded or with women's underwear over the head…".[14] A prisoner gave on January 21, 2004, a sworn statement to the military's Criminal Investigation Division about his time in Abu Ghraib, saying among other things: "Some of the things they did was make me sit down like a dog, … and made me bark like a dog and they were laughing at me… . One of the police was pissing on me and laughing on me." And one of the police he put a part of his stick that he always carries inside my ass and I felt it going inside me about 2 centimeters approximately. "And when I was tied up in my room, one of the girls … she was playing with my dick…"[15]

Let us, with respect to the justification of legal security, and against the background of the examples given, contrast the value of a life of human dignity with the arrogance, insult, and decadence informing legal insecurity.

The arrogance informing legal insecurity lies in considering oneself as being entitled to have the *IPS* of others freely at one's disposal—as being entitled to inflict suffering on others, which is to violate one's own life of human dignity by overestimating oneself: to show *hubris*. Here, however, we must distinguish among the perpetrators between instigators and tools. Violating peoples' *IPS* within the framework of a legal order is indeed a matter of institutionalised violation. But it is always performed by individual human beings, acting either as instigators or as tools. Now it could be said that some tools are not necessarily arrogant, e.g., the judge loyally applying bestial laws or the hangman performing his task. But—unless forced to act as a tool, since, by not complying, he would risk his family's and his own safety—by making himself an instrument for others' arrogance he is degrading himself, thereby violating his own life of human dignity. However, a lot of tools, of course, show arrogance and hence exhibit both *hubris* and self-abasement, e.g., the officials in Abu Ghraib. When perpetrators, which sometimes happens, are later charged with criminal liability, the instigators, not surprisingly, habitually put the blame on the tools ("a few bad apples", as the Bush administration characterised its tools in Abu Ghraib), while the tools habitually throw the blame on the instigators ("we just followed orders", as was the standard defence of Nazi war criminals)—which, at worst, may result in nobody being convicted.

It is no wonder that violence, restraints on movement and activities, intrusion and harassment often go together in one single clump of violations. Besides, this is also the case with violations of the four law-state values taken together. For example, detaining individuals indefinitely is both a violation of their legal certainty and their

[13] Quoted from Mark Danner, "Torture and Truth", pp. 46–47. Originally published in *The New York Times*, May 5, 2004.

[14] Ibid. p. 47.

[15] Mark Danner, "The Logic of Torture", pp. 70–71.

legal security. An obvious example is the use of *secret means of compulsion*, e.g., secret telephone tapping, room bugging, camera surveillance and police control. These devices are not only infringements of *IPS*, but also, being secret, violate the values of legal certainty and legal accessibility.

Arrogance has a tendency to burst its own bounds. It opens doors which never should be opened. Trying to stop the Somalian execution or just to be on the spot, and you might be shot—even if you are an innocent little boy. The more fishes you get into your net, the greater the probability that at least some are terrorists—although, as it happened, the al-Jazeera cameraman was not. Pure arrogance cut loose from any conceivable reasonable goal is particularly manifest with respect to deeds of harassment. To get a prisoner to talk by forcing him to masturbate does not seem to be an especially efficient means to get reliable information. The degradation of prisoners by sexual harassment in Abu Ghraib was multiplied by the camera, thereby making these deeds public—something extremely humiliating for people of Moslim creed. Institutional approval of gross violations of an individual's life of human dignity brings out the worst in men and perverts their morals.

The insult informing legal insecurity hits the victims of such violations and is the reversal of arrogance. The insult lies in being exposed to the arrogance of others. Add to that the powerlessness of the exposed, more or less at the mercy of the officials. The insult can, as we have seen, take several forms, e.g., hitting, or even killing, the victim, frightening him, destroying something valuable to him (e.g, smashing a home as if what is *mine* were worthless) or ridiculing him. Its most prominent features are experience of pain, fear, sorrow and humiliation. With respect to legal insecurity, this pain, fear, sorrow and humiliation get their character of insult by being inextricably amalgamated with the arrogance of the perpetrators.

The decadence informing legal insecurity lies in the perversion of the morals of perpetrators, victims, potential victims, sympathisers of those in power and the rest of the community alike. Not only being exposed but also suffering the risk of being exposed (however unlikely) make people apt to cringe, thereby violating their own life of human dignity.

Excursus on evidence In connection with a discussion of justification I have found it appropriate to say something by way of an excursus about evidence in this last chapter about the four law-state values. Law-state thinking makes strong claims with respect to the production and evaluation of evidence, and that for three reasons. (1) Production and evaluation of evidence play a fundamental role in the particularly *legal* way of conflict-solving. (2) There is a close connection between evaluating evidence and establishing truth. (3) There is a close connection between truth and the idea of a life of human dignity (which is the ultimate justification of the law-state values).

The judicial process (trial, litigation) is in a sense the very backbone of the legal order. Conflicts and claims are tried in individual cases on the basis of the general rules of the legal order. In the judicial process events in the physical world are qualified by such rules and the qualification (interpretation) of these events determines the legal consequences befalling the parties (not least criminal, civil or administrative sanctions). Both the qualification and the choice of individual legal consequences hinge on the assumption that the alleged state of affairs on which they are based is a fact—i.e., that the propositions about what has taken place are true. If these propositions are false, both the qualification of the alleged state of affairs and the choice of sanction are built on sand. The whole legal decision is then a house of cards. And, what is more, a disastrous mistake has been committed, which wrongs human beings.

But it could be called into question whether the evaluation of evidence really is a matter of ascertaining the truth. It could be said that the judge's task is only to ascertain that the standard of proof has been reached with respect to a certain proposition, not that the proposition really is true. However, there is a necessary (conceptual) relationship between the standard of proof and truth. The requirement that a proof presented by a litigant shall at least attain the standard of proof is justified by warranting a certain probability that the state of affairs the proof is intended to be a proof of is a fact—or, in other words, warranting a certain probability that the propositions stating that state of affairs *are true*. What other function would prescribing a standard of proof have? The concept "standard of proof" would lack any sensible meaning if its relationship to the concept "truth" were obliterated. This connection holds even if the law-giver in certain cases contents himself with binding the standard of proof to a rather low degree of probability.

The fact that it is the parties, not the court, who have to produce evidence does not invalidate the thesis that there exists a necessary connection between the standard of proof and truth. It is the task of the court to investigate what the evidence produced has to say about the truth of the propositions concerning the theme of proof. What rules about production of evidence amount to is a distribution among the litigants of the risk of not producing a certain proof. Such rules have no bearing on the connection between the standard of proof and truth.

Our means of "approaching" truth through evidence have become more rational since medieval times. We no longer regard ordeals by fire or water as evidence, nor swearing an oath. But evaluation of evidence in the hands of judges (not to speak of laymen) is, even today, only a little more than amateurish, for lack of a solid scientific foundation.

Further, there is a close connection between truth and the idea of a life of human dignity. If a judge due to disinformation (for instance, based on false testimony) in good faith causes an injustice to a litigant and thus wrongs him, this fact is genuinely tragic. But if the judge due to bias, malevolence, negligence or carelessness brings about such an injustice, "the legal order itself" violates the litigant's life of human dignity, thereby adding insult to tragedy.

Few things, I believe, do harm to human beings more deeply than being judged and treated on the basis of opinions which they know are not true. Therefore, manipulating truth—dishonesty—or careless handling of it is one of the most radical ways of humiliating individuals. All the more so if it is functionaries in the service of law who handle truth in this way.

Malevolence or carelessness on the part of legal functionaries with respect to the production and evaluation of evidence can take forms which violate each of the four basic law-state values. The value of legal equality is violated if a party is unduly discriminated against in the process of the evaluation of evidence. The value of legal certainty is violated if rules such as stating the standard of proof, rules regulating the use of hearsay evidence or rules concerning the right of a witness not to incriminate himself are lacking or are vague. The value of legal accessibility is violated if a litigant is denied the right to produce evidence. The value of legal security is violated if a person is harassed by the police in order to prevent her from giving evidence.

Tying the standard of proof to a low degree of probability can be legitimate in certain situations. But it can also be a token of abuse. Using a low standard of proof with respect to a certain substantive legal rule and a certain class of parties can be a means of depriving members of the class of the adverse parties of their rights or harassing them. Hence, the law-state values violated are (intra-procedural) legal equality, legal security (by harassment) and also legal accessibility, since it then becomes more difficult for a member of the class of the adverse parties to get alleged states of affairs legally examined.

In public discussions on legal affairs it is sometimes argued that a certain loosening of the standard of proof is called for. The reason would be that such a measure would be more effective from the point of view of combating crime. It has, for instance, been said that since it is so very hard to prove the states of affairs involved in crimes of rape, and that therefore many rapists are acquitted, the standard of proof must be lower in order to secure convictions. Yes, it is possible, and even probable, that that will happen. But then the rule stating the lower standard of proof will be efficient in the same way that a sawed-off shotgun is for precision shooting. You might well hit the target but at the expense of also hitting your pet dog, a car tyre or your grandmother, too. Let us think of two courts, A and B, where A allows a low degree of probability with respect to a certain type of crime whereas B requires a high degree. Suppose that court A, with respect to that type of crime during a certain period of time, out of 100 persons prosecuted convicts 70 and acquits 30, while court B, with respect to the same type of crime and the same period of time, out of 100 persons prosecuted convicts 50 and acquits 50. We also suppose that, in both cases, of the 100 persons 80 are in fact guilty and 20 not guilty. This would indicate that court A is more effective than court B as regards crime-combatting. But this conclusion is misleading. What might be called *the function of elimination* of the standard of proof is not taken into consideration. The function of elimination is to secure that the innocent are eliminated and, hence, that those convicted really are guilty. It is a matter of separating the sheep from the goats. If the function of elimination is not effective, the lower level of the legal burden of proof is not an effective tool as regards crime-combating. Of the 70 convicted by court A we know with a lower degree of probability which ones are guilty and which ones are innocent than we know of the 50 convicted by court B which ones of those are guilty and which ones are innocent.

Finally, a few words about the presumption of innocence. It is expressed in the following way in The European Convention for the Protection of Human Rights and Fundamental Freedoms (1950), Art. 6: "Everyone charged with a criminal offence shall be presumed innocent until proved guilty according to law". This procedural principle is a cornerstone of that part of law-state thinking that is directed especially to judges. But it is important to be clear about what this idea can reasonably mean and what it cannot reasonably mean. It cannot reasonably be taken literally. In a trial the judge shall not (initially or later) presume anything at all with respect to the defendant's guilt, not that he is innocent nor that he is guilty. Otherwise he would conduct the trial based on a prejudice. The judge shall commence and continue the trial open-mindedly. He shall be objective. For that reason the term "presumption of innocence" is not particularly well chosen. But what this principle really expresses is, I think, the following four things. (1) The maintenance of the requirement "beyond reasonable doubt". (2) That the burden of proof falls upon the prosecution. (3) The maintenance of the principle *in dubio pro reo*, i.e., if it is doubtful whether the standard of proof is attained or not, the defendant shall be acquitted—the judge shall always give the defendant the benefit of the doubt. (4) Rhetorically to counteract rumours of the type "No smoke without fire." (But, admittedly, the principle can also have the opposite effect.)

It is sometimes uttered (now and then with a touch of malice) that the defendant might well be guilty, although he has been acquitted for lack of evidence. And of course he might. But then it must be borne in mind that, precisely since the standard of proof was not met, *an outsider is not, either intellectually or morally, entitled to believe that the defendant is guilty* (which, of course, does not exclude the existence of different degrees of probability, although not conclusive, of culpability). In that respect the defendant is in the same position as perhaps thousands of other people who could have committed the crime, being in the area at the time and not having an alibi and they, too, if charged, would be acquitted, since the prosecutor's evidence would not meet the standard of proof. No doubt there are exceptions to this, however. For example, a witness who has actually seen the defendant commit the crime might take back his testimony after being threatened by the defendant's cronies. In such cases one might be entitled to believe that the defendant is guilty.

8.3 Value Relations

Two things must be emphasised. (1) Not every infringement of *IPS* is a violation of legal security. (2) There are violations of legal security which must be accepted as due.

It is conceivable that, in an ideal world, every state infringement of *IPS* would also be a violation of legal security, but however that may be, this is not the case in our world. Our human predicament is such that we must allow *certain* state infringements of *IPS* which cannot be adequately described as violations of our legal security. But, worse, we must also in extreme cases allow *certain* violations of legal security.

Hence, within the class of infringements of *IPS* we must distinguish between three different subclasses:

I. Infringements which do not violate legal security (the class *NV*)
II. Infringements which do violate legal security and which are undue (the class *VUD*)
III. Infringements which do violate legal security and which are due (the class *VD*).

As we see, members of *NV*, *VUD* and *VD* are a special kind of actions.

The borderline between infringements of *IPS* violating legal security and such infringements not violating legal security is determined by the help of our "life of human dignity justification" of the value of legal security. If a person's life of human dignity is violated by the infringement, her legal security is violated. If her life of human dignity is not violated, her legal security is not violated.

We can draw the distinction between due and undue infringements on *IPS* in this way. *Due* infringements are those infringements that we can reasonably accept as legal means, even if they violate legal security, since they preserve societal safety. *Undue* infringements are infringements which are not acceptable, since they violate legal security, even if they preserve societal safety.

These distinctions are, of course, vague and are so of necessity. Vagueness pertaining to emotive justifications of this kind cannot be removed by means of conceptual analysis alone. Hence, there are twilight zones between the three classes *NV*, *VUD* and *VD*. These twilight zones can be characterised as *danger zones* in that representatives of decent states might also be tempted to have recourse to infringements of *IPS* within them—infringements which are more far-reaching than is necessary for the purpose in question. For example, a law-giver allows a maximum period of five days before a detained person is brought before a court of law, although four days would be sufficient. Perhaps state infringements of *IPS* within such danger zones, at least in certain minor cases, could be characterised as an over-use rather than abuse of power.[16] However that may be, it is important to formulate good and workable guidelines for the necessary balancing between legal security and other values conflicting with it (which topic will be discussed later in Sect. 8.4).

An example of a member of *NV* (at least at our present level of civilisation) is sentencing a murderer to 20 years imprisonment. To *NV* belong most of the "ordinary" legal punishments and coercive measures in states taking the law-state values seriously. But *NV* is by no means a zone exempt from surveillance from the point of view of the value of legal security. On the contrary, such surveillance must always be there, counteracting the over-use due to overreaction, carelessness, blind routine or meddlesomeness (overcriminalisation). *NV* can be regarded as a zone where permanent necessity prevails. The whole of *NV* is in that respect a danger zone.

An example of a member of *VUD* is waterboarding a prisoner. For every member of *VUD* it is the case that it is not only a violation of someone's legal security but also that it is not acceptable even taking into consideration the need for preserving societal safety. *VUD* is the playground of barbarism.

For every member of *VD* it is the case that it is a violation of someone's legal security, but also that this is reasonably acceptable when considering the need for preserving societal security. An example is the following. "More than 75,000

[16] A suggestion made by Professor Iain Cameron, Uppsala.

refugees from Nazism came to Britain during the 1930s. At the outbreak of war on 3 September 1939, Germans, Austrians and Italians living in Britain were classified as enemy aliens and as such were required to appear before a tribunal to assess their security risk to the country. Most were categorised as 'friendly enemy aliens' and had to report regularly to the local police."[17] This was no doubt a violation of probably most of the aliens' life of human dignity—especially of those who had themselves fled Hitler. But for a nation fighting for its very existence these measures were indeed reasonably acceptable. (Other measures, however, used in Britain from 1940 and afterwards come within the scope of the danger zone between *VD* and *VUD*). While a state of permanent necessity prevails with respect to *NV*, a state of extreme necessity prevails with respect to *VD* (as will be argued below). Like *NV*, also the whole of *VD* can be regarded as a danger zone.

Let *ips* be an individual measure within the set of infringements on *IPS*. *ips* is, let us say, taken into consideration as a legal means by a legislator. Three questions may then arise:

1. Does *ips* violate the value of legal security? (If answered by "no", *ips* is approved in so far as legal security is concerned). If by "yes", the question arises:
2. Is *ips* due? (If "no", *ips* shall not become a part of the law.) If "yes", the question arises:
3. If *ips* violates the value of legal security and *ips* is due: Shall *ips* become a part of the law?

In Sect. 8.4 I shall try to formulate some *legal security principles*, which hopefully can be of some help in the task of balancing the value of legal security and other values or interests in concrete situations—i.e., in answering questions I-III or, in other words, in deciding whether some *ips* shall be placed in *NV* or *VD* or *VUD*. We can distinguish between principles pertaining to I, II and III respectively. But first, a few words on the relation between the value of legal security and other values or interests.

There are two such groups of values, and their relations to the value of legal security are of special importance.

I. It is appropriate, if we embrace the value of a life of human dignity, to look upon respect for a life of human dignity as a moral principle. As such it can be seen as a principle belonging to our private morality and adherence to it is a personal virtue. But it can also appear as a social value, informing the very basis of society, and adherence to it is then a social virtue. We can form an idea of *a humanistic value basis of society* (HVBS, for short), i.e., an idea of what humanism is about when directed towards the state. What would characterise such a HVBS? In what respect can a life of human dignity be a social value or principle and adherence to it a social virtue?

Violations of an individual's life of human dignity performed by the state take essentially three forms: violation of the individual's freedom to live as she wishes as long as she does not harm others unduly, violation of the individual's right to have a

[17] http://en.wikipedia.org/wiki/Concentration_camp.

say in matters of concern to herself, i.e., in the politics of her society, and the state's violating her by violating the law-state values. In other words, HVBS includes liberalism (in the classic sense of holding individual freedom in high esteem), democracy, and the law-state values (legality included). The ideal humanistic state is the liberal-democratic law-state. As for democracy, it can be seen as an expression of the claim of moderation: to have at least one vote like everyone else comports with our self-respect, and to have at most one vote restrains our hubristic tendencies. (Incidentally, the value of democracy consists not only in the public power emanating from the people but also, to no small degree, in the fact that the people are no longer ruled by kings, churches, and landlords.) In a society based on humanism it is a central task of the legal order to guarantee individual freedom and democracy by giving them legal protection, and thereby making them *legal* ideas.

Thus, the values of HVBS are several, and different value relations can hold between them. Legal security is in this respect crucial, since legal insecurity appears in this connection as the great traitor—in the sense corresponding to the value relation "betrayal" (Sect. 3.2.2 above)—due to what violence, restraints of freedom of movement and activities, intrusion, and harassment can do to people. In conflicts between legal security and other values the law-state paradox comes to the fore.

Let us take HVBS* as HVBS with legal security excluded. There are four value relations between legal security (LS) and HVBS* (cf. Sect. 3.2.2. above).

1. Negative counteraction: HVBS* is harmed by realising LS.

This is seldom or never the case.

2. Reinforcement: HVBS* is realised by realising LS.

If LS is upheld and state brutality checked, the more sophisticated values of legal equality, legal certainty, legal accessibility, as well as liberalism and democracy, stand a better chance.

3. Depreciation (betrayal included): HVBS* is harmed by harming LS.

This is a highly important value relation from the point of view of the law-state thinking. If legal insecurity is given free rein it becomes a terrible weapon in the hands of the state which can be used, and, tragically enough, not seldom is used, to terrorise not only private persons but also servants of the law in order to make them violate the HVBS* values.

4. Positive counteraction: HVBS* is realised by harming LS.

This is seldom or never the case.

Let us now have a look at the converse relations.

5. Negative counteraction: LS is harmed by realising HVBS*.

This is seldom or never the case.

6. Reinforcement: LS is realised by realising HVBS*.

This is an important value relation; it is more precarious, however, than value relation (2). Strong adherence to the HVBS* values on the part of those who are in charge of these values can function as a guarantee for LS's being adhered to by those handling state infringements of *IPS*.

7. Depreciation (betrayal included): LS is harmed by harming HVBS*.

If the state does not respect individual freedom and democracy, as well as legal equality, certainty and accessibility, the foundations of HVBS will be so eroded that LS would lie completely unprotected against violations of it.

8. Positive counteraction: LS is realised by harming HVBS*.

This is seldom or never the case.

We see that the important value relations within HVBS are reinforcement and depreciation, while positive and negative counteraction seem in a way irrelevant. This will be compared to the value relations within the other group of values.

II. What we usually have in mind when we think of conflicts between legal security and other values or interests are, I think, conflicts between legal security on the one hand and values related to *societal urgency* on the other, i.e., values pertaining to (i) the external and internal safety of the society, (ii) relief in case of catastrophes and (iii) prevention of crime. It could be a matter of wire-tapping aliens who are regarded as threats to national safety, of demolishing private buildings in order to combat a fire or of initiating capital punishment for murder in a situation where the murder rate in society has increased radically.

It may seem a bit odd to regard prevention of crime as a matter of urgency. This is in line, however, with my view of criminalisation as a last recourse (*ultima ratio*). Criminalisation belongs to a zone where permanent necessity prevails.

Let us look at the value relations between, on the one hand, values related to societal urgency (VSU, for short) and legal safety on the other.

9. Negative counteraction: VSU is harmed by realising LS.

This is the most important value relation in this connection. Infringements, perhaps even undue, on *IPS* are seen as necessary for realising some VSU or, as it is often expressed, for realising some VSU effectively. If we fail to wire-tap aliens, national safety is in jeopardy, if we don't demolish these private buildings, we cannot combat this fire effectively and without initiating capital punishment we cannot reduce the murder rate—or so it is argued.

10. Reinforcement: VSU is realised by realising LS.

This is seldom or never the case.

11. Depreciation (betrayal included): VSU is harmed by harming LS.

This is seldom or never the case.

12. Positive counteraction: VSU is realised by harming LS.

If we allow wire tapping of aliens, national safety stands a better chance, if we demolish these buildings, we can combat the fire effectively, and by initiating capital punishment we reduce the murder rate (effectively)—or so it is argued.

Let us now have a look at the converse relations.

13. Negative counteraction: LS is harmed by realising VSU.

If we wire-tap aliens, their *IPS* are unduly violated, if we demolish these buildings, the owners' *IPS* are unduly violated, and if we initiate capital punishment, the murderers' *IPS* are unduly violated—or so it is argued.

14. Reinforcement: LS is realised by realising VSU.

This is seldom or never the case.

15. Depreciation (betrayal included): LS is harmed by harming VSU.

This is seldom or never the case.

16. Positive counteraction: LS is realised by harming VSU.

If we fail to allow wire-tapping of aliens, their *IPS* are not violated (for that reason), if we abstain from demolishing these buildings, the owners' *IPS* are not violated (for that reason), and if we abstain from capital punishment, the murderers' *IPS* are not violated (for that reason)—or so it is argued.

As we see, while the relevant value relations between legal security and the other values of HVBS are reinforcement and depreciation (betrayal), the relevant value relations between legal security and the VSU values are negative and positive counteraction. I find this illuminating. The difference can be expressed, I think, in the following way. The first set of values, the HVBS values, are by nature intimately linked to each other, they live in a kind of symbiosis. An attack on one of them is, in different ways and more or less, an attack on the others. With respect to the value relations between legal security and VSU (taken as a whole), the situation is quite different. They stand in an antagonistic sort of relationship to each other. Harming one profits the other. No doubt it is useful for law-makers to be aware of this difference.

Conflicts between legal security and the VSU values are often described as conflicts between legal security, on the one hand, and *the effectiveness* of the legal order on the other. This is, in my opinion, a mistake. It is important to separate a certain value from the means of its realisation. Any value, if possible to realise at all, can be realised by better or poorer means. Effectiveness is not an independent value, it is a secondary value, dependent on another value. It has to do with the means of realising some primary value. Prevention of crime can be realised more or less effectively, and so can legal security. Hence, effectiveness must be connected to some specific primary value and cannot be weighed independently against some other value. *The value* of legal security shall not be weighed against the effectiveness of crime prevention, it shall be weighed against *the value* of crime prevention. That this is the case is not contradicted by the fact that it is *the means* of realising crime prevention that can threaten legal security. If, for instance, the latter value in a certain case undoubtedly has greater weight than the former, the effectiveness of their means of realisation might well turn out to be irrelevant. This is, I think, another useful insight for law-makers.

8.4 Principles. Legal Subordination

It is, no doubt, possible to formulate *principles* capable of guiding legal functionaries and politicians on the question of when they are to take a stand on conflicts between legal security and other values. (Much discussed, e.g., is the principle of proportionality, not least the European Union Law variant of it.)

I take, as usual, "principles" to mean guidelines for argumentation, here in matters of weighing and balancing with respect to the value of legal security and values conflicting with it. Principles are themselves a kind of arguments.

Superior to all these principles and the final arbiter, however, is the principle of respecting the individual's life of human dignity.

I shall present three kinds of such principles, ordering principles (or the ordering principle), barring principles, and weighing and balancing principles. *The ordering principle* has an "intellectual" character. It asks of the law-maker that he formulate the problem and the arguments relevant to its solution as exactly as possible. The other two groups are of a more "material" type. *Barring principles* rule out certain values or aims, in the sense that these aims, for one reason or another, do not even deserve to be balanced against legal security. They must never restrict legal safety, i.e., they cannot be balanced against it (numerically speaking, in weighing they have value 0). On the other hand, aims not ruled out by some barrier principle, and the means of the realisation of such aims, are capable of being weighed and balanced against legal security. For such weighing and balancing certain *weighing and balancing principles* are suggested. Such principles can pertain to the shaping of the means and also to the question of the circumstances in which they may be used. If the barring principles allow a certain aim to be balanced against legal security, the weighing and balancing principles help to decide how far the infringement of *IPS* may go.

It is important to distinguish between weighing and balancing. Weighing is to attribute a certain weight to a certain aim or a certain means. As for the means, the most important factor influencing its weight is, of course, its effectiveness as a means to achieve its aim. Balancing is to take all the relevant weights into consideration and to decide on that basis which of the two competing aims shall prevail (more or less).

All principles presented below operate in connection with some specific law-making project, where balancing against legal security may be relevant.

I. The Ordering Principle (OP) Discern the components of the problem. Structure it. Entities to be weighed are the following: (a) the value of legal security (LS), (b) the opposite value, e.g., national safety, (OV), (c) the existing means of realising LS (MLS) and (d) the proposed and other possible means of realising OV (MOV).

OP can be divided into the following "steps":

(i) Identify and formulate clearly the values LS and OV.
(ii) Identify and formulate clearly the arguments for and against LS and OV.
(iii) Identify and formulate clearly the means MLS and MOV.

(iv) Identify and formulate clearly in what way MOV might infringe IPS.
(v) Answer the question: Is MOV without any doubt whatsoever not violating LS? (If the answer is "yes", no further deliberation is necessary.)
(vi) Answer the question: Is MOV due (in the sense indicated on p. 160 above). (If the answer is "obviously not", no further deliberation is necessary. MOV shall not become a legal means.)

(v) and (vi) are "clearance principles", sorting out situations irrelevant from the point of view of balancing.

When this ordering has been performed, the way is prepared for the barring and weighing and balancing principles to do their job, i.e., to be of help in the weighing and balancing argumentation.

II. Barring Principles

(BP1) *The limited scope principle*: Only values pertaining to (i) the external and internal safety of the society, (ii) relief in case of catastrophes, (iii) prevention of crime, and (iv) self-defence can justify violations of legal security. Other values are barred from protection by means involving violations of legal security.

Admittedly, it may in many situations be difficult to draw the line delimiting the scope of those values, or interests. Dictatorships and semi-dictatorships tend to exaggerate (i) and (iii) for purposes of their own. What BP1 forbids are, e.g., violations of legal security for the sake of the economic well-being of the society, for counteracting currency speculation, and for the protection of morals. The European Convention of Human Rights operates, in articles 8 and 9, with, in my opinion, barring rules that are too narrow, barring too little and admitting too much ("the economic well-being of the country, … the protection of health and morals"). The wider prohibitions can be justified by reference to the value of a life of human dignity.

(BP2) *The emergency principle:* Even within a limited scope an emergency must exist. If there is no emergency, the present interest is barred from protection by means of violations of legal security.

(BP3) *The not-as-bad-as-they-are principle* (or *the cruelty principle*): The use of cruel means are not allowed even within a limited scope and even if an emergency exists.

The reason for calling this principle "the-not-as-bad-as-they-are principle" has to do with its justification and is the following. State infringements on *IPS* are mostly directed against criminals. A not uncommon argument then is: Why should we respect them, when they do not respect us? This leads to another question: What consideration should we show the ruthless?

The very *raison d'être* of the legal ordering of society is its civil contributions to it. Vengence shall be a state monopoly and subject to limitations and control determined by humanitarian values and rational deliberation (cf. pp. 19 f. above). The "fight" against crime is not to be taken as a state of war. Legal security must be looked upon in that perspective. The answer to the question "Why should we (the state) respect them, when they do not respect us?" is: It is not the ruthless who shall settle the standard for our behaviour, it is we ourselves. And we shall not be as bad as they are. If we were, the civil contribution of the legal order to society would come to nothing. We might just as well have remained in a "state of nature". In fact, the worse the villain, the greater the weight of the not-as-bad-as-they-are principle. This argument has, of course, a special bearing on cruel means like torture and capital punishment.[18]

Let me say a few words about the latter. The main arguments against it, from the law-state point of view, are the following. (1) If it is the task of the state to abolish private and uninhibited vengeance, i.e., to make vengeance more civilised, the state shall not itself resort to the *worst* form of vengeance—killing. (2) The use of capital punishment requires enormously strong guarantees that the other law-state values (legal equality, legal certainty and legal accessibility) are realised—probably more than is possible. There must not be a shadow of a suspicion that capital punishment is used in an unduly discriminatory way (legal equality), the conditions of capital punishment (the crimes) must be extraordinarily well specified (legal certainty) and, at least equally important, the suspect and later convicted, must have easily and rapidly accessible and highly effective remedies at hand, in charge of competent bodies working without undue delay. After all, once the convicted criminal is dead, he will have had no legal accessibility at all for his own part (which, of course, is especially tragic if in fact he is innocent, which happens now and then in real life). (3) Moreover, capital punishment is to a certain degree necessarily connected to other infringements on *IPS.* Before the execution, the convicted criminal is detained, and detention (especially in those horrid cases where he is detained for a very long time—years perhaps, which has happened) in combination with the agony of death that most of the convicted criminals must feel verges on torture.

III. Weighing and Balancing Principles

(WBP1) *The effectiveness principle*: MOV shall be an effective means of realising OV.

(WBP2) *The minimality principle*: MOV shall never infringe *IPS* to a greater degree than is sufficient to realise OV. If the choice is between two or more different means, the means that infringes *IPS* the least shall be chosen.

It is to be noted that I do not claim that the proposed MOV shall be a necessary condition for attaining OV (*conditio sine qua non*). That seems to me to be an unnecessarily strong requirement.

(WBP3) *The principle of the partial irrelevance of the means*: (a) If OV has lesser weight than, or equal weight as LS, then OV shall not be realised however great the weight (expediency, effectiveness) that MOV has. (b) If the weight of MLS is low, this must never diminish the weight of LS.

But the opposite of (a) does not hold. If OV has greater weight than LS, OV and MOV combined must be balanced against LS. Then it might very well be the case that the disastrous effects of MOV lead to a total preponderance of LS. (b) says that, if the present means of realising LS are less than satisfactory, this must not be used as an argument for attributing less weight to LS in the present situation (rather it is an argument for improving upon the means of safeguarding LS).

[18] Here is the place to recall Nietzsche's famous dictum "Wer mit Ungeheuern kämpft, mag zusehn, dass er nicht dabei zum Ungeheuer wird. Und wenn du lange in einen Abgrund blickst, blickt der Abgrund auch in dich hinein". [He who fights monsters must take care, lest he becomes a monster too thereby. And when you look for a long time into an abyss, the abyss looks into yourself, too.] Friedrich Nietzsche, *Jenseits von Gut und Böse* (1886), aphorism 146.

But is it possible to separate MLS from LS? Do they not coalesce? No doubt it is often difficult to separate them. But they are nevertheless two different things. For instance, the value LS has, as such, a considerable weight with respect to how prisoners are treated. But if, in some society, prisoners are, for petty reasons, subject to solitary confinement, restrictions of correspondence or humiliating bodily searches, MLS are, indeed, defective. Good MLS (MLS having great weight) are rules with rigid claims on things like solitary confinement, restrictions of correspondence, and humiliating bodily searches.

(WBP4) *The comprehensive-view principle*: When taking a stand on some MOV, one shall take into consideration the total level of the infringements on *IPS* that are allowed by the legal system.

There is a limit to the total number of infringements on *IPS* allowed by a legal system. At some point, the citizens might well find themselves trapped in an insidious Big-Brother-is-watching-you kind of society à la George Orwell's *1984*. Demands for limitations of people's *IPS* might, reasonably enough, be put forward as a kind of equality argument. If, for instance, a certain public agency has a right to be informed, on request, of the content of some, otherwise classified data base—there by intruding upon persons' *IPS*—another public agency (or even some private association) might claim access to the data base for the same reason as that which justified the first agency's access to it. And all of a sudden the field may be open for a limitation of people's integrity that was never intended from the start.

(WBP5) *The one-dimensional proportionality principle*: MOV shall be proportional (correspond) to OV.

This commonly used formulation[19] is somewhat vague. Disproportional means are according to WBP5 not allowed. But what does "proportional" mean? The idea seems to be that there must be some kind of reasonable balance between MOV and OV. Let us formulate it more precisely:

(WBP5*) *The one-dimensional proportionality principle* (more precisely formulated): (a) The greater the weight OV has, the more intrusive MOV is allowed to be, and (b) There is a point where the weight of OV is not high enough to justify MOV. If that point is reached or passed, MOV is not allowed.

I call WBP5* "one-dimensional" since it is applicable solely to the relation between OV and MOV. It says, crudely speaking, that the law-maker shall not shoot sparrows with a cannon. But it might be asked whether WBP5* is not already included in the minimality principle, or vice versa. No, this is not the case. It might be the case (i) that although minimal, MOV has passed the crucial point, or (ii) MOV has not passed the crucial point but is not minimal.

(WBP6) *The two-dimensional proportionality principle:* The (positive) weight of MOV as a means to attain OV shall outweigh the (negative) weight of MOV as a means to counteract the realisation of LS.

WBP6 is "two-dimensional", since it applies both to the relation between OV and MOV and to the relation between MOV and LS. WBP6 seems to me to be the core WB-principle. But, it might be asked again, is it not already included in the

[19] See case 66/82 Fromançais v. FORMA [1983] European Court Reports 395.

minimality principle, or vice versa? No. It might be the case (i) that a certain MOV is a minimal one but still does not outweigh the same MOV as a means to counteract the realisation of LS, or (ii) that WBP6 is fulfilled but this MOV is not the minimal MOV that fulfils WBP6. Hence, we need both principles. In discourses within European Union Law WBP5 and WBP6 are commonly lumped together under the name "the proportionality principle", which is a bit confusing.

However, WBP6 might be considered ineffective in another sense. This defect can be cured by the next principle.

(WBP7) *The considerable preponderance principle*: There shall be a considerable preponderance of the positive weight of MOV as a means to attain OV over the negative weight of MOV as a means to counteract the realisation of LS.

It might for good reasons be argued that WBP6 is too weak a principle—even the slightest preponderance of the weight of MOV as a means of attaining OV over the weight of MOV as a means to counteract the realisation (maintenance) of LS is conclusive. This might turn out to be too precarious a form of protection of LS.

(WBP8) *The adjustment principle*: The balance between MOV and OV on the one hand, and MOV and LS on the other, can be adjusted by adding measures of the MLS kind.

Such additions to MLS, aimed at tipping the balance in favour of LS, may be, e.g., that a certain MOV can only be used after permission by a court of law has been granted to the effect that the person exposed to it shall be informed and that classified information handed over to some agency shall be destroyed immediately after it has been used.

(WBP9) *The* in dubio *principle*: If there remains any doubt after WBP1-WBP8 have been taken into consideration, the benefit of the doubt lies with LS.

Thus, we see that some of the principles now formulated are *priority principles* in favour of LS when it comes to balancing. This is the case with WBP3, WBP4, WBP7 and WBP 9.

Let us conclude this presentation of principles for the use of a more rational argumentation in matters concerning infringements on *IPS*—allegedly needed when external or internal national safety, catastrophes, prevention of crime, and self-defence are at risk—by giving an example of how they can be of value. The example chosen belongs to European Union Law: the—controversial—"Directive 2006/24/EC…on the retention of data generated or processed in connection with the provision of publicly available electronic communications services or of public communications networks…" (the Data Retention Directive, here abbreviated DRD).

DRD contains "obligations of providers of publicly available electronic communications services or of public communications networks [i.e., all communication by means of the telephone and Internet] with respect to the retention of certain data which are generated or processed by them, in order to ensure that the data are available for the purpose of the investigation, detection and prosecution of serious crime…". Member states shall ensure that the following categories of data are retained: (a) Data necessary to trace and identify the source of information, e.g., with respect to the telephone, the calling telephone number; with respect to the Internet, the user ID allocated, (b) data necessary to identify the destination of a communication, e.g., the telephone numbers called or the user ID of the intended recipient, (c) data necessary to identify the date, time and duration of a communication, (d) data necessary to identify the type of communication, (e) data necessary to identify users' communication equipment or what purports to be their equipment, and (f) data necessary to identify the location of mobile communication equipment (i.e., where the user is located geographically). No data revealing the content of the communication may be retained. Data shall be retained for periods of not less than six months and not more than 2 years. They shall be destroyed at the end of the period of retention. Compliance with these obligations is warranted by certain remedies, liability, and penalties.

I do not intend to go into detail here. I just wanted to offer a hint of how the principles formulated can be used in practice.

As for OP, I will skip steps (i)-(iv). OV is prevention of serious crimes and MOV are the measures just mentioned. LS is the value of not allowing state intrusion upon the privacy of communication between private individuals. The question put in (v) must obviously be answered by "no", and the question in (vi) by "not obviously not". So we must proceed. BP1 does not bar DRD, since it concerns the prevention of crime. But with respect to BP2 it could be argued that it bars DSD. Do Europeans actually live in a state of emergency with respect to the threat of criminality? BP3 does not bar DRD. The measures proposed, although infringing people's *IPS*, are not "cruel".

We now turn to the WB-principles. Are MOV effective as a means of realising OV (WBP1)? They probably are. But are MOV the effective measure that infringes *IPS* less (WBP2)? This is highly questionable. DRD provides, after all, the state with access to information concerning the questions with whom, where, when and how *each* person communicates with *somebody else*—whether either of them is the suspect of crime or not. Surely, there must be an effective means that infringes less on *IPS* than this to attain OV. Strong reasons speak in favour of limiting the measures. WBP2 is no doubt of great importance in this case. The probability that any individual in Europe will fall victim to a terrorist attack is, after all, extremely low. Does that threat justify, as means, great intrusions upon the privacy of communication of all 500 million or so citizens of the European Union? Is that really the minimal measure? As for WBP3, if LS is considered as having the same weight as OV in this case, then LS "wins", however effective the proposed MOV is. It can reasonably be argued that this is the case here. At least in some member states WBP4 also speaks strongly in favour of LS. In Sweden, for example, other statutes allowing considerable infringements on *IPS* have been implemented, one such being the so-called FRA law (the acronym FRA for *Försvarets radioanstalt*, the Swedish Defence Radio Authority). The FRA law, taking effect on January 1, 2009, is directed against threats to the external and internal safety of the country, especially terrorism. It is applicable to all telephone and Internet traffic on the air or by cable that crosses Swedish borders. Together, the FRA law and DRD allow heavy, arguably too heavy, intrusions upon individuals' private sphere in Sweden.

What help can the proportionality principles provide? WBP5* points in the same direction as WBP2. The positive weight of MOV as a means of attaining OV is no doubt considerable, arguably even redundantly so in proportion to OV (as we found in connection with WBP2). As for WBP6, it can be argued for good reasons that the negative weight of MOV as counteracting the realisation (maintenance) of LS outweighs the positive weight of MOV as a means of attaining OV (for reasons also given in connection with WBP2.) WBP7 points *a fortiori* in the same direction. In order to tip the balance in favour of LS in accordance with WBP8, one could consider adding certain additional MLS measures to the existing ones. One of these could be the setting of a time limit for DRD's being in force and, once the time fixed has elapsed, the undertaking of a serious examination of the actual effects of it. Another could be the requirement for the use of it that an independent court of law authorise such a use. Generally speaking, though, a certain amount of watchfulness might be called for with respect to the law-makers' use of WBP8. There is a risk that measures more cosmetic than efficient might well be added solely in order to accomplish the legislative project. As for WBP9, finally, it is the last resource for the individual law-maker still in doubt.

Let us conclude this chapter by engaging in some reflection on *legal subordination*, i.e., how the realisation of legal safety can be warranted by means of legislation. It could be said that law-state thinking not only contains certain principles about law but also asks for certain principles about law in the law. Of course, where no law exists, no legality can exist either. Legalism demands of "law appliers" that they comply with the law, where there is law to be complied with. But this is not enough for realising the law-state values—and obviously not so with respect to legal security. Some important issues must be incorporated in the law, and the rules so incorporated strictly complied with. This close relationship between legalism and subordination has motivated me to lump them together under the term *nomocracy* (see Sect. 3.4 above).

The claim for legal subordination can be studied by the help of the questions "why?", "what?" and "how?". (i) Why subordinate the conditions of violations of *IPS* to law? In whose interest shall we do that? (ii) Subordination is a relation "X is subordinated to Y". Within our field of discussion, what is X and what is Y? So the question "what?" is twofold. (iii) How shall the protection of people's legal security be shaped in the law?

Why is subordination important? One reason, of course, is that it provides the ordinary citizen and the scheming villain as well with legal certainty (reliable knowledge of how things stand, legally). It is also a necessary condition for legal accessibility. But with respect to legal security alone, the focus is on the legal functionaries. The importance of subordination is linked to them. Subordination places fetters, forged by the law itself, on the legal functionaries by means of legal rules, setting limits for state infringements on *IPS*. When challenged, the functionaries must be able to show that they have *legal authorisation* to do what they are doing. Transgressing the limits must lead to sanctions, also supplied by the law. Without subordination, legal security stands a poor chance.

What shall be subordinated? Mainly four things. (1) The character of the *IPS* infringing measures. (2) The conditions for the use of these measures. (3) The regulation of the measures by which control of *IPS*-infringing authorities is exercised. (4) The regulation of sanctions against individual legal functionaries transgressing the limits of what is allowed.

What shall these things be subordinated to? The answer is simple: Statutory law. Both the case law and the customary law are, for obvious reasons, exceptionally ill-suited for this task.

How shall the protection of legal security be shaped by statutory means? Legal history offers two models: the procedural model and the constitutional model. The procedural model consists in giving specified rules in statutes mainly within the field of (criminal and civil) procedural law about such matters as arrest, detention, search of premises, bodily search, telephone tapping, sequestration etc. (A somewhat unusual example is the English Habeas Corpus Act.) The constitutional model consists in establishing principles of legal security in a written constitution, usually in a catalogue of rights forming a part of such a constitution, which principles can be developed in the form of judicial review at a court of law. These two models are, of course, fully compatible. To suspects, arrested or detained persons—as well as policemen, prosecutors and judges in their daily work—the procedural model, no doubt, is a stronger guarantor of legal security than the constitutional one, with the former's supply of specified, and in the daily work of the legal functionaries familiar, statutory provisions. The constitutional model can be regarded as a complementary measure, giving further guarantees of law-state protection.

A risk with the constitutional model is that its provisions might become a bit vague. This is especially the case when they are formulated as general obligations of the state. It is better, then, to formulate them as prohibitions of certain infringements on *IPS*. This lends greater stringency to the provisions.

On the other hand, a constitution is no place for highly specified rules. For instance, the provision "Application for a detention order shall be made without delay and at the latest 12 o'clock on the third day after the warrant of arrest" (the Swedish Code of Procedure, Chap. 24, Sect. 12) is not particularly well suited to be an article in a constitution.

In Hohfeldian terms, the individual has, especially in the procedural model, certain rights (claims) against the state (with corresponding duties for the state) e.g., the right to be released after having been arrested and then detained for three days, as well as—especially in the constitutional model—certain immunities against the state, e.g., to the effect that the state does not have competence (legal power) to initiate capital punishment by legislation.

Chapter 9
The Organisation of the Law-State

9.1 Introduction

In Sect. 2.2 I characterised a legal order as a relation, which I specified as being between a set of legal norms (*a legal system*) and a system of particular organisations (*a legal organisation*). In this chapter we shall focus on legal organisations and the demands that can be made on them from the point of view of realising the law-state values.

Let me offer a preliminary definition of "legal organisation" in the following way:

(*Lorg*) A legal organisation is the set of all particular organisations that (i) belong to a legal order and (ii) are obligatory according to the legal system of that legal order.

A particular organisation belonging to a legal organisation we call *an authority*.

Lorg will be qualified in Sect. 9.2 in two important respects.

The justification of clause (ii) in *Lorg* is the following. Certain social organisations are products of the legal system in the sense that there are rules in the legal system prescribing the forms for creating these organisations, e.g., a joint stock company or a marriage (if "social organisation" is taken in a very broad sense). In a sense then, a joint stock company, for instance, is a part of a legally regulated organisational system, although of course not an authority. For our purposes it is important to keep apart such products of the legal system and the legal organisation proper. But what is the difference between, e.g., the Supreme Court of the United Kingdom or the Uppsala Public Cleansing Division on the one hand, and Volvo Ltd. on the other, which, all of them, are constituted by legal rules and in many other ways are regulated by legal rules? Clause (ii) is intended to make an acceptable distinction here. That a body is obligatory is taken to mean that the legal system explicitly or implicitly orders that the body shall exist. (Here we disregard the fact that private organisations or individual human beings in exceptional cases can be entrusted with the exercise of public authority.) Authorities are obligatory in this sense (which, of course, does not preclude that the existence of an authority is conditional in the sense that it shall function only under particular circumstances, such as war or danger of war). Joint stock companies or marriages are not obliga-

Å. Frändberg, *From Rechtsstaat to Universal Law-State*, Law and Philosophy Library 109, DOI 10.1007/978-3-319-06784-1_9,

tory in this sense. The legal system does not order them to exist, it only says that if persons want to create such arrangements, this must be done according to the rules of the legal system. In order that such arrangements actually come about, private initiatives are necessary; the initiatives of private persons are in principle free and independent, and they can be carried out by means of contracts and other promissory actions. Authorities, on the contrary, cannot come about in this way.

In Sect. 9.2 we shall say something about the formal properties of legal organisations (their morphology, if you like) and what kind of body legal organisations usually consist of. In Sect. 9.3 we shall, on the basis of what is presented in 9.2, investigate how the law-state values can be realised in so far as the legal organisation is concerned.

9.2 Legal Organisations

An authority is a system of legal relations (positions). Such relations exist between human beings and it is rules in the legal system that regulate how they come into existence and how they cease to exist as well as what their functions are and how these functions shall be performed.

In this respect there is no difference between authorities and other inter-personal relations regulated by the legal system and usually articulated in terms of rights and duties. An authority consists, just like such inter-personal relations, of different kinds of legal positions.[1]

The system of relations forming an authority has, among others, the following important properties.

(1) These relations are *normative relations.* Certain persons have competence to (or shall, may or may not) perform certain actions. Such relations can have this or that deontic status, but a characteristic of authorities is that, among these relations, there is always a core of power relations (competence): to persons in authority are assigned powers over the citizens and the former are in a relation of superiority to the latter.

(2) Authorities are usually *institutions.*[2] The legal system defines a number of "places" (positions) such that if a person fulfils certain qualifications, also usually indicated by the legal system, and certain other circumstances are at hand, then this person has assumed a position in some authority, she has become a person in authority. And as long as she holds this position, her relations—to the public and to other authorities—are connected to the place in question (according to the legal system).

---

[1] For the formal representation of legal positions, see L. Lindahl, *Position and Change*, 1977.

[2] From what follows it should be obvious that I do not use the term "institution" in the same way as is done in N. MacCormick and O. Weinberger, *An Institutional Theory of Law. New Approaches to Legal Positivism*, 1986.

An institution in an ideal-typical form, as I use the term "institution" here, is an organisation such that a person p_1 can be replaced by another person p_2 in any place in the organisation with the consequence that p_2 in the exchange takes over exactly the same relations within the organisation as those p_1 held at that time. In this sense an authority or a joint stock company is an institution (although not in an ideal-typical form). Hence, if the director-general in the former or the managing director in the latter are replaced, no new authority or joint stock company has come into existence. But if a husband divorces his wife and marries another woman, the same marriage does not continue with another place-holder; rather a new marriage has come about. Marriage is not an institution. The institutional form is necessary for achieving permanence in the legal relations tied to more extensive organisations.

In the social life of humankind institutions play a crucial role. They make possible organised co-operation over longer spans of time—longer, indeed, than a lifetime. Institutions are crutches for frail human beings, stumbling along as we make our way through life. The existence of certain institutions is evidently a necessary condition for upholding the law-state values. On the other hand, antiquated institutions can preserve unsatisfactory social states of affairs, also long after those states of affairs have been found intolerable.

(3) The relation-system that structures an authority can be split into three functionally different subsystems, which we shall make use of in the next section when investigating what kinds of organs are necessary for realising the law-state values.
   (a) An authority has an internal structure of relations, which structure solely concerns the relations between the different positions within that authority. An authority is usually hierarchically constructed with a head person at the top.
   (b) When an authority is part of a legal organisation, it takes on certain relations to other organs within that organisation. An authority can be superior or subordinate to another authority, it can have a controlling function with respect to another authority, it can be linked to other authorities in different forms of co-operations, etc.
   (c) Thirdly, and most importantly, authorities are related in a great many (external) ways to private persons, the public. In this connection it is a matter of complicated control and service functions.

An important jurisprudential task is to investigate which types of organs a legal organisation, generally speaking, consists of and to lay bare the typical relations holding between them. A difficulty then is that the legal orders are cultural creations, many of which have existed for centuries and have during that time changed forms—functions which earlier were united within one and the same type of organ have split up into several such types, and new types of organs have emerged. For this reason it is common in jurisprudence to concentrate on what is sometimes called "well-developed" legal orders, having in mind legal orders of the kind we find in current democratic law-states. The analysis can take the form of trying to establish some "minimum content" of legal orders (and, hence, legal organisations), i.e., what kinds of organs a legal order must include in order to be a legal order.[3] Another approach, in a way opposite, is to formulate a so-called ideal-type definition of "legal order": one defines the concept in its strongest conceivable form and then compares actually existing legal orders with the help of this concept.[4]

Lorg defines a very weak concept of "legal organisation". This makes possible a number of distinctions within the framework of this concept. The concept is weak enough to include an organisation consisting exclusively of administrative organs, lacking a judicial function. But are not courts of law—even conceptually—a necessary component of any legal order? Strong reasons can indeed be given for that stand. I agree completely with the view that the judicial function is the central and most important function of a *legal* order. However, purely *administrative order* can, in principle, be regulated in statutory law and its functionaries can adhere to legalism, and in these respects there is an element of law and legality in this order. And the parts of legal orders that are of a purely administrative character are also regarded as falling within the domain of legal science; and its rules, being legal rules, are studied within the discipline of administrative law.

These considerations, though, make it appropriate to distinguish between *legal organisations in a wide sense* and *legal organisations in a strict sense*. This is our first qualification of *Lorg*. The former concept is the one defined by *Lorg*. Here we regard the legal organisation as a system of authorities. The latter takes its point of departure in the judicial function. The legal organisation is seen as including the courts and the organs that are more intimately (although not necessarily) connected to the courts. In the strict sense, a legal organisation is a court-centered organisation.

Such organs that are closely connected to the courts comprise (i) legislative organs, producing the rules that the courts shall apply, (ii) police and prosecution authorities, providing the courts with criminal cases, (iii) executive authorities, executing the judgments of the courts, and (iv) authorities having a controlling function over courts or organs of types (ii)–(iii), or control the administrative authorities with trial at a court as the last resource.

Beyond the legal organisation in the strict sense, then, there are such authorities as the Board of Education, the National Board of Fisheries and the Uppsala Public Cleansing Division. The definition of "legal organisation in a strict sense" can be made more precise by further specifying the relations between (i)–(iv).

However—and now we come to the second qualification of *Lorg*—there is one crucial legal function, intimately connected to the judicial function and performed by a certain body in a well-developed legal order, which is conspicuously missing in both definitions: the function of the advocate, the body of the bar association. It differs from the organs (i)–(iv) in the respect that it is a private body (although there are examples of state bar associations—in Sweden there were, beside the private law firms, so-called public law firms during 1973–1999). When in the following I

[3] See, e.g., J. Raz, *The Concept of a Legal System*, 1. ed., 1970, p. 141.

[4] We find an interesting discussion of these questions in M.P. Golding, *Philosophy of Law*, 1975, ch. 1.

use the term "legal organisation", I use it in the strict sense with the function of the advocate added.

So, in a legal organisation we find the following, typical functions.

1. The law-creating function (performed by legislative assemblies and courts whose decisions have precedential force).
2. The conflict-solving function (performed by courts in civil cases).
3. The breach-of-rule-handling function (performed by police and prosecution authorities and criminal courts in a functional co-operation).
4. The executive function (performed by executive authorities and the correctional system).
5. The controlling function (performed by ordinary courts having the competence of judicial review, constitutional courts, the European Court of Human Rights, *Ombudsmen*, etc.).
6. The party-assisting function (performed *par préférence* by members of private bar associations).

Historically, in the European cultural tradition, functions 1–3 are the oldest and they were, in ancient times, performed by one and the same organ—in the Nordic societies by the *Thing*, where the main focus was on functions 2 and 3. Executive organs did not exist; a court sentence simply gave to the winning party a competence to help himself to his right. Only when the nation-states had been consolidated in Europe did the law-creating function become separated to a greater or lesser degree from the courts, and henceforth performed by absolute rulers or parliamentary assemblies. And only when a strong power of the state emerged could particular executive organs evolve. A more developed civil police organisation—if we except the one created in ancient Rome by Emperor Augustus —is a rather new phenomenon. Controlling organs of type 5 are on the whole products of law-state thinking of the Enlightenment. The role of the advocate is old—a kind of advocate class existed already in ancient Greece—but as a more organised professional category it is of a rather recent origin.

I have argued that a legal order is a relation (or a cluster of relations) between a system of rules (a legal system) and a system of bodies (a legal organisation). Between the legal system and the corresponding legal organisation there is, in existing legal orders, a kind of "balance". Let us regard the two extremes where "the centre of gravity" is on the legal system and on the legal organisation respectively.

Is a legal order possible that consists solely of a legal system and lacks a corresponding legal organisation? Well, this extreme approximates those religious systems that count as legal systems in certain cultures, and are regarded as definitively determined in religious texts once and for all, such as Islam—and which systems "are parasitic upon" the legal organisations of particular states. To a certain extent natural law in the European states during the seventeenth and eighteenth centuries had a similar character– an international, cultural phenomenon "hovering above" the particular legal orders. Also international law has its main focus on the legal system—it has certain law-creating organs and a rudimentary court function, while executive organs are conspicuously missing.

Is a legal order possible that consists solely of a legal organisation but lacks a corresponding legal system? No, that is not possible, since a legal order must at least have a system of rules which constitute and regulate the activity of that legal organisation. But let us assume a legal order with such a minimal legal system, dealing only with the legal organisation (which would be mainly rules of a procedural character). Such an "empty" legal order can most adequately be regarded as a kind of machine, which must be fed by rules from outside the legal order itself. If such rules are found in private contracts or in manners, customs, and the like, the legal order can be characterised as a service order –a rule-enforcement organisation exclusively, enforcing rules created by others than the law-creating bodies of the legal order itself. Such a pure legal order does not, as far as I know, exist, but a legal order approaches such an extreme to the same extent as its legal system contains rules of an optional character, i.e., rules that must yield to rules expressed in contracts, commercial customs, and the like.

9.3 How to Organise a Law-State

I shall conclude this book by presenting some ideas about how a legal organisation should be constructed in order efficiently to contribute to the realisation of the law-state values. It is a question about (i) which types of organs are required, (ii) how these organs shall be constructed and (iii) which legal relations shall exist between themselves, and between them and the public.

As for (i) I shall be very brief. All functions 1–6 described above (p. 177) are important with respect to all four law-state values. With respect to legal equality it is a mere triviality that there must be a law-creating function—bodies creating rules fulfilling the demand of equality in the law—and law-applying authorities which can observe equality before the law. Not least with respect to legal equality and legal security, controlling organs are vital. With respect to legal certainty, legal accessibility and legal security, it is equally trivial that there must be a law-creating function capable of fulfilling the demands of legal certainty, providing individuals with legal remedies and organs to which there is access by means of remedies, and subordinating in statutory form the means allowed for interfering in the individual's personal sphere. Of importance is the existence of an instance that checks drafts from the viewpoint of the law-state values already in the legislative process. For the task of upholding the law-state values an independent advocate class is indispensible.

Let us now turn to (ii) and (iii).

In Sect. 9.2 we split the relation-system that structures an authority into three functionally different subsystems. Let us use this trisecting here.

A. With respect to the internal structure of an organ within a legal order the following demands can be made.

1. *Permanence.* For law-state thinking there is a strong distaste for the creation of legal organs *ad hoc*—i.e., temporary, short-lived organs, established in order to deal with some individual case. This dislike especially concerns courts of law. Legal organs shall be permanent. An insight acquired from experience is that there is a considerable risk concerning such organs, that those in power are tempted to appoint them to biased members. In a permanent organ, on the other hand, knowledge and experience can be stored and made use of in a way that is not possible in temporary organs, which promotes a competent handling of the law in favour of the law-state values. Permanent organs can be subject to continuous control. Legal certainty can benefit from the development of routines (internal practice) within the bounds of valid law. And legality itself—that rules are applied in a uniform way over a long period of time—requires for its accomplishment organs that are permanent during that time. The same argument is applicable to legal equality. Not least of all for the sake of legal security, the permanence of the controlling organs is important. As has been mentioned above, the institutional form is a necessary condition for securing permanence within legal organs.

2. *Internal co-ordination.* Not least of all legal equality and legal certainty demand that every legal organ be consistent in its own handling of the law. This requires internal co-ordination. There are certain techniques for achieving this. One such is the full session (*plenum*), aimed at bringing different opinions into line with one another.

Special problems concerning internal co-ordination may arise when a court includes laymen—juries or lay judges. Let me in this connection add, that I find it, generally speaking, utterly implausible that courts including laymen can contribute more to the promotion of the law-state vales than can courts consisting exclusively of judges trained in the law. (That so-called people's courts are repugnant to the law-state thinking need hardly be mentioned).

3. *Internal control.* In order to maintain internal consistency, certain internal controlling functions may be required. The internal hierarchy of places within the organ must be constructed in such a way that the distance between place-holders at every level in the hierarchy does not obstruct an effective exercise of authority. However, from the viewpoint of the law-states values, it is on the other hand important that the distance be sufficiently great so that higher place-holders are independent from the lower ones to a degree that allows them to control the latter group's exercise of power. This is of special importance with respect to organs which have the right to interfere in the individual's personal sphere by means of violence, where legal security can be endangered. A society taking the law-state values seriously cannot, for example, tolerate police officials who endorse policemen that assault people under arrest. A certain degree of internal distance is necessary in order to prevent false loyalties from informing the work of legal organs. Of importance also, not least of all from the viewpoint of legal accessibility, is the internal control exercised by bar associations over their members.

B. With respect to the relations between different organs within a legal organisation, the following demands can be made.

4. *Independent exercise of authority.* The existence of independent courts of law is regarded, and rightly so, as a cornerstone of the law-state. An important component of that independence is the courts' independence from other organs in the legal organisation (here taken in the wider sense of the word). Ultimately, this independence means that no external organ has a right to make claims about how a court shall decide an individual case—unless that organ itself is a party in litigation. But in addition to that, independence means that it is forbidden on the whole for external organs to try to influence the decision of a court in an individual case. This prohibition also includes the supreme state organ (the parliament).

The law-state arguments for independent courts are that influence from external organs (i) can disturb the consistency that is a condition for legal certainty, (ii) can threaten equality before the law by demands of favouring or disfavouring, and (iii) can threaten legal security when authorities handling violent means ask for the permission of the courts to stretch their competence. Furthermore, (iv) the independence of the courts is a condition for preventing responsibility from slipping away—the courts themselves, and they alone, bear the responsibilty for their decisions. Rules guaranteeing judges irremovability and protection against transfer contribute to their independence.

The same arguments are *mutatis mutandis* applicable to other legal organs as well. As important as the independence of the courts is the police and prosecution authorities' independence of other authorities, the controlling organs' independence of the authorities they shall control and—outside the organisation of authorities—the advocates' independence of, e.g., police and prosecution authorities.

5. *The separation of the legal functions.* Closely linked to the claim of an independent exercise of authority is the idea, which for good reasons can be said to be basic in law-state thinking, of the separation of legal functions. This means, that one and the same organ (authority) shall not exercise several different functions if that leads to a concentration of power or to conflicts of interests, which can threaten the law-state values. *This idea is closely related to the classic separation of power doctrines and can be looked upon as a kind of extension of them.* Of special interest from the point of view of law-state thinking are the following.

(a) *The separation of the legislative law-creating and the judicial functions* (the latter function being the solving of conflicts in civil cases and the handling of the breach of a rule as far as sentencing in criminal cases is concerned). This division is usually justified by the idea of democracy (the popularly elected parliament shall create laws, the courts shall apply them) but it can also be given a law-state justification. Adjudicating parliaments and popular assemblies (which we all know since Socrates was punished by death in 399 BCE) are a threat to all law-state values. That the courts, on their part, besides the pure judicial function, to a certain degree also have a law-creating function, is a necessary consequence of the prohibition of denial of justice.

(b) *The separation between the legislative and the controlling functions.* It is not a good idea to allow an organ to control itself exclusively. This is particularly true in those situations where judicial review is justified, i.e., where legislation must correspond to the constitution. Quite another thing is the preview of legislative drafts during the legislative process, especially from the point of view of the law-state values. In Sweden such a function is performed by The Law Council (*lagrådet*), consisting of judges from the Supreme Court and the Supreme Administrative Court.

(c) *The separation between the judicial and the executive functions.* Executive organs shall execute the decisions of the courts, not retry them. For the sake of legal certainty the public must be able to trust that the courts definitively establish the legal state of affairs.

(d) *The separation between the judicial function and the prosecuting function.* A fusion of these two functions cannot be tolerated in a law-state—it is a threat to all law-state values and attacks its very life-blood. Regard the filmings from the trials against "enemies of the state" in Nazi Germany or eye-witness reports from Soviet dissident trials: screaming judges launching accusations, threats, and sarcasms over the accused in total contempt of things like impartiality and objectivity. The law-state ideal in this respect is the accusatorial (adversary) procedure, not the inquisitorial one, with an impartial and objective judicial function, separated from the role of the party and with parties equal before the court.

(e) *The separation between the judicial function and the police function.* The risk from the law-state viewpoint of police courts is obvious.

(f) *The separation between the police and the prosecution functions.* That a charge of a crime, which has been investigated by the police, is subject to legal scrutiny by a prosecuting authority that is independent of the police and that must give consent before the case is brought before a court, counts as a legal certainty and as a legal security guarantee for the individual. Unwarranted accusations can be removed without a legal process that can be painful to individuals. If this checking function is fused with the pure investigating function there is a risk that the guarantee mentioned is set aside in favour of an ambition to clear up crimes.

(g) *The separation between the party-assisting function* (the advocate function) *and all other functions within the legal organisation.* From the point of view of every law-state value it is of the utmost importance that this function be completely restricted to performing the task of looking after the interests of the client. The client must be able to rely on his adviser. The assignment of roles in a law-state requires that consideration of other interests is the task of other organs. (Compare the lamentable position of the advocates in the Soviet Union.) Attempts on the part of the state to make the advocates sycophants in the service of the state is repugnant to law-state thinking.

Generally speaking, the core of the whole idea of the separation of legal functions is that the legal organisation shall contain built-in counterbalances. A legal organisation is no industrial enterprise, where all functions shall be co-ordinated in order to achieve some common, specified goal. A legal organisation shall be "a principally polarised system"—between its organs and its different functions certain states of tension shall prevail as a matter of principle, in order to guarantee that individuals are not exposed to violations by legal functionaries. This is the doctrine of the separation of powers carried to its extremes. These states of tension within a legal organisation are, in turn, a condition for the development of separate professional roles, which render a psychological internalisation of the law-state values among the servants of the law possible. The personal relationships one can observe in the everyday work in a fairly well developed law-state between lawyers performing different functions within the legal organisation are fascinating in their subtle balance between, on the one hand, a spirit of community among lawyers with respect to what concerns ways of thinking and basic values, and, on the other hand, distance, determined by the different professional roles.

With respect to the traditional separation of powers, the same idea has been expressed in a straightforward way by Justice L. Brandeis of the Supreme Court of the United States in a case where the issue was whether presidential power could be extended in the name of efficiency for certain purposes. The separation of the federal government into three branches, he says, is justified in that it is "not to promote efficiency but to preclude the exercise of arbitrary power. The purpose was not to avoid friction, but, by means of the inevitable friction incident to the distribution of the governmental powers among three departments, to save the people from autocracy".[5]

6. *Control subjection by means of appeal.* That legal organs are independent within the legal organisation does not mean that they are totally and mutually independent in their exercise of authority. On the contrary, not least in the interest of the law-state values, several kinds of dependence relations are necessary between them, especially from the point of view of control: organ o_1 is subjected to the control of organ o_2. One such control relation is that which is established between courts or other authorities when a party appeals from one authority to another. To be sure, this relation is in the first place one between the party and the appellate court and shall be dealt with as such under C below. But an appeal also has the effect that the controlling competence of the appellate court is activated.

Such a control activated by appeal requires of course that there be a hierarchy of instances within the legal organisation. In a law-state at least the supreme instance of such a hierarchy, in matters of individuals' rights, shall be a court of law.

The existence of such a hierarchy also has the indirect advantage, from the viewpoint of legal certainty that pressure towards conformity can come about within the legal organisation.

---

[5] *Myers v United States*, 272 U. S. 52, 1926.

7. *Control subjection by means of judicial review.* I discussed, in Sect. 3.5, judicial review and its relationship to democracy. I argued there that judicial review is no part of the idea of democracy, that they can conflict, and that democracy must yield in so far as the protection of the law-state values is concerned. Grave violations of these values, authorised by democratic decisions, are, in fact, a betrayal of democracy. Even those who are sceptical about judicial review on the grounds that it restricts the rule of democracy and who fear that the courts, if they have extensive judicial review powers, are given too great a political role in society, might think that judicial review is justified at least as regards the protection of the law-state values.

8. *Control subjection by means of legal responsibility.* An imperative law-state demand is that the legal order is equipped with the means of holding legal functionaries responsible for what they do in their different functions. For achieving this purpose three things are necessary: (1) Rules that functionaries can comply with or break, (2) special liability rules, connecting sanctions to the breaking of rules of type 1, i.e., abuse and erroneous decisions in exercising public authority, and (3) organs investigating liability and imposing and executing sanctions. Such sanctions can be—and should be—both criminal (punishment) and civil (damages)—and perhaps administrative ones as well (e.g., fines). All this can be dealt with within the framework of ordinary prosecuting authorities, courts, and executive authorities. But in order to make claims of responsibilty even more efficient we find in many countries special authorities with supervising and prosecuting functions, to which individuals have access, e.g., so-called *Ombudsmen.*

Permanence, we said, is a condition for effective, continuous control, and permanence, in its turn, has as its condition the institutional form. But to claim responsibilty from persons exercising public authority, working within a hierarchically constructed institution, is, on the other hand, beset with certain difficulties. There is something that could be called "the problem of institutional responsibility", meaning the following. Individuals are replaced by others as place-holders within the organ, the places themselves are redefined or cease to exist, and the demarcation between the functions of different organs can be diffuse. For the individual, who wants to claim responsibility, all this can lead to lawlessness. In an institution there is always a risk that the personal responsibility can be watered down or even "absorbed" by the imaginary person, "the Authority", itself: you claim responsibility, seek a responsible person—but there is no one to attach responsibility to. This feature of institutions was exploited to the utmost by the accused in the war crime trials against functionaries among the Nazi organs at the end of World War II. But the phenomenon itself is universal. In a law-state the responsibility must be capable of being individualised.

C. Finally, with respect to the external relations of the organs within the legal organisation to the public, the following demands can be made.

9. *Visibility.* For regimes that consider the law-state values obstacles for an exercise of power undisturbed by inhibitions, the establishment of *secret organs* is a prime device. The secret police, for instance, is one of the totalitarian state's

most effective means. (An only too familiar picture from the political life of the twentieth century: Pale dawn, a block of flats on a quiet street. Tenants anxiously apprehending quick steps up the stairs, and who the visitors are they do not want to know. A door slammed, a car leaving with howling tyres. A flat in disorder, a desperate woman and her children. A husband dragged out of bed and carried away by the secret police. And in the eyes of the state nothing whatever has happened.) In order to bring about a semblance of a law-state, or in order to avoid handling recalcitrant judges and other servants of the law informed by law-state ideas, such regimes often establish secret organs with unlimited power in addition to the ordinary legal organisation, more often than not in military or pseudo-military forms.

But a certain amount of secretiveness also exists in states living up to a high law-state level. Where juries take part in the administration of law it is usually the case that the deliberation of the jury takes place behind closed doors and, furthermore, that its verdict lacks a written justification—no reasons are given—and that its members cannot be held responsible for their verdicts.

The law-state claim of visibility stands out in bold relief when juxtaposed to secretiveness. It should be possible without difficulties to find out which individuals there are who exercise public authority, which competences an authority has, how their decisions can be met, etc. Secretiveness demoralises. Secret exercise of power cannot be controlled. Confronted with secret organs, we are without the safety of law.

10. *Accessibility.* I have treated legal accessibility as one of the four basic law-state values (Chap. 7). More than that is the case with regard to the other basic law-state values, legal accessibility is in the first place a matter of organisation. For this reason I include accessibility in this list of law-state claims on the legal organisation. That visibility is a necessary condition for accessibility is obvious.

An important component of accessibility is the right to appeal to a higher authority, notably a court of law. I am inclined to think that the psychological effect of knowing that when you are convinced that you are in the right, you have at least one more chance to get your case tried, is immense. But it must be borne in mind that also the party who is not in the right has a right to appeal. As a result, the realisation of the legal state of affairs that you try to attain can be delayed for a very long time, with all the negative consequences that that can lead to. Generally speaking, the hierarchy of instances must not, I think, contain more than, say, two or three steps. If there are more, the claim of legal certainty to the effect that legal positions must be authoritatively fixed once and for all within a reasonable period of time is jeopardised.

11. *External independence.* That authorities are independent of other authorities in their exercise of authority is vital. But at least equally important is that they are independent of influential forces outside the legal organisation (in the wider sense of the word). Such forces might be representatives of large interest organisations or enterprises, or private persons in high social positions. Influences from such quarters can be a threat to all law-state values, notably legal equality. The protection against such influences lies in the last resort with the integrity of the persons

exercising public authority. But the conditions for integrity are to no small degree dependent upon how the handling of the law is organised. External independence benefits from a strong legal organisation, whose functionaries enjoy high social prestige. Many factors contribute to securing this: that the servants of the law have a good education, a legal system that supports them in resisting corruption, that they are subject to an effective individual criminal liability, that policemen, prosecutors, judges, etc. are sufficiently well-paid to resist temptation to yield to bribery, and to a great many other things as well.

Index

Å. Frändberg, *From Rechtsstaat to Universal Law-State,* Law and Philosophy Library 109,
DOI 10.1007/978-3-319-06784-1,

MIX
Papier aus verantwortungsvollen Quellen
Paper from responsible sources
FSC® C105338

If you have any concerns about our products,
you can contact us on
ProductSafety@springernature.com

In case Publisher is established outside the EU,
the EU authorized representative is:
Springer Nature Customer Service Center GmbH
Europaplatz 3, 69115 Heidelberg, Germany

Printed by Libri Plureos GmbH
in Hamburg, Germany